Easy German
STEP-BY-STEP

PREMIUM SECOND EDITION

Master High-Frequency Grammar
for German Proficiency—*FAST!*

Ed Swick

New York Chicago San Francisco Athens London Madrid
Mexico City Milan New Delhi Singapore Sydney Toronto

7 8 9 10 11 LBC 28 27 26 25 24

ISBN   978-1-260-45516-8
MHID   1-260-45516-5

e-ISBN   978-1-260-45517-5
e-MHID   1-260-45517-3

McGraw-Hill Education products are available at special quantity discounts to use as premiums and sales promotions or for use in corporate training programs. To contact a representative, please visit the Contact Us pages at www.mhprofessional.com.

McGraw-Hill Language Lab App

This app contains extensive audio recordings (including all the Say It Out Loud sections) to support your study of this book. Go to www.mhlanguagelab.com to access the online version of the application, or download the free mobile app from the Apple app store or Google Play store (for Android devices).

Note: Internet access is required for streaming audio.

I should like to thank my dear friend Stefan Feyen for all his help and suggestions.

Contents

Preface

This book is intentionally called *Easy German Step-by-Step*. It provides two important approaches for learning the German language. The first approach is to explain the makeup of the German language in as simple a form as possible. Learning German or any new language does not have to be an arduous task. That is why this book is designed so the reader can move through the chapters at a comfortable rate and with ease.

The second approach, which works perfectly with the first one, is to provide small amounts of structure and vocabulary at a time. The reader is not burdened with long lists of words to memorize or complicated explanations of grammar. Instead, small doses are provided, which gradually develop into a broader knowledge of a topic. The reader goes through a chapter *step by step* and in time can forge the skills of a competent user of the German language.

The topics of each chapter are initially explained as they relate to English. It is wise to understand a concept in one's native language before attempting to learn and use it in a new language. It makes little sense to learn German past participles if one does not know what a past participle is in his or her own language.

After a concept has been described, German examples of the concept are introduced. They are given in the context of simple sentences, and these sentences are always accompanied by their English translation. The reader needs to know what he or she is saying in German.

Practice comes in two major ways: oral practice by reading sample sentences out loud and written exercises for applying one's new knowledge with a bit of personal creativity. New for this premium second edition, all sample sentences in the Say It Out Loud sections are available as streaming audio recordings via app. In addition, special explanations of some material will accompany practice. These explanations are meant to clarify concepts that are potentially confusing. An example in English would be the word *few*. There is a significant difference between saying <u>*few people know him*</u> and <u>*a few*</u> *people know him.*

In order to avoid memorizing lists of new vocabulary, many words and phrases are repeated regularly in several chapters. Throughout the book the reader is reminded to say everything out loud—a key for developing proficiency.

In addition, a list of new vocabulary is provided at the end of each chapter. This is meant to serve as a resource for quickly finding the meaning of a specific word. Most chapters have a brief text or dialogue for reading. The translation of the text or dialogue does not accompany them. The purpose of the reading section is to provide a vehicle similar to what one finds when visiting a German-speaking country—signs and menus and tickets all written in German without any translation.

At the end of each chapter, there is a *Review Quiz*. Its purpose is to check that the goals of the chapter have been achieved. If the reader is not satisfied with the outcome of the *Review Quiz*, it is wise and simple to repeat the areas of the chapter that need further review.

After Chapters 6 and 13, a *Mastery Check* is provided. The *Mastery Check* serves as an evaluation tool that can help the reader determine how much progress he or she has made. Like a *Review Quiz*, it can serve as a signal to take another look at certain chapters. At the end of the book, the reader will find a *Final Mastery Check*. It is the final evaluation of progress with the whole book.

There are two appendixes at the end of the book. Appendix A lists the old *Fraktur* alphabet. It is presented as a resource should the reader come in contact with old books or other printed materials. *Fraktur* is also used nowadays as a *quaint* way to decorate a sign or advertisement, so it is important to be familiar with it. The name of a typical restaurant written in *Fraktur* might be 𝕵𝖚𝖒 𝕽𝖔𝖙𝖊𝖓 𝕺𝖈𝖍𝖘𝖊𝖓 **(Zum Roten Ochsen)** *The Red Ox Inn.*

Appendix B is a list of German irregular verbs. This is an important resource for checking on the accurate use of verbs.

Do not be intimidated by a new language. Many before you have learned one, and you and many more can do so with the proper effort. Use this book as it is intended for use: go through the material gradually, and *step by step* you will make progress and succeed in achieving your goals.

1

Pronunciation and Cognates

In this chapter, you will be introduced to the German alphabet and the pronunciation of individual letters. An explanation of letter combinations, including consonants and vowels, is also included. Several cognates will be used to provide instant vocabulary and to illustrate how the German pronunciation of these words differs from the English pronunciation.

Some questions that will be answered are as follows:

✓ How do German vowel sounds differ from English vowel sounds?
✓ How do German consonant sounds differ from English consonant sounds?
✓ What special letters are there in the German alphabet, and how are they pronounced?

There is a lot of detail about German pronunciation in this chapter. Do not try to master German pronunciation by the arduous study of this one chapter. Instead, use Chapter 1 as a resource that you can refer to as you go through the other chapters of the book.

The Alphabet

Although this chapter is about the *German alphabet*, it has to be stated right away that there is, in reality, no German alphabet. The Romans developed letters that acted as symbols for the pronunciation of the Latin language. That alphabet, which is well over 2,000 years old, is used for many languages around the world, including German.

The letters of the alphabet, how the letters are pronounced, and sample words illustrating the use of the letters are provided in the chart that follows. The phonetic pronunciation of the word and its meaning follow each word.

1

LETTER	ITS NAME	SAMPLE WORD	PHONETICS	MEANING
Aa	ah	Abend	ah-bent	evening
Bb	bay	bellen	bell-en	bark
Cc	tsay	Couch	couch	couch
Dd	day	da	dah	there
Ee	ay	Ende	en-deh	end
Ff	eff	Frau	frow	woman
Gg	gay	gut	goot	good
Hh	hah	Haus	house	house
Ii	ee	ideal	ee-day-ahl	ideal
Jj	yawt	ja	jah	yes
Kk	kah	Kind	kint	child
Ll	ell	laut	lout	loud, noisy
Mm	emm	Maus	mouse	mouse
Nn	enn	nah	nah	near
Oo	oh	oben	oh-ben	up there
Pp	pay	Pest	pest	plague
Qq	koo	Quark	kwahrk	curd cheese
Rr	air	rot	rote	red
Ss	ess	sieben	zee-ben	seven
Tt	tay	Tante	tun-teh	aunt
Uu	oo	Kuh	koo	cow
Vv	fow	Vati	fah-tee	daddy
Ww	vay	was	vuss	what
Xx	ix	extra	extra	extra
Yy	uepsilon	Typ	**tue**p	type
Zz	tset	Zelle	tsell-eh	cell

This alphabet chart has provided the names of the letters that a German uses to identify the letters. When a German recites the alphabet, he or she will say, "ah, bay, tsay, day, ay, eff, . . ." and so on. But these names are not necessarily the pronunciation of the letters. Consider the English letter Ww, which is called *double u*. When a word with this letter occurs, the name *double u* is not pronounced. No one pronounces the word *went* as *doubleuent*. German is the same; the names of some letters do not give a clue as to their pronunciation.

When dealing with letters and their pronunciation consider the similarity of how German and English speakers pronounce the same letter. That word *similarity* is important because several letters sound very much alike in both languages, but *they are not identical*. When the English pronunciation is used where the German pronunciation is needed, the word will in all likelihood be understood, but the speaker will have a foreign accent.

A good example is the letter Ll (*ell*). The English Ll is pronounced with the tip of the tongue placed against the alveolar ridge—that raised area behind the upper teeth. The German Ll is pronounced with the tongue placed behind the alveolar ridge. The two sounds are quite distinct. Compare the following words that are spelled the same or similarly in both languages but are pronounced differently.

Say It Out Loud

Practice saying the German words with the tongue placed behind the alveolar ridge.

English		German	
bell	*instrument for ringing*	bell	*bark*
fell	*past of fall*	fell	*fur*
flipper	*limb used for swimming*	Flipper	*pinball machine*
hell	*Hades*	hell	*bright*
killer	*murderer*	Killer	*killer, hit man*
lout	*boor*	laut	*loud*

Note: Audio recordings by native German speakers of all Say It Out Loud sections are available via app to model your pronunciation.

It is important to understand right away that German words end with *voiceless consonant sounds*. The final letter may be a voiced consonant, but it is pronounced voiceless. There are three primary German consonants that are affected by this:

Voiced Consonant	Voiceless Consonant Counterpart
b bay	p pay
d day	t tay
g gay	k kah

Consider the following examples that illustrate how a word ends with a voiced consonant but is pronounced with the voiceless counterpart:

Word	Pronunciation	Meaning
Gib	geep	*give*
Kind	kint	*child*
Tag	tuck	*day*

Step 1: Consonants

Let's look at all the consonants and the nuances of their pronunciation. You will discover that there are few sounds that will be new to your ear.

Bb

This letter is pronounced like English at the beginning or middle of a word. For example:

German Word	Pronunciation	Meaning
Boot	bote	*boat*
bellen	bell-en	*bark*
oben	oh-ben	*up there, above*
Farbe	far-beh	*color*

At the end of a word, Bb changes to its voiceless counterpart Pp.

Korb	corp	*basket*
Gib	geep	*give*

Cc

This consonant is used as the symbol for the sound Kk in words that tend to come from foreign sources. For example:

Camping	kem-ping	*camping*
Charakter	kah-rahk-tuh	*character*

Sometimes there are two spellings for such foreign words, one with Cc and one with Kk.

Cassette/Kassette	kah-set-teh	*cassette*
Casino/Kasino	kah-zee-no	*casino*

It is most common for Cc to occur in combination with other consonants. These combinations will be taken up later in this chapter.

Dd

This consonant is pronounced voiced at the beginning and in the middle of a word.

dumm	doom	*dumb*
das	duss	*that*
beide	bye-deh	*both*
wieder	vee-duh	*again*

At the end of a word, Dd changes to its voiceless counterpart Tt.

| Bad | baht | *bath* |
| Hand | hahnt | *hand* |

Ff

This consonant sound is like English.

| faul | fowl | *lazy* |
| Schaf | shahf | *sheep* |

Say It Out Loud

Pronounce each German word, paying attention to the pronunciation of the consonants B, C, D, and F.

Boot, Bank, aber, beste	*boat, bank, but, best*
Dort, dies, Danke, leider	*there, this, thanks, unfortunately*
Fallen, darf, werfen, Freitag	*fall, may, throw, Friday*

Gg

The voiced consonant is found at the beginning and in the middle of words. For example:

| gegen | gay-gen | *against* |
| Bogen | boh-gen | *curve, bend* |

It changes to its voiceless counterpart Kk at the end of words.

| Tag | tuck | *day* |
| klug | klook | *smart* |

Hh

At the beginning of words, Hh is an aspirated sound like the English letter.

| halt | huhlt | *halt, stop* |
| Heu | hoy | *hay* |

Most often it is not pronounced in the middle of a word unless it is part of a combination of consonants.

gehen	gay-en	*go*
sehen	zay-en	*see*
zieht	tseet	*pulls*

Jj

This letter is pronounced like the English Yy. For example:

jung	yoong	*young*
jagen	yah-gen	*hunt*

There are a few foreign words in which the consonant Jj sounds like the English consonant Jj, for example, **Jazz** and **Jogging**.

Kk

This consonant has the same pronunciation no matter its position in a word. As in English, it is often accompanied by Cc.

Klasse	kluh-seh	*class*
schicken	shick-en	*send*
buk	book	*baked* (old-fashioned)

Ll

This consonant is similar to English but with the tongue placed behind the alveolar ridge.

liegen	lee-gen	*lie, recline*
Keller	kell-uh	*cellar*
will	vill	*want*

Mm

This is a bilabial consonant; it is pronounced as in English by placing the lips together.

Mund	moont	*mouth*
atmen	aht-men	*breathe*
schwimm	shvim	*swim*

Nn

Like its English counterpart, this is a nasal consonant.

nein	nine	*no*
rennen	ren-nen	*run*
braun	brown	*brown*

Say It Out Loud

Pronounce each German word, paying attention to the pronunciation of the consonants G, H, J, K, L, M, and N.

gut, gelb, Magen, Freitag	*good, yellow, stomach, Friday*
Hut, heben, lehren, haben	*hat, lift, teach, have*
Jodler, Junge, Jahr, Jurist	*yodeller, boy, year, lawyer*
klein, Wecker, Kissen, kurz	*little, alarm clock, pillow, short*
Mag, muss, warm, Sturm	*like, must, warm, storm*
nett, Nase, Donner, Gewinn	*nice, nose, thunder, gain/win*

Pp

This is another bilabial consonant and is similar to English.

Park	park	*park*
Lippe	lip-peh	*lip*
klapp	klup	*lift up, turn down*

Qq

This letter is most often combined with Uu, and together they are pronounced like *kv*.

Qualität	kvah-lee-tate	*quality*
quer	kvair	*sideways*

Rr

This consonant can be pronounced as a *trilled Rr*, which is similar to its sound in Italian or Russian, or it can be pronounced similar to a French or *guttural Rr*. At the end of a word, it resembles a *schwa* sound like a final British Rr.

Reise	rye-zeh	*trip*
sparen	shpah-ren	*save*
Bruder	broo-duh	*brother*
Schwester	shves-tuh	*sister*

More information on how to pronounce the guttural Rr will be given later in the chapter.

Ss

At the beginning or in the middle of a word, this consonant is pronounced like Zz. If it is a double ss, it is pronounced *Ss*.

singen	zing-en	*sing*
leise	lye-zeh	*soft, quiet*
Schloss	shlawss	*palace*

Tt

This consonant is pronounced like the English Tt. When it is followed by Hh, this usually indicates a foreign word, but it is still pronounced like *Tt*.

tanken	tunk-en	*fill up with gas*
raten	rah-ten	*advise*
Theorie	tay-oh-ree	*theory*

Vv

This consonant is most often pronounced like an Ff, but in many foreign words it sounds like an English Vv.

viel	feel	*much*
vor	fore	*before*
Version	vare-zee-one	*version*
Vase	vah-zeh	*vase*

Ww

This letter stands for the English consonant sound Vv.

Wasser	wuss-uh	*water*
Volkswagen	folks-vah-gen	*Beetle, people's car*
wiegen	vee-gen	*weigh*
wo	voe	*where*

Xx

This consonant is found in few words, many of which have a foreign origin. It sounds much like the English Xx.

Sex	zecks	*sex*
X-Beine	icks-bye-neh	*knock knees*
X-Strahlen	icks-shtrah-len	*X-rays*

Zz

This letter is always pronounced like the letters *ts* in the English word *hats*. But unlike English, German frequently uses this letter to begin a word. In the middle or at the end of a word it is sometimes accompanied by *t*.

Zeit	tsyte	*time*
Zug	tsook	*train*
Walzer	vultz-uh	*waltz*
Platz	plutz	*place, space*

Say It Out Loud

Pronounce each German word, paying attention to the pronunciation of the consonants P, Q, R, S, T, V, W, X, and Z.

Party, Preis, Tapete, Kupfer	*party, prize, wallpaper, copper*
Quark, qualifizieren, Quittung, Quorum	*curd cheese, qualify, receipt, quorum*
Rollschuh, recht, fahren, Butter	*roller skate, right, drive, butter*
Suppe, sagen, messen, Besen	*soup, say, measure, broom*
Treu, Flirt, Flotte, Bart	*loyal, flirtation, fleet, beard*
verkehrt, voll, vier, vulgar	*wrong, full, four, vulgar*
warum, wer, Verwendung, anderswo	*why, who, use, elsewhere*
zu, Blitz, kratzen, Zeppelin	*to, lightning, scratch, Zeppelin*

There are three special letter combinations that do not follow a pattern that is used in English. They are **pf**, **sp**, and **st**.

The combination **pf** is unusual for English speakers, because both letters are pronounced in words, and at many times words can begin with this combination. Practice saying the following words:

pfeifen	*whistle*
Pflanze	*plant*
tapfer	*brave*
Pferd	*horse*

The combinations **sp** and **st** are not difficult for English speakers. The confusion lies with the fact that they are both pronounced as if they began with the sound **sh. Sp** is pronounced *shp*, and **st** is pronounced *sht*. For example, **sparen** (shpah-ren) *save* and **stehen** (shtay-en) *stand*. Practice saying the following words:

spielen	*play*
Speise	*food*
Sport	*athletics*
sprechen	*speak*
verstehen	*understand*
Stuhl	*chair*
Stechen	*sting*
Strafe	*punishment*

Step 2: Vowels

German vowels are similar to English vowels and are therefore easy to pronounce. Let's look at each vowel and at the nuances of its pronunciation.

Aa

This vowel is pronounced with a long *ah* sound before a single consonant and with a short *uh* before a double consonant. If the vowel **a** precedes an **Hh**, it is pronounced long.

German Word	Pronunciation	Meaning
alt	ult	*old*
Frage	frah-geh	*question*
tragen	trah-gen	*carry*
fallen	fuh-len	*fall*
stehlen	shtay-len	*steal*

Ee

The long vowel sound of this letter is **ay** (as in *stay*) and precedes a single consonant. The short vowel sound is pronounced **eh** and precedes double consonants.

essen	ess-en	*eat*
lesen	laze-en	*read*
egal	ay-gahl	*no difference*
besser	bess-uh	*better*

Ii

Like other vowels, this one is pronounced with the long **ee** before single consonants and with the short **ih** before double consonants.

Italien	ee-tah-lee-en	*Italy*
isst	isst	*eats*
wider	wee-duh	*against*
Bild	bilt	*picture*

Oo

The long vowel **oh** is used before single consonants and the short vowel **aw** before double consonants. If it precedes **h**, it is pronounced long.

oder	oh-duh	*or*
soll	zawl	*should*
Bohnen	bone-en	*beans*
Monat	mone-aht	*month*
stottern	shtaw-tun	*stutter*

Uu

The long Uu is pronounced *oo* as in *moon,* and the short Uu is pronounced *oo* as in *look*. Uu is always long before the letter **h**.

tun	toon (*moon*)	*do*
Mutter	moo-tuh (*look*)	*mother*
Schuh	shoo (*moon*)	*shoe*
Mund	moont (*look*)	*mouth*

Yy

This vowel should be practiced carefully, because it is a sound that does not occur in English. It is simple to describe what to do, but to teach the muscles of the mouth to make the correct sound requires effort. Two different actions must be done simultaneously. First, purse the lips to say a long **oo.** Then say the vowel **ee.** The sound may seem weird to you at first, but it is the correct one for this letter. The phonetic symbol for this sound is **ue.** Let's practice some words.

Symbol	**zue**m-bole	*symbol*
Gymnasium	**gue**m-nah-zee-oom	*preparatory school*
Typ	**tue**p	*type*

German uses an umlaut to alter the sound of three vowels. Let's look at how these three vowels changed when written with an umlaut.

Ää

With an umlaut added, the vowel sounds very much like Ee. Consider the following words and their pronunciation.

älter	ell-tuh	*older*
Väter	fay-tuh	*fathers*
Krähe	kray-eh	*crow*

Öö

This vowel sound can be a little tricky, but there is an easy way to arrive at the correct pronunciation. Say the English word *her* and string out the sound for a couple of extra seconds. Do that again, but do not pronounce the final *r.* The resulting sound is the closest to how Öö is pronounced. Practice the following words:

mögen	m(er)-gen	*like*
Schlösser	shl(er)-suh	*palaces*
schön	sh(er)n	*nice, pretty*

Üü

This vowel is pronounced like the German vowel **Yy.** Practice the following words:

über	**ue**-buh	*over*
Tür	t**ue**-uh	*door*
Flüsse	fl**ue**ss-eh	*rivers*

Say It Out Loud

Pronounce each word or phrase, paying attention to the various consonant and vowel sounds.

im Januar	*in January*
kaufen	*sell*
kleiner	*smaller*
langsam	*slow*
lernen	*learn*
mein Bruder	*my brother*
meine Frau	*my wife*
sagen	*say*
schön	*nice, pretty*
sehr bald	*very soon*
Sommer	*summer*
wann	*when*
wo ist der Zug?	*Where is the train?*
zu Hause	*at home*

Letter Combinations

English combines letters to act as symbols of some specific sounds. For example, *s* and *h* are combined to symbolize the fricative or rushing sound of words like *shush* and *shower.* A *t* and an *h* combine to stand for a unique English sound, in which the tongue is placed between the teeth combined with a rush of air. It is in such words as *think* and *with.*

German also combines letters to symbolize special sounds. Some combinations are clusters of consonants, and others are combinations of vowels. Let's take a look.

Consonants

CH

This combination of two consonants is very common in German but unlike any sound in English. To make this sound, the back of the tongue is raised close to the roof of the mouth and air is allowed to rush through that narrow opening. This provides a rasping sound. It can be heard in a Scottish word like *loch*. This sound is not difficult to make but requires practice and effort. The phonetic symbol for this sound will be **ch**. Practice these examples.

German Word	Pronunciation	Meaning
ach	ah**ch**	*oh, alas*
ich	ee**ch**	*I*
nach	nah**ch**	*after, to*
stechen	shteh**ch**-en	*sting*

Words that end in **-ig** pronounce this letter combination in many regions as if it were written as **ich**. Consider, for example, **König** k(er)-ni**ch** *king* and **ständig** shten-di**ch** *constant*.

SCH

These letters stand for the English sound symbolized by *sh*. Practice the following words with this sound:

Schule	shoo-leh	*school*
waschen	wush-en	*wash*
schicken	shick-en	*send*
Tisch	tish	*table*

TSCH

This combination of consonants is used primarily to stand for the sound *ch* in a few foreign words. One such word in German is **Tschechien** cheh**ch**-ee-en *Czech Republic*.

Vowels

AA

A double *a* in a word means that the sound is pronounced long—*ah*. For example:

German Word	Pronunciation	Meaning
Haar	hahr	*hair*
Paar	pahr	*pair, couple*

AU

This combination is the sound *ow* as in the English word *how*. Practice these words:

Frau	frow	*woman*
blau	blow	*blue*

ÄU

These two vowels are the symbol for the sound *oy* as in the English word *toy*.

Fräulein	froy-line	*young woman* (politically incorrect)
bräunen	broy-nen	*tan*

EE

This double vowel means that the vowel sound is pronounced long. For example:

Tee	tay	*tea*
Schnee	shnay	*snow*

EU

This vowel combination is similar to **äu** and is pronounced *oy*.

Freude	froy-deh	*joy*
scheu	shoy	*shy*

EI

This vowel combination is pronounced like *y* in *try*.

frei	fry	*free*
neine	nine	*no*

IE

This double vowel is pronounced like a long *ee*.

sieben	zee-ben	*seven*
zieh	tsee	*pull*

OO

The double o indicates a long *oh* sound. For example, the word **Boot** bote *boat*.

Say It Out Loud

Pronounce each word or phrase, paying attention to the pronunciation of the consonant combinations:

auf Wiedersehen	*good-bye*
bauen	*build*
Beere	*berry*
brauchen	*need*
Das ist scheußlich.	*That is dreadful.*
gute Musik	*good music*
Guten Tag!	*Hello. Good day.*
ich auch	*me (I), too*
im Frühling	*in the spring*
Käfig	*cage*
neue Sportler	*new athletes*
Schönheit	*beauty*
Süßigkeiten	*sweets*
Tschau!	*So long!*
verkaufen	*sell*

German has a special letter that does not exist in English. It is called **ess-tset** and looks like this: **ß**. It comes from an old printing form called *Fraktur*. You can see the entire Fraktur alphabet in Appendix A, which you can use as an aid when you read texts printed in the old style.

In Fraktur, there were two forms for the letter *Ss*: *Ss*, with which you are already familiar, and, ſ, which was used in the middle of words. This form of the letter was combined with the Fraktur letter *Zz* and became ß. In modern German print it is ß. It is not a *B*. See Appendix A for the complete Fraktur alphabet.

The letter ß is used in place of a double **s** *when it follows a long vowel sound.* A double **s** is written *when it follows a short vowel sound.*

Compare the following pairs of words, written in Fraktur and modern German printing.

Amerika	Amerika	*America*
Deutschland	Deutschland	*Germany*
Volkswagen	Volkswagen	*Volkswagen*
Kindergarten	Kindergarten	*kindergarten, nursery school*

Practice saying the following words:

Schloss, Kissen, muss, essen	*palace, pillow, must, eat*
heißen, Fuß, aßen, reißen	*be called, foot, ate, rip*
schießen, Kuss, groß, lassen	*shoot, kiss, big, let*
wissen, biss, außer, fließen	*know, bit, except, flow*

Wondering About This? The German *Rr*

The sound of the guttural German Rr is sometimes hard to reproduce. Here's a little trick to help. First, be sure you can form the German **ch** sound properly. A good test is pronouncing the word **ach.** Remember that the back of the tongue is raised to near the roof of the mouth, and air is allowed to rush through that narrow opening. The place at the roof of the mouth where the speaker can feel the friction of the air when saying **ach** is the same place where the guttural Rr is produced.

The English (particularly the American) Rr is made by a sound in the throat while the jaw is tensed. The German Rr is not so tense. Say **ach** several times. Then say **rah** with the sound being made at that spot on the roof of the mouth where **ach** is said but *do not let your jaw move.* Practice by repeating **ach-rah** many times. In time, you will become comfortable with this new sound. Remember that a final Rr or -er sounds like a British Rr or -er and resembles *uh.*

Say It Out Loud

Pronounce each German word, paying attention to the pronunciation of the consonant Rr.

Rad, Bruder, Ring, Rose	*wheel, brother, ring, rose*
krank, Frau, Freund, früh	*sick, woman, friend, early*
später, Lehrer, Rohr, stören	*later, teacher, cylinder, disturb*
bringen, Tür, Wahrheit, Straße	*bring, door, truth, street*

Step 3: Cognates

Cognates are words that are identical or similar in various languages because they come from the same source. Many such words are of Latin origin. They are easy to recognize in writing, but their pronunciation differs from language to language. This is certainly true of German and English.

A large group of cognates ends in **-tion**. That stem of the word is pronounced **tsee-one** in German. Let's look at a few words that have the stem **-tion** and how they are pronounced in German. The German meaning is usually identical to the English meaning.

German Word	Pronunciation	Meaning
Konstitution	kone-stee-too-tsee-one	*constitution*
Position	poe-zih-tsee-one	*position*
Qualifikation	kvah-lee-fee-kah-tsee-one	*qualification*
Situation	zih-too-ah-tsee-one	*situation*
Variation	vah-ree-ah-tsee-one	*variation*

The stem ending **-isch** is commonly used in German. Its English counterpart is **-ic** or **-ical**.

biologisch	bee-oh-loh-gish	*biological*
historisch	hiss-tore-ish	*historic*
hysterisch	h**ue**-stare-ish	*hysterical*
logisch	loh-gisch	*logical*
romantisch	roh-mahn-tish	*romantic*

Many words end in **-ist**. This stem usually means that a person is involved in a profession or regular activity.

Artist	ahr-tist	*artist*
Kapitalist	kah-pee-tah-list	*capitalist*
Komponist	kome-poh-nist	*composer*
Maschinist	mah-shee-nist	*machinist*
Pianist	pee-ah-nist	*pianist*

Some words end in **-tät**, which is written in English as **-(i)ty.**

Qualität	kvah-lee-tate	*quality*
Souveränität	zoo-vair-aye-nee-tate	*sovereignty*
Spezialität	shpeh-tsee-ah-lee-tate	*speciality*
Universität	oo-nee-vair-zee-tate	*university*

Say It Out Loud

Pronounce each word, paying attention to how the German and English pronunciation of these words differ.

Afrika und Europa	*Africa and Europe*
Apotheke	*apothecary, drugstore*
Diktator	*dictator*
ein amerikanischer Tourist	*an American tourist*
ein Biergarten	*a beer garden*
ein deutscher Jurist	*a German lawyer*
ein Komputer	*a computer*
ein Tiergarten	*a zoo*
große Elefanten	*big elephants*
Hamburg und München	*Hamburg and Munich*
hundert Euro	*hundred euros*
in Berlin	*in Berlin*
in der Schweiz	*in Switzerland*
klassische Sinfonie	*classical symphony*
Mobiltelefon	*mobile (cell) phone*
Präsident	*president*

Review Quiz 1

Choose the letter of the word or sound that best completes each sentence.

1. The letter ß has the sound of _____
   - a. z
   - b. ss
   - c. s
   - d. tz

2. The English word *her* can help in learning to pronounce the vowel sound in _____
   - a. Schön
   - b. Fließen
   - c. Mein
   - d. Tür

3. The final letter in the word **Lampe** is pronounced like _____
   - a. eh
   - b. ah
   - c. uh
   - d. eu

4. The consonant combination of **tsch** is pronounced in English like _____
   a. th   c. st
   b. sh   d. ch

5. To pronounce **Üü**, purse your lips for the vowel sound **oo** but say _____
   a. eh   c. yoo
   b. uu   d. ee

6. To pronounce the guttural **Rr**, you should first learn to pronounce _____
   a. er   c. ach
   b. rer   d. sch

7. The first syllable of **spielen** is pronounced _____
   a. shpee   c. spell
   b. speh   d. shep

8. *Circus* in German is **Zirkus.** The first letter in the German word is
   pronounced _____
   a. z   c. ts
   b. zt   d. ß

9. The vowel combination **äu** is pronounced like the German vowel
   combination _____
   a. eu   c. ei
   b. ae   d. au

10. German words tend to end in _____
    a. short vowels   c. long vowels
    b. voiced consonants   d. voiceless consonants

2

Gender and *heißen*

This chapter will introduce you to the German concept of gender. In addition, the definite articles and the **der**-words will be explained and practiced.

Some questions that will be answered are as follows:

✓ How does the German concept of gender differ from the English concept?
✓ What is the gender difference between animate and inanimate nouns?
✓ What is the relationship of **der**-words to the definite articles?

The concept of gender is found in most European languages, but that concept is not static. There are many similarities of how gender functions in European languages, but there are also distinct differences. This is particularly true in the case of German and English.

English gender has evolved to a point where actual sexual gender dominates the concept. In the English language, all things male are masculine, and all things female are feminine. Inanimate objects—books, rocks, cars, shoes, and so on—are neuter.

English often does something unique when determining the gender of an animal. If an animal is identified by an indefinite article (*a, an*), it is referred to by the neuter pronoun *it*. For example:

*A horse is a farm animal. **It** can pull a plow or a heavily loaded wagon.*

But if the animal is identified with the definite article (*the*), it can be referred to by a gender pronoun (*he, she*).

*The horse seems quite tired. **She** needs time to rest and feed.*

*The colt is only a day old, but **he** is already very active and curious.*

It is possible, however, to use *it* at all times with animals.

German Gender

German gender is only partially determined by the sex of a person or animal. In general, males are masculine, and females are feminine. But inanimate objects are not always considered neuter, and males and females are not always considered masculine and feminine, respectively. More frequently than determining gender by sex, the formation of a noun determines gender, and this is a concept that English speakers sometimes find difficult to grasp in the beginning. Be assured that in a short time you will accept the concept and use it with ease.

Step 1: Masculine

The masculine definite article is **der** (*the*). Most nouns that identify a male use **der** as their definite article. Look at the list of nouns that follows, and pronounce each one with the help of the phonetics. An accent mark is provided when the stress is located on the final syllable. Check the meaning of the noun to see why it is considered masculine:

Noun	Phonetics	Meaning
der Bauer	dair bow-uh	*the farmer*
der Bruder	dair broo-duh	*the brother*
der Herr	dair hair	*the gentleman, Mr.*
der Jurist	dair yoo-ríst	*the lawyer*
der Lehrer	dair lay-ruh	*the teacher*
der Onkel	dair ohn-kel	*the uncle*
der Pilot	dair pee-lóht	*the pilot*
der Sohn	dair zone	*the son*
der Vater	dair fah-tuh	*the father*

Just like in the English-speaking world, young boys are addressed with their first name. Some traditional and contemporary names for boys are as follows:

Name	Phonetics
Alex	ah-lex
Andreas	ahn-dray-uss

Felix	fay-lix
Frank	frahnk
Lars	lahs
Martin	mah-teen
Peter	pay-tuh
Stefan	shteh-fahn
Thomas	toe-mahs

You can use these names to say *hello* and *good-bye* to someone: **Guten Tag** and **Auf Wiedersehen**.

Say It Out Loud

Say each sentence out loud, using the phonetics to help you pronounce each one correctly:

Guten Tag, Felix.	goo-ten tuck fay-lix	*Hello, Felix.*
Auf Wiedersehen, Martin.	owf vee-duh-zay-en mah-teen	*Good-bye, Martin.*
Guten Tag, Peter.	goo-ten tuck pay-tuh	*Hello, Peter.*
Auf Wiedersehen, Andreas.	owf vee-duh-zay-en ahn-dray-ahs	*Good-bye, Andreas.*
Guten Tag, Thomas.	goo-ten tuck toe-mahs	*Hello, Thomas.*
Auf Wiedersehen, Frank.	owf vee-duh-zay-en frahnk	*Good-bye, Frank.*
Guten Tag, Lars.	goo-ten tuck lahs	*Hello, Lars.*
Auf Wiedersehen, Stefan.	owf vee-duh-zay-en shteh-fahn	*Good-bye, Stefan.*

Last names are used with both males and females. Some of the commonly used German surnames are as follows:

Surname	Phonetics
Braun	brown
Dorf	dohrf
Keller	kell-uh
Klein	kline

Surname	Phonetics
Neufeld	noy-felt
Rieger	ree-guh
Schäfer	shay-fuh
Schmidt	shmitt
Schneider	shneye-duh

Adult men are most frequently addressed with the title **Herr** (*Mr.*). You can say *good day* to greet these men, which is **Guten Tag** and is used in general to mean *hello*. You can also say **Guten Morgen** (*good morning*), **Guten Abend** (*good evening*), and **Gute Nacht** (*good night*).

Say It Out Loud

Say each sentence out loud, using the phonetics to help you pronounce each one correctly:

Guten Tag, Herr Schmidt.	goo-ten tuck hair shmitt	*Hello, Mr. Schmidt.*
Guten Morgen, Herr Neufeld.	goo-ten maw-gen hair noy-felt	*Good morning, Mr. Neufeld.*
Guten Abend, Herr Schneider.	goo-ten ah-bend hair shny-duh	*Good evening, Mr. Schneider.*
Gute Nacht, Herr Keller.	goo-teh nah**ch**t hair kell-uh.	*Good night, Mr. Keller.*
Guten Tag, Herr Schäfer.	goo-ten tuck hair shay-fuh	*Hello, Mr. Schäfer.*
Guten Morgen, Herr Klein.	goo-ten maw-gen hair kline	*Good morning, Mr. Klein.*
Guten Abend, Herr Braun.	goo-ten ah-bend hair brown	*Good evening, Mr. Braun.*
Gute Nacht, Herr Dorf.	goo-teh nah**ch**t hair dohrf	*Good night, Mr. Dorf*

The German word **wo** means *where* and is used to ask where someone or something is. For example:

Question	Phonetics	Meaning
Wo ist Felix?	voh ist fay-lix	*Where is Felix?*
Wo ist Herr Klein?	voh ist hair kline	*Where is Mr. Kline?*

Wo ist Thomas?	voh ist toe-mahs	*Where is Thomas?*
Wo ist Herr Schneider?	voh ist hair shneye-duh	*Where is Mr. Schneider?*

You can answer the question by saying that the person is **hier** (*here*):

Herr Braun ist hier.	hair brown ist hee-uh	*Mr. Brown is here.*
Stefan ist hier.	shteh-fahn ist hee-uh	*Stefan is here.*
Herr Keller ist hier.	hair kell-uh ist hee-uh	*Mr. Keller is here.*
Peter ist hier.	pay-tuh ist hee-uh	*Peter is here.*

Of course, these boys and men can be in more places than just here. Let's look at some of the words and phrases that give them a few more interesting places to be:

Question	Phonetics	Meaning
bei Felix	bye fay-lix	*at Felix's house*
bei Peter	bye pay-tuh	*at Peter's house*
da	dah	*there*
im Garten	im gah-ten	*in the garden/yard*
in Berlin	in bare-léen	*in Berlin*
in der Schweiz	in dair shveyetse	*in Switzerland*
in Hamburg	in hahm-boork	*in Hamburg*
zu Hause	tsoo how-zah	*at home*

Say It Out Loud

Say each sentence out loud, and notice that two or three lines provide a miniature conversation:

Guten Tag, Herr Keller.	goo-ten tuck hair kell-uh	*Hello, Mr. Keller.*
Wo ist Thomas?	voh ist toe-mahs	*Where is Thomas?*
Thomas ist zu Hause.	toe-mahs ist tsoo how-zeh	*Thomas is home.*
Guten Abend, Herr Braun.	goo-ten ah-bent hair brown	*Good evening, Mr. Brown.*
Wo ist Herr Klein?	voh ist hair kline	*Where is Mr. Kline?*
Herr Klein ist in Berlin.	hair kline ist in bare-léen	*Mr. Klein is in Berlin.*
Guten Morgen, Alex.	goo-ten maw-gen ah-lex	*Good morning, Alex.*

Wo ist Martin?	voh ist mah-teen	*Where is Martin?*

Martin ist bei Felix.	mah-teen ist
	  bye fay-lix
		Martin is at
		  Felix's house.

Gute Nacht,
  Herr Schäfer.
	goo-teh nah**ch**t
	  hair shay-fuh
		Good night,
		  Mr. Schäfer.

Gute Nacht, Lars.	goo-teh nah**ch**t lahs	*Good night, Lars.*

Like English, German uses **Gute Nacht** (*good night*) as a way of saying good-bye at night or when someone is retiring. **Auf Wiedersehen** is the most common way of saying good-bye and means something close to *until I see you again*. That verb *see* is important in this phrase. You cannot use it when speaking on the telephone. When you say good-bye to a telephone caller, you say **auf Wiederhören**, which means approximately, *until I hear your voice again*. A more casual way of saying good-bye, which can even be used on the telephone, is with the word **tschüß**. It is used where English speakers say *so long* or *see you later*. It comes from the French word **adieu**, and was in fashion in the German-speaking world in the early nineteenth century. Over time, its pronunciation became corrupted, and in twentieth-century Germany it is pronounced *chuess*. Look at the following examples of people saying good-bye:

Auf Wiedersehen,
  Herr Keller.
	owf vee-duh-zay-en
	  hair kell-uh
		Good-bye,
		  Mr. Keller.

Gute Nacht, Alex.	goo-teh nah**ch**t
	  ah-lex
		Good night,
		  Alex.

Auf Widerhören,
  Herr Schmidt.
	owf vee-duh-h(er)-ren
	  hair shmitt
		Good-bye,
		  Mr. Schmidt.

Tschüß, Andreas.	chuess ahn-dray-us	*So long, Andreas.*

It was stated earlier that the gender of a noun is often determined not by its meaning but by the formation of the word. For example, a noun that ends in **-er** is often masculine even when that noun does not refer to a male. This is also true of nouns that end in **-el** and **-en**. Pronounce each of the following nouns, and check out their meaning:

Noun	Phonetics	Meaning
der Keller	dair kell-uh	*the cellar, basement*
der Wecker	dair veck-uh	*the alarm clock*
der Löffel	dair l(er)-fell	*the spoon*
der Mantel	dair munn-tell	*the coat*
der Boden	dair boh-den	*the floor*
der Wagen	dair vah-gen	*the car*

Determining gender in German is sometimes a compelling task. The previous statement about nouns ending in **-er**, **-el**, and **-en** was made with the intentional adverb *often*. German likes to break its own rules, and you will discover words of other genders with these same endings. But the endings **-er**, **-el**, and **-en** *tend* to put such nouns in the masculine column.

Ihr and *mein*

The adjectives **Ihr** and **mein** are *your* and *my*, respectively, and can modify any masculine noun. Take note how they are used in the following sentences:

Noun	Phonetics	Meaning
Guten Abend, Herr Braun.	goo-ten ah-bent hair brown	*Good evening, Mr. Braun.*
Guten Abend, Alex.	goo-ten ah-bent ah-lex	*Good evening, Alex.*
Ist Ihr Sohn zu Hause?	ist eer zohn tsoo how-zeh	*Is your son at home?*
Mein Sohn ist bei Felix.	mine zohn ist bye fay-lix	*My son is at Felix's house.*
Guten Morgen, Herr Schmidt.	goo-ten maw-gen hair shmitt	*Good morning, Mr. Schmidt.*
Ist Ihr Vater in der Schweiz?	ist eer fah-tuh in dair shveyetze	*Is your father in Switzerland?*
Mein Vater ist in Berlin.	mine fah-tuh ist in bare-léen	*My father is in Berlin.*
Guten Tag, Herr Keller.	goo-ten tuck hair kell-uh	*Good day, Mr. Keller.*
Ist Ihr Mantel hier?	ist eer munn-tell hee-uh	*Is your coat here?*
Mein Mantel ist im Garten.	mine munn-tell ist im gah-ten	*My coat is in the garden.*
Wo ist Ihr Bruder?	voh ist eer broo-duh	*Where is your brother?*
Mein Bruder ist bei Peter.	mine broo-duh ist bye pay-tuh	*My brother is at Peter's house.*
Wo ist Ihr Wecker?	voh ist eer veck-uh	*Where is your alarm clock?*
Mein Wecker ist zu Hause.	mine veck-uh ist tsoo how-zeh	*My alarm clock is at home.*

Perhaps you have noticed that some words are always capitalized. German has a very simple rule: capitalize all nouns. This is different from English, because we only capitalize proper nouns. In German, first names, surnames, and all other nouns are capitalized. The adjective **Ihr** is also always capitalized when it means *your*. Some examples of capitalization include:

Martin der Lehrer	*teacher*
Herr Braun mein Wagen	*car*
Alex Keller Ihr Bruder	*brother*
Thomas der Bauer	*farmer*

Exercise 2.1

Complete each sentence with any appropriate word or phrase from this chapter:

1. Mein _____ ist im Garten.

2. Wo ist Ihr _____?

3. Guten _____, Herr Schneider.

4. _____ Wiedersehen, Thomas.

5. Ihr _____ ist in Hamburg.

6. Ist _____ zu Hause?

7. Mein Onkel ist bei _____.

8. Stefan _____ hier.

9. Ist der Bauer in _____?

10. _____ Lehrer ist in Amerika.

Step 2: Feminine

The feminine definite article is **die** (*the*). It is used to modify most nouns that describe females. For example:

Noun	Phonetics	Meaning
die Bäuerin	dee boy-uh-rin	*the female farmer*
die Frau	dee frow	*the woman, Mrs., Ms.*
die Kellnerin	dee kell-nuh-rin	*the waitress*
die Lehrerin	dee lay-ruh-rin	*the female teacher*

die Mutter	dee moo-tuh	*the mother*
die Schwester	dee shves-tuh	*the sister*
die Tante	dee tun-teh	*the aunt*
die Tochter	dee taw**ch**-tuh	*the daughter*

Wondering About This? The Ending *-in*

Perhaps you noticed in the previous list of feminine nouns that three of them ended in **-in**. That little ending is a signal that the noun in question will always be feminine. And it is most often the feminine counterpart of a masculine noun that is identical except for that ending. Look at these examples:

Noun	Phonetics	Meaning
die Bäuerin/der Bauer	boy-uh-rin/bow-uh	*farmer*
die Lehrerin/der Lehrer	lay-ruh-(rin)	*teacher*
die Kellnerin/der Kellner	kell-nuh-(rin)	*waitress/waiter*
die Juristin/der Jurist	yoo-rist-(in)	*lawyer*
die Studentin/der Student	shtoo-dent-(in)	*student*
die Wirtin/der Wirt	veert-(in)	*landlady/landlord*

If you know a feminine noun that ends in **-in**, you can be certain that there is a masculine counterpart to that noun.

Let's look at some names for females. Some are traditional, and others are contemporary:

Name	Phonetics
Angela	ahn-geh-luh
Gabi	gah-bee
Ingrid	een-greet
Monika	moe-nee-kuh
Sonja	zone-yuh
Susanne	zoo-zuh-neh
Tina	tee-nuh
Ursula	oor-zoo-luh

You can address a young girl by her first name, but an adult woman is addressed with the title **Frau** (*frow*) and her last name. **Frau** not only means *woman* and *wife*; it is the only title that is presently considered politically correct for both married and single women. Therefore, it also means *Mrs., Miss,* and *Ms.*

Many nouns that describe an inanimate object are feminine—that is, they use **die** as their definite article. Many such nouns end in **-e**:

Noun	Phonetics	Meaning
die Lampe	dee lum-peh	*the lamp*
die Schule	dee shoo-leh	*the school*
die Küche	dee k**ue-ch**-eh	*the kitchen*
die Tür	dee **tue**-uh	*the door*
die Decke	dee deck-eh	*the blanket*
die Milch	dee mil**ch**	*the milk*
die Uhr	dee oo-uh	*the clock*
die Straße	dee shtrah-she	*the street*
die Tasche	dee tush-eh	*the (hand)bag*

When you modify feminine nouns with **Ihr** and **mein**, they change to **Ihre** and **meine**. The meaning has not changed, but the gender has. Just as the definite article ends in **-e**, the adjectives also end in **-e**: **Ihre Schule** *your school* and **meine Uhr** *my clock*.

Say It Out Loud

Say each sentence out loud, using the phonetics to help you pronounce each one correctly:

Guten Morgen, Frau Benz.	goo-ten maw-gen frow bents	*Good morning, Ms. Benz.*
Guten Morgen, Tina.	goo-ten maw-gen tee-nuh	*Good morning, Tina.*
Wo ist Ursula?	voh ist oor-zoo-luh	*Where is Ursula?*
Ursula ist in Berlin.	oor-zoo-luh ist in bare-léen	*Ursula is in Berlin.*
Guten Abend, Frau Schneider.	goo-ten ah-bent frow shneye-duh	*Good evening, Ms. Schneider.*
Guten Abend, Gabi.	goo-ten ah-ben gah-bee	*Good evening, Gabi.*
Ist Angela zu Hause?	ist ahn-geh-luh tsoo how-zeh	*Is Angela at home?*

Ja, Angela ist im Garten.	yah ahn-geh-luh ist im gah-ten	*Yes, Angela is in the garden.*
Guten Tag, Frau Keller.	goo-ten tuck frow kell-uh	*Hello, Ms. Keller.*
Guten Tag, Sonja.	goo-ten tuck zone-yuh	*Hello, Sonja.*
Wo ist Ihre Tasche?	voh ist eer-eh tush-eh	*Where is your purse?*
Meine Tasche ist hier.	mine-eh tush-eh ist hee-ah	*My purse is here.*

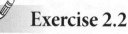 **Exercise 2.2**

*Provide the definite article for each noun (**der** or **die**). Then reword the phrase with the correct form of **Ihr** and **mein**. For example:*

<u>der</u> Vater	<u>Ihr Vater</u>	<u>mein Vater</u>
1. _____ Onkel	_____	_____
2. _____ Tante	_____	_____
3. _____ Tasche	_____	_____
4. _____ Wagen	_____	_____
5. _____ Lehrerin	_____	_____
6. _____ Mantel	_____	_____
7. _____ Schwester	_____	_____
8. _____ Sohn	_____	_____
9. _____ Tochter	_____	_____

 Step 3: Neuter

Neuter nouns are always modified by the definite article **das** (*the*). As in English, many neuter nouns are inanimate objects, but some neuter nouns refer to people. This usually occurs when the noun is a *diminutive*—that is, a noun that describes something small or in its infancy. Two suffixes tell that something is diminutive: **-chen** and **-lein**. For example, the noun **Frau** was often formed as a diminutive with **-lein**: **Fräulein** froy-line. This suggested that the meaning was *little woman*. The same word formerly was used as the title *Miss*. Practice saying the following neuter nouns:

Noun	Phonetics	Meaning
das Auto	duss ow-toe	*the car, automobile*
das Haus	duss howss	*the house*
das Kind	duss kint	*the child*
das Mädchen	duss mayt-**ch**en	*the girl*
das Buch	duss boo**ch**	*the book*
das Röslein	duss r(er)ss-line	*the little rose*
das Geld	duss gelt	*the money*
das Land	duss lunt	*the land, country*
das Fenster	duss fen-stuh	*the window*

When you modify a neuter word with **Ihr** or **mein**, no additional ending is needed, for example, **das Kind, Ihr Kind, mein Kind** and **das Auto, Ihr Auto, mein Auto**.

Say It Out Loud

Say each sentence out loud, using the phonetics to help you pronounce each one correctly:

Das Haus ist groß.	duss howss ist grohss	*The house is big.*
Das Land ist groß.	duss lunt ist grohss	*The country is big.*
Das Fenster ist groß.	duss fen-stuh ist grohss	*The window is big.*
Das Auto ist klein.	duss ow-toe ist kline	*The car is little.*
Das Buch ist klein.	duss boo**ch** ist kline	*The book is little.*
Das Kind ist klein.	duss kint ist kline	*The child is little.*
Wo ist das Mädchen?	voh ist duss mayt-**ch**en	*Where is the girl?*
Das Mädchen ist zu Hause.	duss mayt-**ch**en ist tsoo how-zeh	*The girl is at home.*
Wo ist das Geld?	voh ist duss gelt	*Where is the money?*

Das Geld ist hier.	duss gelt ist hee-uh	*The money is here.*
Ist Ihr Kind im Garten?	ist eer kint im gah-ten	*Is your child in the garden?*
Ja, mein Kind ist im Garten.	yah mine kint ist im gah-ten	*Yes, my child is in the garden.*

Exercise 2.3

*Provide the definite article for each noun (**der**, **die**, or **das**). Then reword the phrase with the correct form of **Ihr** and **mein**. For example:*

<u>der</u> Vater   *Ihr Vater*   *mein Vater*

1. _____ Mutter   _____   _____

2. _____ Buch   _____   _____

3. _____ Pilot   _____   _____

4. _____ Röslein   _____   _____

5. _____ Geld   _____   _____

6. _____ Jurist   _____   _____

7. _____ Lehrerin   _____   _____

8. _____ Tante   _____   _____

9. _____ Schwester   _____   _____

10. _____ Auto   _____   _____

Heißen

The verb **heißen** is important because it is used in a special way to give one's name. There is another phrase that looks much like English: **Mein Name ist Alex.** *My name is Alex.* But it is just as likely that a German will use **heißen** to give his or her name. This special verb has the meaning *be called*. In German, you are saying: *I am called, you are called, he is called,* and so on. Let's look at some phrases with this verb.

Say It Out Loud

Say each sentence out loud, paying attention to the use of the verb **heißen**:

Sie heißen Frau Keller.	*Your name is Ms. Keller.*
Heißen Sie Herr Benz?	*Is your name Mr. Benz?*
Nein, ich heiße Alex Schmidt.	*No, my name is Alex Schmidt.*
Heißen Sie Angela?	*Is your name Angela?*
Ja, ich heiße Angela.	*Yes, my name is Angela.*
Nein, ich heiße Tina.	*No, my name is Tina.*
Wie heißen Sie?	*What is your name?*
Ich heiße Thomas.	*My name is Thomas.*
Wie heißt das Mädchen?	*What is the girl's name?*
Das Mädchen heißt Sonja.	*The girl's name is Sonja.*
Wie heißt der Junge?	*What is the boy's name?*
Der Junge heißt Andreas.	*The boy's name is Andreas.*

You certainly noticed that the verb **heißen** made changes to its ending. These changes were *conjugational endings*. English has conjugational endings for the various persons (first person, second person, and third person singular and plural), but most English verbs have no additional ending except for the third personal singular, which requires an *-s* ending. For example:

	Singular	**Plural**
First person:	I sing	we sing
Second person:	you sing	you sing
Third person:	he sing**s**	they sing
	she sing**s**	the girls sing
	it sing**s**	
	the girl sing**s**	

German also has conjugational endings. You encountered three of them with the verb **heißen**:

ich heiß<u>e</u>	*my name is/I am called*
Sie heiß<u>en</u>	*your name is/you are called*
der Junge heiß<u>t</u>	*the boy's name is/the boy is called*

Take note that the pronoun **Sie** (*you*) is always capitalized. More will be explained about conjugations in Chapter 3.

Exercise 2.4

Fill in the blank with any appropriate word. For example:

Mein <u>Vater</u> heißt Peter Schmidt.

1. Das Mädchen _____ in Berlin.

2. Wie _____ Sie?

3. Ihre _____ heißt Sonja.

4. Ist _____ Bruder im Garten?

5. Ist das _____ groß?

6. Mein _____ heißt Martin.

7. _____ ist Ihr Auto?

8. _____ heiße Angela Schneider.

9. Der _____ heißt Andreas Braun.

10. Wie heißen _____?

Review Quiz 2

Choose the letter of the word or phrase that best completes each sentence.

1. Meine _____ ist in der Schweiz.
   - a. Onkel
   - b. Geld
   - c. Tochter
   - d. Fenster

2. Wo _____ Ihr Lehrer?
   - a. ist
   - b. heißt
   - c. mein
   - d. Lehrerin

3. Ist Ihre Mutter _____?
   - a. zu Hause
   - b. Garten
   - c. Hamburg
   - d. mein

4. Wie heißt _____?
   - a. in Berlin
   - b. die Kellnerin
   - c. Sie
   - d. ich

5. _____ Herr Benz in München?

    a. Wo   c. Heißt

    b. Ist   d. Heißen

6. Mein _____ ist Pilot.

    a. Schwester   c. Buch

    b. Frau Schäfer   d. Bruder

7. Ist mein _____ in Berlin?

    a. Onkel   c. Ihr

    b. Küche   d. in der Schweiz

8. Mein Haus ist _____.

    a. wie   c. Straße

    b. groß   d. heißen

9. _____ heißen Sie?

    a. Wo   c. Frau Neufeld

    b. Thomas   d. Wie

10. Mein Buch ist _____.

    a. klein   c. wie

    b. Haus   d. Ihre

New Vocabulary

auf Wiederhören	*good-bye (on the telephone)*
auf Wiedersehen	*good-bye*
Auto *(n.)*	*car, automobile*
Bauer *(m.)*	*farmer*
Bäuerin *(f.)*	*female farmer*
bei	*by, at, at the house of*
Boden *(m.)*	*the floor*
Buch *(n.)*	*book*
da	*there*
Decke *(f.)*	*blanket*
Fenster *(n.)*	*window*

Frau (*f.*)	*woman, Mrs., Ms.*
Garten (*m.*)	*garden*
Geld (*n.*)	*money*
groß	*big*
Gute Nacht	*good night*
Guten Abend	*good evening*
Guten Morgen	*good morning*
Guten Tag	*good day, hello*
Haus (*n.*)	*house*
heißen	*be named, be called*
hier	*here*
Ihr	*your*
Jurist (*m.*)	*lawyer*
Keller (*m.*)	*the cellar, basement*
Kellnerin (*f.*)	*waitress*
Kind (*n.*)	*child*
klein	*little, small*
Küche (*f.*)	*kitchen*
Lampe (*f.*)	*lamp*
Land (*n.*)	*land, country*
Lehrer (*m.*)	*teacher*
Lehrerin (*f.*)	*female teacher*
Löffel (*m.*)	*the spoon*
Mädchen (*n.*)	*girl*
Mantel (*m.*)	*the coat*
mein	*my*
Milch (*f.*)	*milk*
Mutter (*f.*)	*mother*
Pilot (*m.*)	*pilot*
Röslein (*n.*)	*little rose*
Schule (*f.*)	*school*
Schweiz (*f.*)	*Switzerland*
Schwester (*f.*)	*sister*

Sohn (*m.*)	*son*
Straße (*f.*)	*street*
Tante (*f.*)	*aunt*
Tasche (*f.*)	*(hand)bag*
Tochter (*f.*)	*daughter*
Tür (*f.*)	*door*
Uhr (*f.*)	*clock*
Vater (*m.*)	*father*
Wagen (*m.*)	*car*
Wecker (*m.*)	*the alarm clock*
wo	*where*
zu Hause	*at home*

3

Nominative Pronouns, *der*-Words, and the Verb *sein*

This chapter provides your first look at the German personal pronouns. The conjugation of the verb **sein** in the present tense is also introduced.

Some questions that will be answered are:

✓ What are the German personal pronouns, and how are they used?
✓ How are **der**-words used?
✓ How is the verb **sein** conjugated in the present tense?
✓ How is the verb **sein** used with the personal pronouns?
✓ How is the verb **sein** used with nouns?

The English personal pronouns are used in place of nouns and names. They make sentences less wordy and awkward sounding and make the doer of an action specifically first, second, or third personal singular or plural. The English personal pronouns are *I*, *you*, *he*, *she*, *it*, *we*, and *they*.

Let's assume there is a man named John. It would seem strange to use his name every time someone wanted to state something that John is doing or did. For example:

> *John lived in Washington. John married a girl from his high school. John has two children.*

English is more flexible than that. It provides third person singular pronouns (*he, she, it*) that can replace a name or noun and make speech or writing flow less awkwardly. For example:

> *John lived in Washington. He married a girl from his high school. He has two children.*

All of the English personal pronouns are used in this way.

German Personal Pronouns

German personal pronouns function in much the same way: they are replacements for names and nouns and make the language flow easily while retaining the idea of who the doer of an action is without continually naming that person. The personal pronouns are:

	Singular		Plural	
First person:	ich	*I*	wir	*we*
Second person:	du	*you*	ihr	*you*
	Sie	*you* (formal)	Sie	*you* (formal)
Third person:	er	*he, it*	sie	*they*
	sie	*she, it*		
	es	*it, he, she*		

Step 1: Third Person Pronouns and Gender

In Chapter 2, you discovered how the gender of a noun is determined and thereby which of the definite articles (**der, die, das** *the*) to use with a noun. The main lesson of German gender is that it is not necessarily sexual gender. Often the formation of the word can determine the gender. For example:

Masculine		Feminine		Neuter	
der Bruder	*brother*	die Tante	*aunt*	das Mädchen	*girl*
der Keller	*cellar*	die Lampe	*lamp*	das Haus	*house*

When the concept of German gender is understood, it is time to add the third person pronouns to the equation. These pronouns conform to the gender of the noun and, like nouns, do not always reflect the sexual gender of the noun. If a masculine noun refers to an inanimate object, its pronoun replacement must be masculine (**er**), even though the meaning of the noun is an inanimate object and not a male. The same thing occurs with feminine and neuter nouns. That is the reason for the translation of **er, sie**, and **es** as *he* and *it*, *she* and *it*, and *it* and *he* and *she* for masculine, feminine, and neuter, respectively. Let's look at some example sentences that illustrate this use of gender with pronouns.

Say It Out Loud

Say each sentence out loud, while paying close attention to the gender of the nouns and pronouns.

Der Lehrer ist zu Hause.	*The teacher is at home.*
Er ist zu Hause.	*He is at home.*
Der Tisch ist in der Küche.	*The table is in the kitchen.*
Er ist in der Küche.	*It is in the kitchen.*
Die Frau ist im Garten.	*The woman is in the garden.*
Sie ist im Garten.	*She is in the garden.*
Die Tasche ist im Garten.	*The handbag is in the garden.*
Sie ist im Garten.	*It is in the garden.*
Das Kind ist bei Sonja.	*The child is at Sonja's house.*
Es ist bei Sonja.	*He/She is at Sonja's house.*
Der Wagen ist alt.	*The car is old.*
Er ist alt.	*It is old.*
Die Decke ist da.	*The blanket is there.*
Sie is da.	*It is there.*
Das Mädchen heißt Monika.	*The girl's name is Monika.*
Es heißt Monika.	*Her name is Monika.*

Notice in each of the preceding sentences that the verb used with the noun is the same as the one used with the pronoun: **Die Decke <u>ist</u> da. Sie <u>ist</u> da. Das Mädchen <u>heißt</u> Monika. Es <u>heißt</u> Monika.**

Exercise 3.1

*Provide the pronoun (**er, sie, es**) that is the appropriate replacement for the noun. For example:*

der Vater	<u>er</u>
1. die Mutter	_____
2. das Buch	_____
3. der Wagen	_____

4. der Richter   _____

5. die Lehrerin   _____

6. das Röslein   _____

7. das Bad   _____

8. die Vase   _____

9. der Tisch   _____

10. die Schule   _____

When **Ihr(e)** or **mein(e)** are used in place of the definite article, the pronoun that replaces the noun phrase still conforms to the gender of the noun. For example:

Der Wagen ist da. *The car is there.*	Er ist da. *It is there.*
Ihr Wagen ist da. *Your car is there.*	Er ist da. *It is there.*
Mein Wagen ist da. *My car is there.*	Er ist da. *It is there.*

Say It Out Loud

*Read each sentence out loud, paying attention to how **mein** and **Ihr** are used:*

Der Mann ist alt.	*The man is old.*
Mein Vater ist alt.	*My father is old.*
Das Kind ist im Garten.	*The child is in the garden.*
Ihr Kind ist im Garten.	*Your child is in the garden.*
Wo ist die Decke?	*Where is the blanket?*
Wo ist meine Decke?	*Where is my blanket?*
Der Pilot ist in der Schweiz.	*The pilot is in Switzerland.*
Ihr Sohn ist in der Schweiz.	*Your son is in Switzerland.*
Ihre Schwester ist in Berlin.	*Your sister is in Berlin.*
Ist das Auto alt?	*Is the car old?*
Ist Ihr Auto zu Hause?	*Is your car at home?*
Wie heißt die Frau?	*What is the woman's name?*
Meine Frau heißt Angela.	*My wife's name is Angela.*
Heißt der Junge Alex?	*Is the boy's name Alex?*
Heißt das Mädchen Tina?	*Is the girl's name Tina?*

Let's learn some new adjectives that will come in handy when using the German already introduced.

Say It Out Loud

Say each sentence out loud, paying attention to the adjective shown in bold.

Das Mädchen ist **jung**.	*The girl is young.*
Ist Ihr Wagen **neu**?	*Is your car new?*
Das Haus ist **weiß**.	*The house is white.*
Mein Hut ist **schwarz**.	*My hat is black.*
Ist Ihre Bluse **rot**?	*Is your blouse red?*
Der Bleistift ist **kurz**.	*The pencil is short.*
Die Straße Ist **lang**.	*The street ıs long.*
Mein Rock ist **grün**.	*My skirt is green.*
Ist Ihr Hemd **blau**?	*Is your shirt blue?*
Welche Farbe hat das Kleid?	*What color is the dress?*
Das Kleid ist **gelb**.	*The dress is yellow.*

Exercise 3.2

Reword each sentence by changing the personal pronoun to any appropriate noun with its correct definite article. For example:

Es ist alt.

Das Auto ist alt.

1. Er ist jung.

   _____

2. Sie ist lang.

   _____

3. Es ist rot.

   _____

4. Er ist neu.

   _____

5. Sie ist schwarz.

_____

6. Es ist klein.

_____

7. Er ist groß.

_____

8. Sie ist gelb.

_____

9. Es ist blau.

_____

10. Er ist weiß.

_____

 ## Step 2: *Der*-Words

A small group of words called **der**-words follows the gender pattern of the definite articles. You have already encountered one of these words: **welcher** (*which, what*). The other three **der**-words are **dieser** (*this*), **jener** (*that*), and **jeder** (*each, every*). When they modify a masculine noun, they end in **-er** just like the definite article **d<u>er</u>**. For example:

der Mantel	*the coat*
welcher Mantel	*which (what) coat*
dieser Mantel	*this coat*
jener Mantel	*that coat*
jeder Mantel	*each (every) coat*

Perhaps you are beginning to see just how important gender is in speaking and writing German correctly. But have no fear. If you ever make a mistake with gender, it is not a terrible sin. You will still be understood and be able to communicate. With time and practice, your accuracy will develop, and conforming to how German uses gender becomes quite natural.

The feminine definite article ends in **-e**. When the **der**-words modify feminine nouns, they end in **-e**. The neuter definite article ends in **-s**. When the **der**-words modify neuter nouns, they end in **-es**. Let's practice some sentences with feminine and neuter nouns.

Say It Out Loud

Say each sentence out loud, paying attention to the gender endings on the ***der****-words:*

Die Frau ist alt.	*The woman is old.*
Welche Frau ist jung?	*Which woman is young?*
Diese Frau ist meine Mutter.	*This woman is my mother.*
Jene Frau heißt Angela.	*That woman's name is Angela.*
Das Haus ist weiß.	*The house is white.*
Welches Haus ist groß?	*Which house is big?*
Dieses Haus ist neu.	*This house is new.*
Jenes Haus ist klein.	*That house is small.*
Ist jedes Haus alt?	*Is every house old?*

Exercise 3.3

*Provide the missing **der**-words for the noun given. For example:*

Auto	*das*	welches welch—	*dieses* dies—	*jenes* jen—	*jedes* jed—
1. Wagen	der	_____	_____	_____	_____
2. Küche	_____	_____	_____	jene	_____
3. Mantel	_____	_____	_____	_____	jeder
4. Bluse	die	_____	_____	_____	_____
5. Buch	_____	_____	_____	jenes	_____
6. Garten	_____	welcher	_____	_____	_____
7. Rock	der	_____	_____	_____	_____
8. Bleistift	_____	_____	_____	_____	jeder
9. Schule	_____	_____	diese	_____	_____
10. Kind	_____	welches	_____	_____	_____

Say It Out Loud

Say each sentence out loud, paying attention to the questions and their answers:

Welche Farbe hat Ihr Wagen?	*What color is your car?*
Mein Wagen ist rot.	*My car is red.*
Ist Ihr Wagen neu oder alt?	*Is your car new or old?*
Er ist neu.	*It is new.*
Ist diese Bluse gelb oder weiß?	*Is this blouse yellow or white?*
Diese Bluse ist gelb.	*This blouse is yellow.*
Welches Haus ist klein?	*Which house is little?*
Jenes Haus ist klein.	*That house is little.*
Wie heißt dieses Mädchen?	*What is this girl's name?*
Dieses Mädchen heißt Tina.	*This girl's name is Tina.*
Jenes Mädchen ist schön.	*That girl is pretty.*
Jedes Mädchen ist schön.	*Every girl is pretty.*
Welche Farbe hat das Hemd?	*What color is the shirt?*
Das Hemd ist braun.	*The shirt is brown.*
Ist dieses Hemd neu oder alt?	*Is this shirt new or old?*

There are two more third person pronouns that are important for asking questions: **wer** (*who*) and **was** (*what*). Notice in the sentences that follow, that the definite article **das** is used to mean *that* in questions and answers.

> **Wondering About This?** *welche Farbe*
> Let's take a moment to look at this question: **Welche Farbe hat das Hemd?** It is translated as: *What color is the shirt?* But it must be obvious to you that it does not exactly mean that word for word. The actual German words translate as *What color does the shirt have?* It is a special usage when asking about colors. But the answer has a word-for-word translation, because the word **Farbe** (*color*) is not used in the answer: **Das Hemd ist rot.** *The shirt is red.*

Say It Out Loud

*Say each sentence out loud, paying attention to how **wer** and **was** are used:*

Wer ist das?	*Who is that?*
Das ist mein Freund.	*That is my friend.*
Ist das Ihr Bruder?	*Is that your brother?*

Nein, das ist mein Vetter.	*No, that is my cousin.* (male cousin)
Wer ist das?	*Who is that?*
Das ist meine Freundin.	*That is my girlfriend.*
Ist das Ihre Schwester?	*Is that your sister?*
Nein, das ist meine Cousine.	*No, that is my cousin.* (female cousin)
Was ist das?	*What is that?*
Das ist mein Fotoapparat.	*That is my camera.*
Ist Ihr Fotoapparat alt?	*Is your camera old?*
Nein, er ist neu.	*No, it is new.*
Was ist das?	*What is that?*
Das ist der Laptop.	*That is the laptop.*
Ist das mein Laptop?	*Is that my laptop?*
Ja, das ist Ihr Laptop.	*Yes, that is your laptop.*

A Useful Little Phrase

You already know the words **was** and **ist**. They can be used in a special way that is quite simple to say but has a meaning different from the meaning of the words themselves.

    Was ist?   *What is it? What's up?*

Think of the English translation: *What's up?* In that example, the meaning of the question is not derived from the meaning of those two words. That's quite similar to what German is doing. In several of the chapters that follow, other such *idioms* will be included.

Exercise 3.4

*Use the cue words given to create a question and an answer. Use a pronoun (**er, sie, es**) as the subject in the answer. For example:*

Haus/weiß

Welche Farbe hat das Haus?

Es ist weiß.

1. Hemd/blau

_____

_____

2. Bluse/grün

_____

_____

3. Fotoapparat/schwarz

_____

_____

4. Wagen/rot

_____

_____

5. Vase/gelb

_____

_____

The Verb *sein*

The verb **sein** is the German infinitive that means *be* in English. German infinitives end in **-n** or **-en**. English infinitives are sometimes preceded by the fragment word *to*: *be* or *to be*, *come* or *to come*. An infinitive is the base form of a verb. To use it in sentences, it has to be *conjugated*. That word simply means that specific endings are used with specific personal pronouns. Let's look at the conjugation of *be* in English. You'll notice that the verb *be* does not appear in this *irregular* conjugation:

	Singular	Plural
First person:	*I am*	*we are*
Second person:	*you are*	*you are*
Third person:	*he is*	*they are*
	she is	
	it is	

You could say *I are* instead of *I am* and be understood, but the conjugation illustrates which verb is appropriate for the pronoun *I*.

Now let's look at the conjugation of the German verb **sein**, which also is an irregular conjugation:

	Singular		**Plural**	
First person:	ich bin	*I am*	wir sind	*we are*
Second person:	du bist	*you are*	ihr seid	*you are*
	Sie sind	*you are*	Sie sind	*you are*
Third person:	er ist	*he is*	sie sind	*they are*
	sie ist	*she is*		
	es ist	*it is*		

This chapter has stressed the use of **ist** in sentences. Now let's look at how the other personal pronouns are used with the verb **sein**.

Say It Out Loud

*Say each sentence out loud, paying attention to the verb **sein** and the personal pronouns:*

Bin ich in Hamburg?	*Am I in Hamburg?*
Nein, du bist in Berlin.	*No, you are in Berlin.*
Er ist mein Freund.	*He is my friend.*
Ist sie Ihre Freundin?	*Is she your girlfriend?*
Ist Ihr Hemd grün?	*Is the shirt green?*
Ja, es ist grün.	*Yes, it is green.*
Sind Sie zu Hause, Frau Bauer?	*Are you at home, Ms. Bauer?*
Nein, ich bin im Park.	*No, I'm at the park.*
Wo sind wir?	*Where are we?*
Wir sind in der Küche.	*We are in the kitchen.*
Ihr seid im Garten.	*You are in the garden.*
Sind sie klein oder groß?	*Are they little or big?*
Sie sind klein.	*They are little.*

Wondering About This? *du, ihr,* and *Sie*

We need to clear up any confusion about **du**, **ihr**, and **Sie** with a capital **S** and **sie** with a small **s**.

All three pronouns (**du**, **ihr**, **Sie**) mean *you* in modern English. There was a time when English had other forms for this second person pronoun: *thou, thee,* and *ye*. But today English always uses the plural form of *you* for both singular and plural meanings. That's why *you* is always followed by a plural verb, such as *are*.

German still has more than one pronoun in the second person. **Du** is always singular and informal and is used with close friends, children, and family members. **Ihr** is the plural of **du**. **Sie** is always formal and can be singular or plural, just like *you*. It is used with strangers, people of authority, and just to be polite.

The pronoun **Sie** is never confused with **sie**, because of the way it is used. The pronoun **sie** with a singular verb (**ist**) always means *she* or *it*, and **sie** with a plural verb (**sind**) always means *they*. Both are spelled with a small **s** except at the beginning of a sentence.

Perhaps it seems a bit complicated, but in time it becomes quite natural and easy to use.

Nouns are either third person singular or third person plural. That means that they use only the conjugated forms **ist** or **sind** of the infinitive **sein**. For example:

Die Frau **ist** zu Hause.	*The woman is at home.*
Thomas und Sonja **sind** zu Hause.	*Thomas and Sonja are at home.*

Say It Out Loud

Say each sentence out loud, paying attention to the questions and their answers:

Ist Herr Braun in München?	*Is Mr. Brown in Munich?*
Nein, er ist in Heidelberg.	*No, he is in Heidelberg.*
Wo bin ich?	*Where am I?*
Du bist im Keller.	*You are in the cellar.*
Sind Sie Richterin, Frau Bauer?	*Are you a judge, Ms. Bauer?*
Nein, ich bin Lehrerin.	*No, I am a teacher.*
Sind Erik und Monika Amerikaner?	*Are Erik and Monika Americans?*
Nein, sie sind Deutsche.	*No, they are Germans.*
Was sind das?	*What are those?*
Das sind deutsche Autos.	*Those are German cars.*
Kinder, wo seid ihr?	*Children, where are you?*
Wir sind im Garten.	*We are in the garden.*
Tina und Erik sind in Hamburg.	*Tina and Erik are in Hamburg.*
Ist Ihr Haus in Berlin?	*Is your house in Berlin?*
Die Kinder sind in der Küche.	*The children are in the kitchen.*

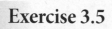

Exercise 3.5

Complete the sentences with the correct form of the verb **sein**. *For example:*

Er *ist* mein Freund.

1. _____ ihr Deutsche oder Amerikaner?

2. Ich _____ bei Erik.

3. Wo _____ es?

4. Du _____ jung.

5. Der Lehrer und die Lehrerin _____ alt.

6. Wir _____ im Keller.

7. Sie (*they*) _____ braun und weiß.

8. Ihr _____ groß.

9. _____ du Amerikanerin?

10. Guten Abend. _____ Sie Frau Keller?

You now know enough German to do some actual reading. It is always a good practice to say everything out loud, so as you read you may want to speak in a full voice. Most chapters will have a text to read in German, and none will be accompanied by a translation.

Let's Read

Read the following dialogue, and determine the meanings of the lines on your own.

TINA: Guten Tag, Andreas.

ANDREAS: Guten Tag, Tina.

TINA: Wer ist das?

ANDREAS: Das ist meine Cousine. Sie ist Amerikanerin.

TINA: Wo ist Thomas?

ANDREAS: Mein Bruder ist zu Hause.

TINA: Auf Wiedersehen.

ANDREAS: Tschüß, Tina.

Review Quiz 3

Choose the letter of the word or phrase that best completes each sentence:

1. Ist das Ihr _____?
   a. Mutter
   b. Vetter
   c. Cousine
   d. Lehrerin

2. Ist die Bluse blau? Nein _____ ist gelb.
   a. sie
   b. es
   c. er
   d. Sie

3. Wir _____ im Park.
   a. ist
   b. seid
   c. bin
   d. sind

4. Das ist meine Tante. _____ ist alt.
   a. Er
   b. Sie
   c. Ihr
   d. Es

5. Kinder, seid _____ im Garten?
   a. du
   b. Sie
   c. ihr
   d. mein

6. Wer ist _____?
   a. Sie
   b. das
   c. im
   d. ich

7. Wo _____ ich?
   a. bin
   b. ist
   c. seid
   d. bist

8. Mein Hemd ist weiß. _____ ist neu.
   a. Du
   b. Sie
   c. Ihr
   d. Es

9. Meine Freundin ist _____.
   a. Amerikanerin
   b. was
   c. Ihr Lehrer
   d. Kinder

10. _____ ist das?
    a. Sie sind
    b. Was
    c. Monika und Andreas
    d. Sein

New Vocabulary

alt	*old*
blau	*blue*
Bleistift (*m.*)	*pencil*
Bluse (*f.*)	*blouse*
braun	*brown*
Cousine (*f.*)	*cousin (female)*
dieser	*this*
Farbe (*f.*)	*color*
Fotoapparat (*m.*)	*camera*
Freundin (*f.*)	*girlfriend*
gelb	*yellow*
grün	*green*
Hut (*m.*)	*hat*
jeder	*each, every*
jener	*that*
jung	*young*
Kleid (*n.*)	*dress*
kurz	*short*
lang	*long*
Laptop (*n.*)	*laptop*
neu	*new*
rot	*red*
schön	*pretty, nice*
schwarz	*black*
Schwester (*f.*)	*sister*
sein (bin, bist, ist, sind, seid)	*be (am, are, is)*
Vetter (*m.*)	*cousin*
was	*what*
weiß	*white*
welcher	*which, what*
wer	*who*

4

Ein-Words, *haben*, and the Present Tense

This chapter illustrates the form and use of **ein**-words and possessive adjectives. The conjugation of the verb **haben** as well as other present tense verbs will be introduced.

Some questions that will be answered are:

✓ How are **ein-**words different from **der-**words?
✓ How does gender affect the possessive adjectives?
✓ How is **haben** conjugated?
✓ What are the conjugational endings of the regular present tense?

Ein-Words

In Chapter 2, you came face-to-face with **der**-words. Another category of words is called **ein**-words because they follow the pattern of the indefinite article **ein** (*a, an*). Just like **der**-words, the **ein**-words conform to the German rules of gender.

All masculine and neuter words use **ein** as their indefinite article. Let's look at some examples:

ein Apfel (der)	*an apple*
ein Bleistift (der)	*a pencil*
ein Mann (der)	*a man*
ein Student (der)	*a student*
ein Stuhl (der)	*a chair*
ein Buch (das)	*a book*

ein Kind (das)	*a child*
ein Sweatshirt (das)	*a sweatshirt*
ein Telefon (das)	*a telephone*
ein Tier (das)	*an animal*

The feminine definite article ends in **-e**. Likewise, the feminine indefinite article ends in **-e: eine** (*a, an*). Let's look at some feminine nouns accompanied by the indefinite article:

eine Tante (die)	*an aunt*
eine Zeitung (die)	*a newspaper*
eine Schule (die)	*a school*
eine Stadt (die)	*a city*
eine CD (die) tsay-day	*a CD*
eine Uhr (die)	*a clock*
eine Landkarte (die)	*a map*
eine Apfelsine (die)	*an orange*
eine Dame (die)	*a lady*
eine Großmutter (die)	*a grandmother*

Be aware that **ein/eine** also means *one*: **ein Buch** *a book/one book* and **eine Schule** *a school/one school*.

Say It Out Loud

*Say each sentence out loud, paying attention to the use of **ein** and **eine**:*

Ich habe eine Zeitung.	*I have a newspaper.*
Ich habe ein Sweatshirt.	*I have a sweatshirt.*
Ein Kind lernt Deutsch.	*A child is learning German.*
Ein Junge lernt Englisch.	*A boy is learning English.*
Ist das eine CD?	*Is that a CD?*
Eine Schule ist in dieser Straße.	*A school is on this street.*
Eine Bibliothek ist in dieser Straße.	*A library is on this street.*
Ein Student wohnt in dieser Straße.	*A student lives on this street.*
Eine Studentin wohnt hier.	*A (female) student lives here.*
Ein Apfel schmeckt gut.	*An apple tastes good.*
Eine Apfelsine schmeckt gut.	*An orange tastes good.*

Exercise 4.1

*Reword each noun with the appropriate indefinite article (**ein, eine**). For example:*

das Haus	*ein Haus*
1. der Student	_____
2. die Landkarte	_____
3. die CD	_____
4. das Mädchen	_____
5. der Stuhl	_____
6. das Tier	_____
7. die Stadt	_____
8. die Bibliothek	_____
9. das Telefon	_____
10. der Bleistift	_____

Say It Out Loud

*Read each sentence out loud, paying attention to the use of **ein** and **eine**:*

Schmeckt eine Apfelsine gut?	*Does an orange taste good?*
Schmeckt ein Apfel gut?	*Does an apple taste good?*
Eine Studentin lernt Deutsch.	*A student is learning German.*
Ein Student lernt Spanisch.	*A student is learning Spanish.*
Ist das eine Bibliothek?	*Is that a library?*
Nein, das ist eine Schule.	*No, that is a school.*
Ich habe eine Landkarte von Deutschland.	*I have a map of Germany.*
Ich habe eine deutsche Zeitung.	*I have a German newspaper.*
Eine Großmutter ist alt.	*A grandmother is old.*
Ist ein Großvater jung?	*Is a grandfather young?*
Nein, ein Großvater ist auch alt.	*No, a grandfather is also old.*
Ist ein Kind auch alt?	*Is a child also old?*
Nein, ein Kind ist jung.	*No, a child is young.*
Ein Pilot wohnt in dieser Straße.	*A pilot lives on this street.*
Eine junge Dame wohnt in dieser Straße.	*A young lady lives on this street.*

Kein

The adjective **kein/keine** (*no*, *not any*) is an **ein**-word and follows the pattern of **ein/eine**: **kein** modifies masculine and neuter nouns, and **keine** modifies feminine nouns. For example:

Ist das ein Park?	*Is that a park?*
Nein, das ist kein Park.	*No, that is not a park.*
Ist das eine Apfelsine?	*Is that an orange?*
Nein, das ist keine Apfelsine.	*No, that is not an orange.*
Haben Sie ein Telefon?	*Do you have a telephone?*
Nein, ich habe kein Telefon.	*No, I have no (don't have a) telephone.*
Haben Sie eine Uhr?	*Do you have a clock?*
Nein, ich habe keine Uhr.	*No, I have no (don't have a) clock.*

Step 1: Possessive Adjectives

Possessive adjectives modify nouns and tell to whom something belongs. In English, a specific possessive adjective refers to a specific personal pronoun. For example:

	Singular Pronoun/Possessive	Plural Pronoun/Possessive
First person:	*I my*	*we our*
Second person:	*you your*	*you your*
Third person:	*he his*	*they their*
	she her	
	it its	

Singular nouns use *his*, *her*, and *its* according to the gender of the noun. All plural nouns use *their*.

You use the appropriate possessive adjective to tell to whom something belongs. For example:

***My** book is there. (**I** own the book.)*

***Your** house is big. (**You** own the house.)*

***Her** blouse is nice. (**She** owns the blouse.)*

German possessive adjectives work in the same way, while conforming to the German rules of gender usage. It is important to remember that the possessive adjectives are **ein**-words. They modify nouns just like **ein/eine** and **kein/keine**. The German possessive adjectives are:

	Singular **Pronoun/Possessive**		**Plural** **Pronoun/Possessive**	
First person:	ich mein	*my*	wir unser	*our*
Second person:	du dein	*your*	ihr euer	*your*
	Sie Ihr (formal)	*your*	Sie Ihr (formal)	*your*
Third person:	er sein	*his, its*	sie ihr	*their*
	sie ihr	*her, its*		
	es sein	*its, his, her*		

Say It Out Loud

*Say each sentence out loud, paying attention to how the possessive adjectives use the same gender endings as **ein/eine** and **kein/keine**:*

Wessen Apfelsine ist das?	*Whose orange is that?*
Meine Mutter ist Lehrerin.	*My mother is a teacher.*
Ist deine Cousine in der Stadt?	*Is your cousin in the city?*
Wo ist sein Buch?	*Where is his book?*
Ist ihre Zeitung in der Küche?	*Is her newspaper in the kitchen?*
Wessen Landkarte ist das?	*Whose map is that?*
Unser Telefon ist kaputt.	*Our phone is broken.*
Eure Großmutter ist sehr alt.	*Your grandmother is very old.*
Ist ihr Bleistift kaputt?	*Is your pencil broken?*
Wessen Uhr ist das?	*Whose clock is that?*

The word **wessen** (*whose*) requires no ending changes for gender. Look at the following examples:

Wessen Bruder ist das? (masculine)	*Whose brother is that?*
Wessen Haus ist das? (neuter)	*Whose house is that?*
Wessen Bluse ist das? (feminine)	*Whose blouse is that?*

When the possessive adjective **Ihr** is capitalized, it refers only to **Sie** and means *your*. When the possessive adjective **ihr** is written with a small **i**, it can mean *her* or *their*, and the difference in meaning is determined by how the possessive adjective is used in a sentence. For example:

Sie ist zu Hause. Ihr Vater ist mein Freund.	She is at home. **Her** father is my friend.

In this example, **ihr** refers to singular **sie** (*she*) and therefore means *her*. Let's look at another example:

Sie sind zu Hause. Ihr Vater ist mein Freund.	They are at home. **Their** father is my friend.

In this example, **ihr** refers to plural **sie** (*they*) and therefore means *their*.

Take note that the feminine of **euer** drops the **e** that stands before **r** and becomes **eure** with an **-e** ending added, but the feminine of **unser** just adds the ending **-e**: **unsere**.

Exercise 4.2

*Reword each noun with the appropriate definite article (**der**, **die**, **das**) and the possessive adjective provided in parentheses. For example:*

ein Haus (mein)	*das Haus*	*mein Haus*
1. ein Student (unser)	_____	_____
2. eine Landkarte (sein)	_____	_____
3. eine CD (dein)	_____	_____
4. ein Kleid (Ihr)	_____	_____
5. ein Stuhl (ihr *her*)	_____	_____
6. ein Tier (ihr *their*)	_____	_____
7. eine Stadt (euer)	_____	_____
8. eine Bibliothek (unser)	_____	_____
9. einTelefon (mein)	_____	_____
10. ein Bleistift (dein)	_____	_____

Step 2: The Verb *haben*

The verb **haben** means *have* and is very important because it is a *high-frequency* verb and has many uses. In most cases, it is used in the same way as the English verb *have*: it is both a transitive verb that means that someone possesses something, or it can act as an auxiliary. This chapter deals only with the transitive verb. Auxiliaries will be taken up in a later chapter.

The present tense conjugation of **haben** is only slightly irregular. Let's look at the present tense of **haben**:

	Singular		**Plural**	
First person:	ich habe	*I have*	wir haben	*we have*
Second person:	du hast	*you have*	ihr habt	*you have*
	Sie haben	*you have*	Sie haben	*you have*
Third person:	er hat	*he has*	sie haben	*they have*
	sie hat	*she has*		
	es hat	*it has*		

Interestingly, the conjugation of **haben** is similar to the conjugation of *have* in older English. Look at how similar the second and third person singular conjugations are of **haben** and old English *have*: **du hast** *thou hast* and **er hat** *he hath*. It is easy to see that English and German are brother and sister languages and once shared many of the same words and grammar.

Say It Out Loud

*Say each sentence out loud, paying attention to the conjugation of the verb **haben**:*

Ich habe eine neue Landkarte.	*I have a new map.*
Du hast kein Geld.	*You have no money.*
Er hat meine Zeitung.	*He has my newspaper.*
Hat sie ein Kleid?	*Does she have a dress?*
Wo ist das Kind? Es hat mein Buch.	*Where is the child? He has my book.*
Wir haben keine Zeit.	*We have no time.*
Habt ihr eine Apfelsine?	*Do you have an orange?*
Sie haben kein Bier.	*They don't have any beer.*
Haben Sie eine Schwester?	*Do you have a sister?*
Nein, ich habe keine Schwester.	*No, I don't have a sister.*

If the subject of the verb **haben** is a noun rather than a personal pronoun, use **hat** and **haben** as its conjugation because nouns are either third person singular or plural. For example:

Er hat kein Geld.	*He has no money.*
Mein Freund hat kein Geld.	*My friend has no money.*
Wessen Bluse hat sie?	*Whose blouse does she have?*
Wessen Bluse hat Tanja?	*Whose blouse does Tanja have?*
Sie haben keine Zeit.	*They have no time.*
Tina und Erik haben keine Zeit.	*Tina and Erik have no time.*

Exercise 4.3

*In the blank provided, give the correct conjugation of **haben** for the subjects shown. For example:*

Er *hat* mein Hemd.

1. Sie (*she*) _____ eine neue Bluse.

2. Wir _____ kein Geld.

3. Ich _____ eine Schwester.

4. Herr Braun _____ keine Zeit.

5. _____ du keine Landkarte?

6. Herr Schmidt und Frau Keller _____ keine Kinder.

7. _____ Sie eine Zeitung oder ein Buch?

8. Wo ist das Mädchen? Es _____ mein Sweatshirt.

9. _____ sie (*they*) kein Bier?

10. Unsere Großmutter _____ kein Telefon.

11. _____ Andreas ein neues Hemd?

12. _____ ihr kein Geld?

13. Du _____ seine CD.

14. Mein Vetter und meine Cousine _____ ein Haus in Berlin.

15. Ich _____ eine Uhr im Keller.

Say It Out Loud

Read each sentence out loud, paying attention to the questions and answers:

Haben Sie eine Zeitung, Herr Bauer?	*Do you have a newspaper, Mr. Bauer?*
Nein, ich habe keine Zeitung.	*No, I don't have a newspaper.*
Hat Frau Bauer eine Zeitung?	*Does Ms. Bauer have a newspaper?*
Nein, sie ist nicht zu Hause.	*No, she is not at home.*
Hast du ein Buch?	*Do you have a book?*
Ja, ich habe ein Buch.	*Yes, I have a book.*
Hat der Student auch ein Buch?	*Does the student have a book, too?*
Nein, er hat kein Buch.	*No, he doesn't have a book.*
Was habt ihr, Kinder?	*What do you have, children?*
Wir haben eine Katze.	*We have a cat.*
Sie heißt Muschi.	*Her name is Muschi.*

Wondering About This? Asking Questions

You have probably noticed that German asks questions in a slightly different way than in English. In English, a question that uses the verb *be* begins with a conjugation of that verb followed by the subject:

Is he a judge?

Are these people your friends?

With most other verbs, a form of *do* is used as the auxiliary of a verb to form a question:

Do you have enough money?

Does that girl live on this street?

German is simpler. Questions are formed by placing the conjugated verb in front of the subject:

Ist er Richter?	*Is he a judge?*
Haben Sie kein Geld?	*Don't you have any money?*
Wohnt der Junge hier?	*Does the boy live here?*

The same kind of word order is used if the question begins with an interrogative word (**was, wo, wessen**):

Was hast du im Keller?	*What do you have in the cellar?*
Wo wohnt Frau Schneider?	*Where does Ms. Schneider live?*
Wessen Haus ist das?	*Whose house is that?*

Present Tense

So far, you have learned the present tense of the verbs **sein** and **haben**. Now it is time to meet other verbs and their present tense conjugation. Some verbs in the present tense have minor irregularities, but in this chapter you will encounter only verbs that follow a regular pattern.

The conjugational endings for the verb **haben** are, for the most part, the same endings for other verbs in the present tense. They are:

	Singular	**Plural**
First person:	ich -e	wir -en
Second person:	du -st	ihr -t
	Sie -en	Sie -en
Third person:	er -t	sie -en
	sie -t	
	es -t	

Don't forget that **wer** and **was** are third person singular pronouns and follow the ending patterns of **er**, **sie**, and **es**.

The infinitive **wohnen** means *live* or *reside*. In order to add conjugational endings to the verb, first the infinitive ending **-en** must be removed, leaving only the stem of the verb **wohn-**. The present tense conjugational endings are added to this stem. This verb in its present tense conjugation looks like this:

	Singular		**Plural**	
First person:	ich wohne	*I live*	wir wohnen	*we live*
Second person:	du wohnst	*you live*	ihr wohnt	*you live*
	Sie wohnen	*you live*	Sie wohnen	*you live*
Third person:	er wohnt	*he lives*	sie wohnen	*they live*
	sie wohnt	*she lives*		
	es wohnt	*it lives*		

Let's practice this verb with places where someone might live.

Say It Out Loud

Say each sentence out loud, paying attention to the conjugational endings used:

Ich wohne in der Schillerstraße.	*I live on Schiller Street.*
Wohnst du auch in der Schillerstraße?	*Do you also live on Schiller Street?*

Er wohnt in der Schweiz.	*He lives in Switzerland.*
Wohnt sie auch in der Schweiz?	*Does she also live in Switzerland?*
Das Mädchen? Es wohnt in Amerika.	*The girl? She lives in America.*
Wir wohnen in Deutschland.	*We live in Germany.*
Wohnt ihr in Österreich?	*Do you live in Austria?*
Nein, wir wohnen in Italien.	*No, we live in Italy.*
Wohnen Sie bei Peter?	*Do you live at Peter's house?*
Die Kinder? Sie wohnen bei Tante Luise.	*The children? They live at Aunt Luise's house.*
Wer wohnt oben?	*Who lives upstairs?*

A brief list of infinitives follows. Each one follows the conjugational pattern in the present tense of **wohnen**:

fliegen	*fly*
gehen	*go (on foot)*
hören	*hear*
kaufen	*buy*
lernen	*learn*
machen	*do, make*
schreiben	*write*
trinken	*drink*
verkaufen	*sell*
verstehen	*understand*

In the case of each verb, the infinitive ending **-en** is dropped, which leaves the stem of the verb. Then the conjugational endings appropriate to the personal pronouns are added to the stem: **-e**, **-st**, **-t**, and **-en**. Let's look at a couple of examples:

	fliegen		**lernen**	
ich	fliege	*I fly*	lerne	*I learn*
du	fliegst	*you fly*	lernst	*you learn*
er, sie, es	fliegt	*he, she, it flies*	lernt	*he, she, it learns*
wir	fliegen	*we fly*	lernen	*we learn*
ihr	fliegt	*you fly*	lernt	*you learn*
Sie	fliegen	*you fly*	lernen	*you learn*
sie *pl.*	fliegen	*they fly*	lernen	*they learn*

Note that when the pronoun **sie** is followed by *s.*, it stands for *singular*, and the pronoun means *she*. When the pronoun **sie** is followed by *pl.*, it stands for *plural*, and the pronoun means *they*. These abbreviations will be used with the pronoun **sie** to provide you with the appropriate meaning. You will see **sie** *s.* and **sie** *pl.*

A Useful Little Phrase

The verb **gehen** means *go*. It is used idiomatically to ask how someone is. If you are on an informal basis with someone (**du, ihr**), you ask: **Wie geht's?** *How are you?* If you have a formal relationship with someone (**Sie**), you ask: **Wie geht es Ihnen?** *How are you?* There are several logical responses:

Wie geht es Ihnen, Herr Benz?	*How are you, Mr. Benz?*
Es geht mir gut, danke. Und Ihnen?	*I am well, thanks. And you?*
Wie geht es Ihnen, Frau Keller?	*How are you, Ms. Keller?*
Es geht mir schlecht. Und Ihnen?	*I'm not doing well. And you?*
Wie geht's, Andreas?	*How are you, Andreas?*
Danke, sehr gut.	*Thanks, very well.*
Wie geht's, Gabi?	*How are you, Gabi?*
Nicht schlecht.	*Not bad.*

Say It Out Loud

Read each sentence out loud, paying attention to the present tense conjugation:

Thomas fliegt nach Berlin.	*Thomas is flying to Berlin.*
Wir fliegen nach Hause.	*We are flying home.*
Gehst du auch nach Hause?	*Are you going home, too?*
Ich gehe mit Andreas und Monika.	*I am going with Andreas and Monika.*
Hören Sie Radio, Frau Keller?	*Are you listening to the radio, Ms. Keller?*
Ich höre Musik.	*I hear music.*
Die Richterin kauft ein Kleid.	*The judge is buying a dress.*
Was kauft ihr, Kinder?	*Children, what are you buying?*
Lernen sie Deutsch oder Spanisch?	*Are they learning German or Spanish?*
Wir lernen Italienisch.	*We are learning Italian.*

Was machst du?	*What are you doing?*
Ich mache nichts.	*I'm not doing anything.* (*I do nothing.*)
Tina schreibt eine Postkarte.	*Tina is writing a postcard.*
Ich schreibe nichts.	*I'm not writing anything.* (*I write nothing.*)
Was trinken Sie, Herr Bauer?	*What are you drinking, Mr. Bauer?*
Ich trinke Bier. Was trinkst du?	*I'm drinking beer. What are you drinking?*
Ich trinke nichts.	*I'm not drinking anything.*
Er verkauft sein Auto.	*He sells his car.*
Wer verkauft dieses große Haus?	*Who is selling this big house?*
Verstehst du Deutsch?	*Do you understand German?*
Ich verstehe Deutsch aber nicht gut.	*I understand German but not well.*

Wondering About This? Translating the Present Tense

English has a complication in the present tense that German does not. English has two ways to express a present tense meaning: one describes a habitual or repeated action, and the other describes an incomplete or ongoing action. For example:

Habitual or Repeated Action

I go to school.	This is what I do every day.
She cooks supper every evening.	This is what she does every evening.
Dad works as a bus driver.	This is his daily occupation.

Incomplete or Ongoing Action

I am going to school.	I am on my way there but have not yet arrived.
She is cooking supper.	She is in the process of making supper, which is not yet ready.
Dad is working as a bus driver.	This is his temporary job. His customary profession is real estate agent.

German has only one present tense formation, which has already been introduced. The English translation, however, can be either of the English versions, depending upon what the English speaker wishes to infer. For example:

Sie kauft eine Bluse.	*She buys a blouse. She is buying a blouse.*
Er lernt Deutsch.	*He learns German. He is learning German.*

Exercise 4.4

Fill in the blank with the verb provided in parentheses with the appropriate conjugational ending. For example:

(haben) Der Mann *hat* kein Geld.

1. (sein) Ihr _____ in der Schillerstraße.

2. (hören) _____ Sie Radio?

3. (gehen) Ich _____ nach Hause.

4. (fliegen) Herr Bauer und Frau Schmidt _____ nach Hamburg.

5. (kaufen) _____ du ein Sweatshirt?

6. (verkaufen) Der kleine Junge _____ eine Katze.

7. (schreiben) Wer _____ eine Postkarte?

8. (trinken) Das Kind _____ kein Bier.

9. (verstehen) _____ sie *s.* Deutsch oder Englisch?

10. (lernen) Was _____ sie *pl.* in der Schule?

The word **kein/keine** (*no/not any*) is an adjective. It is used differently from the adverb **nicht** (*not*). **Kein/keine** responds negatively to the use of **ein/eine**. For example:

Ist das *eine* Universität?	*Is that a university?*
Nein, das ist *keine* Universität.	*No, that is not a university.*
Das ist eine Schule.	*That is a school.*

Nicht is the negative adverb that negates a verb or phrase. For example:

Ist Thomas zu Hause?	*Is Thomas at home?*
Nein, er ist <u>nicht</u> zu Hause.	*No, he is not at home.*
Fliegen Sie nach Frankfurt?	*Are you flying to Frankfurt?*
Nein, ich fliege <u>nicht</u> nach Frankfurt.	*No, I am not flying to Frankfurt.*

A further explanation of **nicht** will be continued in other chapters.

Let's Read

Read the following text and determine its meaning on your own:

Das Mädchen ist meine Freundin. Sie heißt Marianne Schiller. Sie wohnt in Heidelberg in Deutschland. Sie hat eine Schwester. Ihre Schwester heißt Tina. Tina wohnt nicht zu Hause. Sie wohnt bei Frau Gretel Bauer. Frau Bauer ist ihre Tante. Marianne versteht kein Englisch, aber sie versteht Italienisch und Spanisch.

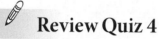

Review Quiz 4

Choose the letter of the word or phrase that best completes each sentence.

1. Ist das dein _____?

   a. Schule

   b. Bleistift

   c. Schwester

   d. Universität

2. Mein Bruder wohnt _____ Schweiz.

   a. im

   b. in der

   c. nach

   d. zu Hause

3. Herr Schneider, ist diese junge Dame _____ Frau?

   a. eure

   b. dein

   c. ihr

   d. Ihre

4. Wir haben kein _____.

   a. Bier

   b. Kinder

   c. CDs

   d. Richterin

5. _____ ihr nicht nach München?

   a. Wo wohnt

   b. Fliegt

   c. Kauft

   d. Verkaufen

6. _____ du keine Zeit?

   a. Lernst

   b. Haben

   c. Bin

   d. Hast

7. Meine Schwester ist _____ zu Hause.

     a. nicht   c. kein

     b. nach   d. keine

8. Ich _____ kein Deutsch.

     a. verstehe   c. mache

     b. wohne   d. verkaufe

9. Ein Apfel _____ gut.

     a. machen   c. machst

     b. schmecken   d. schmeckt

10. _____ Radio.

     a. Haben sie   c. Was macht

     b. Ich höre   d. Ihr schreibt

New Vocabulary

Apfel (*m.*)	*apple*
Apfelsine (*f.*)	*orange*
Bibliothek (*f.*)	*library*
Bleistift (*m.*)	*pencil*
Buch (*n.*)	*book*
CD (*f.*)	*CD*
Dame (*f.*)	*lady*
dein	*your (informal)*
Deutsch	*German*
Englisch	*English*
euer	*your (informal plural)*
Geld	*money*
Großmutter (*f.*)	*grandmother*
gut	*good, well*
haben	*have*
Herr (*m.*)	*Mr., gentleman*
ihr	*her, its, their*
Junge (*m.*)	*boy*
kaputt	*broken, kaput*
kein	*no, not any*

Kind (*n.*)	*child*
Landkarte (*f.*)	*map*
lernen	*learn*
Mann (*m.*)	*man*
nicht	*not*
schlecht	*bad, badly*
schmecken	*taste*
Schule (*f.*)	*school*
sehr	*very*
sein	*his, its*
Stadt (*f.*)	*city*
Student (*m.*)	*student*
Stuhl (*m.*)	*chair*
Sweatshirt (*n.*)	*sweatshirt*
Tante (*f.*)	*aunt*
Telefon (*n.*)	*telephone*
Tier (*n.*)	*animal*
Uhr (*f.*)	*clock*
unser	*our*
wessen	*whose*
Wie geht es Ihnen?	*How are you? (formal)*
Wie geht's?	*How are you? (informal)*
wohnen	*live, reside*
Zeit (*f.*)	*time*
Zeitung (*f.*)	*newspaper*

5

Irregular Present Tense and *werden*

This chapter continues the introduction of the German present tense. The conjugation of the verb **werden** and the irregular present tense will be introduced. The regular present tense will be reviewed.

Some questions that will be answered are:

✓ How does German form the irregularities of the present tense?
✓ What pronouns are affected by these irregularities?
✓ How is **werden** conjugated?
✓ How is **werden** used with the impersonal **es** (*it*)?

Irregular Present Tense

Irregularities occur not only in German but also in English. The two most common irregularities in the English present tense are *be* and *have*. For example:

be		*have*	
I am	*we are*	*I have*	*we have*
you are	*you are*	*you have*	*you have*
he/she/it is	*they are*	*he/she/it has*	*they have*

Clearly, the English verb *be* has the more irregular conjugation, consisting of three changes to the verb (*am*, *are*, *is*). The verb *have* has only two forms (*have*, *has*).

Present tense irregularities in German occur in a similar way. You have already encountered two of them in Chapters 3 and 4 with the verbs **sein** and **haben**:

sein

First person:	ich bin	*I am*	wir sind	*we are*
Second person:	du bist	*you are*	ihr seid	*you are*
	Sie sind	*you are*	Sie sind	*you are*
Third person:	er ist	*he is*	sie sind	*they are*
	sie ist	*she is*		
	es ist	*it is*		

haben

First person:	ich habe	*I have*	wir haben	*we have*
Second person:	du hast	*you have*	ihr habt	*you have*
	Sie haben	*you have*	Sie haben	*you have*
Third person:	er hat	*he has*	sie haben	*they have*
	sie hat	*she has*		
	es hat	*it has*		

Before we look at some present tense irregularities, let's review the present tense conjugational endings that will occur even when a verb has an irregularity. The verb **kommen** means *come*. In order to conjugate this verb in the present tense, drop the infinitive ending **-en** to form the stem **komm-**. Then the endings appropriate for each person are added to the stem. Look at the following sentences that illustrate the present tense conjugational endings:

Ich komme aus Amerika.	*I come from America.*
Du kommst aus Deutschland.	*You come from Germany.*
Er kommt aus Österreich.	*He comes from Austria.*
Sie kommt aus Italien.	*She comes from Italy.*
Wir kommen nach Hause.	*We come home.*
Kommen Sie mit?	*Are you coming along?*
Kommen sie nach Hause?	*Are they coming home?*
Wer kommt mit?	*Who is coming along?*

Step 1: Irregularities Formed with an *Umlaut*

There are three types of present tense conjugational irregularities. One of these types adds an umlaut to the stem of the verb, *but only with the second and third persons singular.* The conjugational endings added to the stem are identical to the regular conjugational endings. Two verbs that add an umlaut in the present tense are **fahren** (*drive, travel*) and **laufen** (*run*). Look at their formation in the present tense:

	fahren		**laufen**	
ich	fahre	*I drive*	laufe	*I run*
du	fährst	*you drive*	läufst	*you run*
er	fährt	*he drives*	läuft	*he runs*
sie	fährt	*she drives*	läuft	*she runs*
es	fährt	*he/she/it drives*	läuft	*he/she/it runs*
wir	fahren	*we drive*	laufen	*we run*
Sie	fahren	*you drive*	laufen	*you run*
ihr	fahrt	*you drive*	lauft	*you run*
sie	fahren	*they drive*	laufen	*they run*
wer	fährt	*who drives*	läuft	*who runs*

Say It Out Loud

Say each sentence out loud, paying attention to the irregularities that occur:

Fahren Sie nach Hause?	*Are you driving home?*
Nein, ich fahre nach München.	*No, I'm driving to Munich.*
Fährt Ihre Schwester mit?	*Is your sister going (driving) along?*
Nein, sie fährt nicht mit.	*No, she's not going along.*
Wohin fährt sie?	*Where is she driving to?*
Sie fährt nach Polen.	*She's driving to Poland.*
Wir fahren nach Frankreich.	*We're driving to France.*
Fahrt ihr mit dem Auto?	*Are you going (driving) by car?*
Nein, wir fahren mit dem Bus.	*No, we're going by bus.*
Wohin laufen die Kinder?	*Where are the children running?*

Thomas läuft in den Garten.	*Thomas is running into the garden.*
Aber Tina läuft nach Hause.	*But Tina is running home.*
Wohin läufst du?	*Where are you running?*
Ich laufe zum Park.	*I'm running to the park.*
Wer läuft zum Cafe?	*Who's running to the café?*
Der Kellner läuft zum Cafe.	*The waiter is running to the café.*

In German, **wo** can occur in more than one form, for example, **wo** and **wohin**. **Wo** is used to ask *where someone or something is located*:

Wo ist dein Bruder?	*Where is your brother?*
Wo ist die Universität?	*Where is the university?*

Wohin is used to ask *where to* or *to what destination*. It accompanies *verbs of motion* that describe movement from one place to another. Three commonly used verbs of motion are **gehen** *go*, **fahren** *drive*, and **laufen** *run*. Let's look at some example sentences:

Wohin gehen Sie?	*Where are you going? (What is your destination?)*
Wohin fährt der Mann?	*Where is the man driving? (What is the man's destination?)*
Wohin laufen die Kinder?	*Where are the children running? (What is their destination?)*

Exercise 5.1

In the blank provided, give the conjugation of the infinitive given in parentheses for the subject of the sentence. For example:

(haben) *Hast* du die Uhr?

1. (gehen) Der Pilot _____ zum Cafe.

2. (fahren) Ich _____ nicht nach Berlin.

3. (laufen) Wohin _____ die Studentin?

4. (sein) Ich _____ sein Freund.

5. (fahren) Wir _____ nach Frankreich.

6. (kommen) Wer _____ mit?

7. (haben) Meine Schwester _____ keine Kinder.

8. (laufen) _____ du zum Park?

9. (kommen) Erik und Monika _____ auch mit.

10. (fahren) _____ ihr mit dem Bus?

11. (haben) Wer _____ mein Buch?

12. (sein) _____ das Mädchen Amerikanerin?

13. (kommen) Ich _____ aus Deutschland.

14. (fahren) Du _____ mit dem Auto.

15. (laufen) Wohin _____ der Junge?

Say It Out Loud

Read each sentence out loud, paying attention to the present tense irregularities:

Wo wohnt Frau Schneider?	*Where does Ms. Schneider live?*
Sie wohnt in der Hauptstadt.	*She lives in the capital.*
Fahren Sie nach Berlin?	*Are you driving to Berlin?*
Ja, ich fahre mit dem Auto nach Berlin.	*Yes, I'm going by car to Berlin.*
Meine Tante wohnt auch da.	*My aunt lives there, too.*
Wohin fährst du, Lars?	*Where are you driving, Lars?*
Ich fahre nach Paris.	*I'm driving to Paris.*
Meine Freunde wohnen da.	*My friends live there.*
Woher kommen sie? Aus Frankreich?	*Where are they from? From France?*
Nein, sie kommen aus Österreich.	*No, they come from Austria.*
Wie heißt der neue Student?	*What is the new student's name?*
Er heißt Simon Neufeld.	*His name is Simon Neufeld.*
Woher kommt er?	*Where does he come from?*
Er kommt aus Amerika.	*He comes from America.*
Aber seine Familie ist deutsch.	*But his family is German.*

Wondering About This? *wo, wohin,* and *woher*

Did you notice another formation of **wo** in the previous practice? There are three forms with **wo**: **wo**, **wohin**, and **woher**. Each has a specific function: *location*, *movement to a place*, and *movement away from a place*. Let's look at some examples:

Location

Wo ist die Lampe?	*Where is the lamp? (Where is it located?)*
Wo wohnt Sonja?	*Where does Tina live? (What is the location of her residence?)*

Movement to a Place

Wohin gehen Sie?	*Where are you going? (To what place are you going?)*
Wohin läuft das Kind?	*Where is the child running? (To what place is the child running?)*

Movement Away from a Place

Woher kommt diese Frau?	*Where does this woman come from? (From what place does she come?)*
Woher kommst du?	*Where do you come from? (From what place do you come?)*

Step 2: Irregularities Formed with a Shift from *-e-* to *-i-*

The second type of present tense irregularity occurs with certain verbs that have the vowel **e** in their stem. That vowel shifts to an **i** but only in the second and third persons singular. Some verbs with this kind of irregularity are:

Infinitive		Shift from -e- to -*i*-
brechen	*break*	bricht
essen	*eat*	isst
geben	*give*	gibt
helfen	*help*	hilft
nehmen	*take*	nimmt
sprechen	*speak*	spricht
vergessen	*forget*	vergisst

Let's look at the full conjugation of three of these verbs. One of the examples is **nehmen** (*take*) that also changes the **h** to another **m** in the second and third persons singular:

	essen		**geben**		**nehmen**	
ich	esse	*I eat*	gebe	*I give*	nehme	*I take*
du	isst	*you eat*	gibst	*you give*	nimmst	*you take*
er	isst	*he eats*	gibt	*he gives*	nimmt	*he takes*
sie	isst	*she eats*	gibt	*she gives*	nimmt	*she takes*
es	isst	*he/she/it eats*	gibt	*he/she/it gives*	nimmt	*he/she/it takes*
wir	essen	*we eat*	geben	*we give*	nehmen	*we take*
Sie	essen	*you eat*	geben	*you give*	nehmen	*you take*
ihr	esst	*you eat*	gebt	*you give*	nehmt	*you take*
sie	essen	*they eat*	geben	*they give*	nehmen	*they take*
wer	isst	*who eats*	gibt	*who gives*	nimmt	*who takes*

 In the second person singular (**du**), the conjugation ending **-st** is not added to the stem of the verb if the stem ends in **-s**, **-ss**, **-z**, or **-ß**. Only a **-t** is added to the stem. For example:

essen	du isst	*you eat*
heißen	du heißt	*your name is*
küssen	du küsst	*you kiss*
reizen	du reizt	*you annoy*

Say It Out Loud

*Say each sentence out loud, paying attention to the vowel shift from **-e-** to **-i-**:*

Ich esse gern im Park.	*I like eating in the park.*
Was isst du gern?	*What do you like to eat?*
Ich esse gern Bratwurst.	*I like eating bratwurst.*
Essen Sie gern im Restaurant?	*Do you eat in a restaurant?*
Nein, wir essen gern zu Hause.	*No, we like eating at home.*
Wo isst Ihr Sohn gern?	*Where does your son like to eat?*
Mein Sohn isst gern in der Küche.	*My son likes to eat in the kitchen.*

Sprichst du gern Englisch?	*Do you like speaking English?*
Nein, ich spreche gern Deutsch.	*No, I like speaking German.*
Was nimmt der Mann?	*What is the man taking?*
Der Mann nimmt eine Apfelsine.	*The man is taking an orange.*
Wer hilft Thomas?	*Who is helping Thomas?*
Niemand hilft Thomas.	*No one is helping Thomas.*
Unsere Tochter bricht sich den Finger.	*Our daughter breaks her finger.*
Herr Braun vergisst sein Geld.	*Mr. Braun forgets his money.*

The word **gern** is used idiomatically to indicate that someone is *fond of* doing something or *likes* doing something. In a statement, it follows the verb; in a question, it follows the subject. Let's look at a couple more examples:

Ich lerne gern Italienisch.	*I like learning Italian.*
Er trinkt gern Kaffee.	*He likes drinking coffee.*
Sprichst du gern Deutsch?	*Do you like speaking German?*
Wir fahren gern nach Hamburg.	*We like driving to Hamburg.*

When **gern** is paired with the verb **haben**, the general meaning is *like*, and the person or object that someone likes is followed by **gern**. For example:

Monika hat Simon gern.	*Monika likes Simon.*
Ich habe Bier nicht gern.	*I don't like beer.*

Step 3: Irregularities Formed with a Shift from *-e-* to *-ie-*

This irregularity is similar to the previous one. The vowel **-e-** in the stem shifts to **-ie-** in the irregular present tense conjugation. Again, this occurs only in the second and third persons singular. Here are some verbs that follow this pattern:

Infinitive		**Shift from -e- to -ie-**
befehlen	*order*	befiehlt
empfehlen	*recommend*	empfiehlt
geschehen	*happen*	geschieht
lesen	*read*	liest
sehen	*see*	sieht
stehlen	*steal*	stiehlt

The verb **geschehen** is used only with third person subjects because only *it* or *events* can happen. For example:

Es geschieht jeden Tag.	*It happens every day.*
Was geschieht im Winter?	*What happens in winter?*
Hier geschehen keine Unfälle.	*Accidents don't happen here.*

Let's look at the full conjugation of three of these verbs:

	befehlen		**sehen**		**stehlen**	
ich	befehlen	*I order*	sehe	*I see*	stehle	*I steal*
du	befiehlst	*you order*	siehst	*you see*	stiehlst	*you steal*
er	befiehlt	*he orders*	siehst	*he sees*	stiehlt	*he steals*
sie	befiehlt	*she orders*	siehst	*she sees*	stiehlt	*she steals*
es	befiehlt	*he/she/it orders*	siehst	*he/she/it sees*	stiehlt	*he/she/it steals*
wir	befehlen	*we order*	sehen	*we see*	stehlen	*we steal*
Sie	befehlen	*you order*	sehen	*you see*	stehlen	*you steal*
ihr	befehlt	*you order*	seht	*you see*	stehlt	*you steal*
sie	befehlen	*they order*	sehen	*they see*	stehlen	*they steal*
wer	befiehlt	*who orders*	siehst	*who sees*	stiehlt	*who steals*

Exercise 5.2

In the blank provided, give the conjugation of the infinitive given in parentheses for the subject of the sentence. For example:

(haben) <u>Hast</u> du die Uhr?

1. (fahren) Wer _____ nach München?

2. (sprechen) Mein Vater _____ Deutsch und Italienisch.

3. (kommen) _____ ihr mit?

4. (sehen) _____ du das neue Auto?

5. (essen) Monika _____ gern im Restaurant.

6. (haben) _____ sie *s.* die Lehrerin gern?

7. (geschehen) Was _____ im Sommer?

8. (lesen) _____ Sie ein Buch?

9. (empfehlen) Wer _____ dieses Restaurant?

10. (haben) _____ ihr kein Geld?

11. (befehlen) Was _____ der General?

12. (geben) Ich _____ Thomas meine Uhr.

13. (helfen) Wir _____ Frau Keller.

14. (vergessen) Der Richter _____ sein Buch.

15. (essen) Die Kinder _____ gern Pudding.

Say It Out Loud

Read each sentence out loud, paying attention to the present tense irregularities:

Er trinkt gern Kaffee und Milch.	*He likes to drink coffee and milk.*
Wer isst in der Küche?	*Who is eating in the kitchen?*
Ich empfehle die Bratwurst nicht.	*I do not recommend the bratwurst.*
Siehst du die Berge?	*Do you see the mountains?*
Das sind die Alpen.	*Those are the Alps.*
Niemand spricht gern Englisch.	*No one likes speaking English.*
Was vergessen sie?	*What do they forget?*
Gibst du Thomas Geld?	*Do you give Thomas money?*
Sie hilft Simon und Monika.	*She is helping Simon and Monika.*
Martin nimmt meine Zeitung.	*Martin takes my newspaper.*
Der alte Mann stiehlt ein Auto.	*The old man steals a car.*
Esst ihr oft im Cafe?	*Do you often eat in a café?*
Herr Lautrec kommt aus Frankreich.	*Mr. Lautrec comes from France.*
Wohin fährst du heute?	*Where are you driving today?*
Ich fahre heute in die Schweiz.	*I am driving to Switzerland today.*
Was geschieht heute?	*What happens today?*
Heute ist mein Geburtstag.	*Today is my birthday.*

Conjugation of *werden*

The verb **werden** has several uses in German. One of its primary uses is as the verb *become* or *get*. The irregular conjugation of this verb resembles closely the vowel shift from **-e-** to **-i-** with a couple of spelling changes that require minimal explanation. Let's look at the full conjugation of **werden** in the present tense:

	werden	
ich	werde	*I become*
du	wirst	*you become*
er	wird	*he becomes*
sie	wird	*she becomes*
es	wird	*he/she/it becomes*
wir	werden	*we become*
Sie	werden	*you become*
ihr	werdet	*you become*
sie	werden	*they become*
wer	wird	*who becomes*

When the stem of a verb ends in **-d** or **-t**, an extra **e** is added to the second person plural (**ihr**) and the third person singular (**er/sie/es**) stem of the verb. This is the reason for the spelling of **werden** in the previous conjugation: **ihr werdet**.

Say It Out Loud

*Say each sentence out loud, paying attention to the irregularities of the verb **werden**:*

Ich werde Arzt.	*I am becoming a doctor.*
Wird Ihre Frau auch Ärztin?	*Is your wife also becoming a doctor?*
Nein, sie wird Zahnärztin.	*No, she is becoming a dentist.*
Die Kinder werden sehr krank.	*The children get very sick.*
Werden sie heute wieder gesund?	*Will they get well again today?*
Meine Freundin wird nicht Lehrerin.	*My girlfriend isn't becoming a teacher.*
Sie wird Sängerin.	*She is becoming a singer.*
Wann wird Martin wieder gesund?	*When will Martin get well again?*
Im Winter wird er wieder gesund.	*He'll get well again in winter.*
Werdet ihr Sportler?	*Are you becoming athletes?*
Ja, wir werden Fußballspieler.	*Yes, we are becoming soccer players.*
Spielt ihr gut oder schlecht?	*Do you play well or badly?*
Wir spielen sehr gut.	*We play very well.*

A simple but important rule to remember is that when something other than the subject begins a sentence, the verb precedes the subject. This is true no matter what begins the sentence. It can be a single word or a phrase. For example:

<u>Heute</u> fahren wir nach Hause.   *We are driving home today.*

<u>Im Sommer</u> wohne ich in Bonn.   *I live in Bonn in the summer.*

The Impersonal *es*

German and English are part of the family of Germanic languages. Those languages have a unique feature: the impersonal pronoun **es** (*it*). For example, in English you say that *it* is raining, *it* is cold out today, and *it* is getting hot. It is not clear to whom or what *it* is referring. It is the impersonal subject of the sentence and is the accepted way of describing weather and other conditions.

Let's look at some German sentences that illustrate the impersonal **es** with **werden** as well as with sentences that use the impersonal pronoun **es** with a variety of other verbs.

Say It Out Loud

Say each sentence out loud, paying attention to the impersonal pronoun **es***:*

Es wird sehr kalt.	*It is getting very cold.*
Heute wird es heiß.	*It is getting hot today.*
Es wird warm.	*It is getting warm.*
Es wird nicht kühl.	*It is not getting cool.*
Wird es wieder regnerisch?	*Is it getting rainy again?*
Wird es wieder sonnig?	*Is it getting sunny again?*
Wird es jetzt dunkel?	*Is it getting dark?*
Nein, es wird jetzt hell.	*No, it is getting light now.*
Es regnet.	*It is raining.*
Schneit es?	*Is it snowing?*
Es blitzt.	*There is lightning.*
Es donnert wieder.	*It is thundering again.*
Es geschieht jeden Tag.	*It happens every day.*
Es riecht.	*It smells.*

Exercise 5.3

Fill in the blank with the correct word or phrase provided in parentheses. For example:

Ich <u>werde</u> Zahnarzt. (wirst, werde, wird, werden)

1. _____ wird es wieder kalt. (Er, Sommer, Heute, Winter)

2. Mein Freundin _____ Sängerin. (wird, seid, jetzt, in der Hauptstadt)

3. Im Sommer _____ sehr heiß. (wird es, ihr werdet, es ist, sie sind)

4. Es blitzt und _____. (hell, dunkel, regnerisch, donnert)

5. Wird _____ wieder gesund? (wir, du, sie, Sie)

6. _____ wird es sehr kalt. (Alpen, Im Winter, Woher, Wohin)

7. Meine kleine Schwester wird _____. (krank, neu, dunkel, heute)

8. Wird der Mann _____ gesund? (wieder, regnet, ist, sind)

9. Im Winter _____ es oft. (lauft, schneit, kühl, sonnig)

10. Heute regnet _____. (er, wir, wo, es)

Some Useful Phrases

It is important in learning any language to know the numbers. In German, the first 20 cardinal numbers are:

1 eins	6 sechs	11 elf	16 sechzehn
2 zwei	7 sieben	12 zwölf	17 siebzehn
3 drei	8 acht	13 dreizehn	18 achtzehn
4 vier	9 neun	14 vierzehn	19 neunzehn
5 fünf	10 zehn	15 fünfzehn	20 zwanzig

Note the difference in spelling between 6 (**sechs**) and 16 (**sechzehn**) and 7 (**sieben**) and 17 (**siebzehn**).

The numbers are used in basic arithmetic and to show quantities. Let's practice using the numbers.

Say It Out Loud

Read each sentence out loud, paying attention to how the numbers are used:

Wie viel ist zwei plus/und drei?	*How much is two plus/and three?*
Zwei plus/und drei ist fünf.	*Two plus/and three is five.*
Wie viel ist sieben plus/und vier?	*How much is seven plus/and four?*
Sieben plus/und vier ist elf.	*Seven plus/and four is eleven.*
Wie viel ist neunzehn weniger/minus sechs?	*How much is 19 minus 6?*
Neunzehn weniger/minus sechs ist dreizehn.	*Nineteen minus six is thirteen.*
Wie viel ist zwölf weniger/minus zwei?	*How much is 12 minus 2?*
Zwölf weniger/minus zwei ist zehn.	*Twelve minus two is ten.*
Ich habe ein Hemd.	*I have one shirt.*
Wir haben drei Kinder.	*We have three children.*
Wer hat zwanzig Euro?	*Who has 20 euros?*
Wie viel ist zwei plus/und drei?	*How much is two plus/and three?*
Zwei plus/und drei ist fünf.	*Two plus/and three is five.*
Wie viel ist sieben plus/und vier?	*How much is seven plus/and four?*
Sieben plus/und vier ist elf.	*Seven plus/and four is eleven.*
Wie viel ist neunzehn weniger/minus sechs?	*How much is 19 minus 6?*
Neunzehn weniger/minus sechs ist dreizehn.	*Nineteen minus six is thirteen.*
Wie viel ist zwölf weniger/minus zwei?	*How much is 12 minus 2?*
Zwölf weniger/minus zwei ist zehn.	*Twelve minus two is ten.*

Wondering About This? *plus, und, weniger, minus,* and *eins*

In German addition, you can use either **plus** or **und** to express the statement of addition, and in subtraction, you can use either **weniger** or **minus** to express the statement:

Eins plus eins ist zwei.

Eins und eins ist zwei.

Acht weniger vier ist vier.

Acht minus vier ist vier.

Eins is used alone as a number. **Ein/eine** can mean *a/an* or *one* and modifies a noun. For example:

Vier plus eins ist fünf.   *Four plus one is five.*

Er hat ein Buch.   *He has a book. He has one book.*

Sie sieht eine Dame.   *She sees a lady. She sees one lady.*

Exercise 5.4

Give each equation in words. Then provide the answer. For example.

6 – 4 = ?

Wie viel ist sechs minus vier?

Sechs minus vier ist zwei.

1. 20 – 8 = ?

_____

_____

2. 8 + 3 = ?

_____

_____

3. 19 – 18 = ?

_____

_____

4. 3 + 4 = ?

_____

_____

5. 17 – 15 = ?

_____

_____

Review Quiz 5

Choose the letter of the word or phrase that best completes each sentence.

1. Heute _____ unsere Tante nach Frankreich.

   a. kommst

   b. gehen

   c. fährt

   d. lauft

2. Es _____ jeden Winter.

   a. geschieht

   b. werden

   c. ist

   d. seid

3. Was gibst _____ Martin?

   a. er

   b. ihr

   c. sie *s.*

   d. du

4. Heute _____ zum Park.

   a. gehe ich

   b. sie läuft

   c. sie laufen

   d. wir gehen

5. Im Winter wird mein Sohn oft _____.

   a. regnerisch

   b. krank

   c. dunkel

   d. woher

6. _____ gehen Sie heute, Herr Bauer?

   a. Wie viel

   b. Wohin

   c. Was

   d. Wer

7. Acht plus neun ist _____.

   a. zwanzig

   b. fünf

   c. vierzehn

   d. siebzehn

8. _____ wird wieder heiß.

   a. Sommer

   b. Es

   c. Sie

   d. Sie *s.*

9. _____ ist zwölf weniger sieben?

    a. Was   c. Wie viel

    b. Fünf   d. Wo

10. _____ kommt Herr Schäfer?

    a. Wo   c. Wie viel

    b. Wer   d. Woher

New Vocabulary

Alpen (*pl.*)	*Alps*
Amerika	*America*
Arzt (*m.*)	*doctor, physician*
Ärztin (*f.*)	*doctor, physician*
befehlen	*order, command*
Berg (*m.*)	*mountain*
blitzen	*lightning*
Bratwurst	*bratwurst, sausage*
brechen	*break*
Deutschland	*Germany*
donnern	*thunder*
dunkel	*dark*
empfehlen	*recommend*
essen	*eat*
fahren	*drive, travel*
Familie (*f.*)	*family*
Frankreich	*France*
Fußballspieler (*m.*)	*soccer player*
geben	*give*
Geburtstag (*m.*)	*birthday*
geschehen	*happen*
gesund	*healthy, well*
Hauptstadt (*f.*)	*capital city*
heiß	*hot*
helfen	*help*
hell	*light, bright*
heute	*today*
Italien	*Italy*

jetzt	*now*
kalt	*cold*
kommen	*come*
kühl	*cool*
küssen	*kiss*
laufen	*run*
lesen	*read*
nach Hause	*home, homeward*
nehmen	*take*
Österreich	*Austria*
regnen	*rain*
regnerisch	*rainy*
reizen	*annoy*
Sängerin (f.)	*singer*
schlecht	*bad*
schneien	*snow*
sehen	*see*
sehr	*very*
Sommer (m.)	*summer*
sonnig	*sunny*
spielen	*play*
Sportler (m.)	*athlete*
sprechen	*speak*
stehlen	*steal*
Tag (m.)	*day*
Unfall (m.)	*accident*
vergessen	*forget*
warm	*warm*
weniger	*minus, less*
werden	*become, get*
wie viel	*how much*
wieder	*again*
Winter (m.)	*winter*
woher	*(from) where*
wohin	*(to) where*
Zahnarzt (m.)	*dentist*
Zeitung (f.)	*newspaper*

6

Accusative Case: Direct Objects and Prepositions

In this chapter, you will discover the form and use of the German accusative case. How direct objects and prepositions are linked to this case will also be discussed. The formation of the plural of masculine nouns will be introduced.

Some questions that will be answered are:

✓ How do nouns and pronouns differ in the accusative case?
✓ When is the accusative case used?
✓ How is the accusative case used with prepositions?
✓ How is the plural of masculine, feminine, and neuter nouns formed?

Accusative Case

The accusative case is the Latin name for what is called the *objective case* in English. One of the main functions of the objective or accusative case is the identification of the *direct object* in a sentence. Don't let the name *direct object* stymy you. Finding it in a sentence is really a simple matter. Just ask *whom* or *what* of the subject and its verb, and the answer is the direct object. Let's look first at short sentences to identify the direct object. They will be followed by longer sentences, in which the direct object is easily found by asking the same kinds of questions.

Two Short Sentences

*John kissed Mary behind the garage. (**Whom** did John kiss?) **Mary = direct object***

*I found some keys on the floor. (**What** did I find?) **some keys = direct object***

91

Two Longer Sentences

*During the summer, we spent a week in Canada with our relatives. (**What** did we spend?)* **a week = direct object**

*After the dance last week, my brother took his girlfriend to the park where he proposed. (**Whom** did my brother take?)* **his girlfriend = direct object**

This explanation is meant only to show how to *identify* a direct object in a sentence, but in English a noun used as the subject of a sentence is identical to the same noun used as the direct object of a sentence. For example:

*Subject: **The boy** spoke in German.*

*Direct object: Charles saw **the boy** at the park.*

Being able to identify direct objects will be important when you encounter them in German.

The **der**-words and **ein**-words you have already learned are, for the most part, the same when they are used in the nominative case (subject of a sentence) and the accusative case (direct object of a sentence). Feminine and neuter nouns are identical in both cases. Only masculine nouns make a change in the accusative case. Let's compare the **der**-words and **ein**-words in the two cases. Take note of how the masculine differs in them.

Der-Words

	Masculine	Feminine	Neuter
Nominative case	der Lehrer	die Lampe	das Kind
Accusative case	<u>den</u> Lehrer	die Lampe	das Kind

Ein-Words

	Masculine	Feminine	Neuter
Nominative case	ein Stuhl	eine Tochter	ein Buch
Accusative case	<u>einen</u> Stuhl	eine Tochter	ein Buch

Remember that all **der**-words and **ein**-words conform to the illustrated endings. Refer to Chapters 2 and 4 to review **der**-words and **ein**-words.

When a masculine noun is used as a direct object, both **der**-words and **ein**-words change the ending to **-en**: der ➔ den and ein ➔ einen.

Step 1: Direct Object Nouns

To identify the direct object in a German sentence, ask **wen** (*whom*) or **was** (*what*) of the subject and verb in the sentence. For example:

Mein Vater hat ein Buch.	*My father has a book.*	(Was hat mein Vater?)	ein Buch = direct object
Thomas sieht seinen Freund.	*Thomas sees his friend.*	(Wen sieht Thomas?)	seinen Freund = direct object

You should have noticed that the masculine direct object (**seinen Freund**) had an **-en** ending on the **der**-word **sein**. This occurs with all masculine nouns. For example:

Thomas sieht den Garten.	*Thomas sees the garden.*
Thomas sieht einen Tisch.	*Thomas sees a table.*
Thomas sieht meinen Onkel.	*Thomas sees my uncle.*

As the verb that accompanies the direct object changes, the accusative case direct object remains:

Thomas fotografiert den Garten.	*Thomas photographs the garden.*
Thomas kauft einen Tisch.	*Thomas buys a table.*
Thomas besucht meinen Onkel.	*Thomas visits my uncle.*

Say It Out Loud

Read each sentence out loud, paying attention to the use of the direct objects.

Kaufen Sie eine Bluse?	*Are you buying a blouse?*
Nein, ich kaufe keine Bluse.	*No, I'm not buying a blouse.*
Ich kaufe ein Kleid.	*I'm buying a dress.*
Trinkst du ein Glas Bier?	*Are you drinking a glass of beer?*
Nein, ich trinke ein Glas Wein.	*No, I'm drinking a glass of wine.*
Das Kind trinkt keine Milch.	*The child isn't drinking any milk.*
Was isst Tina?	*What is Tina eating?*
Sie isst einen Apfel.	*She is eating an apple.*
Warum essen die Männer keine Suppe?	*Why aren't the men eating soup?*
Wen besuchen Sie in Berlin?	*Whom are you visiting in Berlin?*
In Berlin besuche ich meinen Freund.	*I'm visiting my friend in Berlin.*
Er kauft ein Haus am Fluss.	*He's buying a house on the river.*
Wen küssen die Frauen?	*Whom are the women kissing?*
Sie küssen die Kinder.	*They're kissing the children.*
Was brauchst du?	*What do you need?*
Ich brauche einen Bleistift.	*I need a pencil.*

Exercise 6.1

*Create a question with **wen** or **was** that asks about the underlined direct object in the sentence. For example:*

Sie sieht <u>einen Freund</u>. *Wen sieht sie?*

Er hat <u>ein Buch</u>. *Was hat er?*

1. Ich kaufe <u>einen Wagen</u>. _____

2. Mein Bruder besucht <u>seine Freundin</u>. _____

3. Erik hat <u>dieses Mädchen</u> gern. _____

4. Der Herr küsst <u>ihren Finger</u>. _____

5. Wir brauchen <u>das Geld</u>. _____

6. Die Frau isst <u>eine Apfelsine</u>. _____

7. Wir sehen <u>seine Schwester</u>. _____

8. Die Mädchen besuchen <u>diese Schule</u>. _____

9. Sie besuchen <u>ihre Großmutter</u>. _____

10. Ich trinke <u>Kaffee und Tee</u>. _____

There are many verbs that can be followed by a direct object. A few of the high-frequency *transitive* verbs that do just that are:

Infinitive	Sample Sentence	English
bauen	Ich baue ein Haus.	*I build a house.*
kennen	Wir kennen den Lehrer.	*We know the teacher.*
lehren	Frau Benz lehrt Klavier.	*Ms. Benz teaches piano.*
lernen	Welche Sprache lernt er?	*What language is he learning?*
schreiben	Schreibst du eine Postkarte?	*Are you writing a postcard?*
verkaufen	Tina verkauft ihre Bluse.	*Tina sells her blouse.*
verstehen	Sie versteht kein Wort.	*She doesn't understand a word.*

Exercise 6.2

Reword each sentence with the words in parentheses. For example:

Er hat ein- _____.

(der Bleistift) *Er hat einen Bleistift.*

(die Landkarte) *Er hat eine Landkarte.*

   Wer verkauft dies- _____?

1. (das Auto) _____

2. (der Wagen) _____

   Meine Mutter schreibt kein- _____.

3. (die Postkarte) _____

4. (der Brief *letter*) _____

   Die Männer (*men*) bauen ein- _____.

5. (die Schule) _____

6. (das Theater) _____

   Die Kinder verstehen dies- _____ nicht.

7. (der Arzt) _____

8. (die Lehrerin) _____

   Wir besuchen unser- _____ in Österreich.

9. (die Tante) _____

10. (der Sohn) _____

Wondering About This? Plural Nouns

When the noun subject of a sentence is in the plural, the verb must be plural. Compare the following pairs of sentences:

Das Kind liest ein Buch.	*The child reads a book.*
Die Kinder lesen ein Buch.	*The children read a book.*
Die Frau hat kein Geld.	*The woman has no money.*
Die Frauen haben kein Geld.	*The women have no money.*
Der Mann versteht Tina nicht.	*The man doesn't understand Tina.*
Die Männer verstehen Tina nicht.	*The men don't understand Tina.*

When a pronoun replaces a plural noun, it is always plural **sie** (*they*). This is true of both animates and inanimates: **die Kinder → sie**.

Step 2: Direct Object Pronouns

When it comes to direct object pronouns, English and German are similar. You have already encountered the German personal pronouns in the nominative case. Just like English, they have counterparts in the accusative case. Note how many are the same in both cases. For example:

		Singular		**Plural**					
		Nominative/Accusative		**Nominative/Accusative**					
First person:	ich	*I*		mich	*me*	wir	*we*	uns	*us*
Second person:	du	*you*		dich	*you*	Sie	*you*	Sie	*you*
				ihr	*you*	euch	*you*		
Third person:	er	*he*		ihn	*him*	sie	*they*	sie	*them*
	sie	*she*		sie	*her*	sie	*they*	sie	*them*
	es	*it*		es	*it*	sie	*they*	sie	*them*

The direct object pronoun is identified by asking **wen** (*whom*) or **was** (*what*) of the subject and verb. The answer is the direct object. Let's look at some example sentences:

Karl besucht mich.	*Karl visits me.*	(Wen besucht Karl?)	mich = direct object
Sonja vergisst dich.	*Sonja forgets you.*	(Wen vergisst Sonja?)	dich = direct object
Wir kennen ihn.	*We know him.*	(Wen kennen wir?)	ihn = direct object
Ich verkaufe sie.	*I sell it.*	(Was verkaufe ich?)	sie = direct object
Erik schreibt es.	*Erik writes it.*	(Was schreibt Erik?)	es = direct object
Sie fotografiert uns.	*She photographs us.*	(Wen fotografiert sie?)	uns = direct object
Niemand versteht Sie.	*No one understands you.*	(Wen versteht niemand?)	Sie = direct object
Die Männer sehen euch.	*The men see you.*	(Wen sehen die Männer?)	euch = direct object
Die Frauen kaufen sie.	*The women buy them.*	(Was kaufen die Frauen?)	sie = direct object

Say It Out Loud

Read each sentence out loud, paying attention to the direct object pronouns.

Lernen Sie es?	*Are you learning it?*
Niemand kennt mich.	*No one knows me.*
Martin verkauft ihn.	*Martin sells it.*

Die Kinder besuchen sie.	*The children visit her/them.**
Die Touristen fotografieren dich.	*The tourists photograph you.*
Meine Freundin empfiehlt es.	*My girlfriend recommends it.*
Er gibt sie Thomas.	*He gives it/them to Thomas.**
Meine Cousine schreibt ihn.	*My cousin is writing it.*
Wer trinkt es?	*Who drinks it?*
Sechs Männer bauen ihn.	*Six men are building it.*
Herr Keller kennt euch.	*Mr. Keller knows you.*
Der Amerikaner versteht Sie nicht.	*The American doesn't understand you.*

*The context of a text or conversation would determine the meaning of **sie**.

 ## Exercise 6.3

In the blank provided, give the missing form of the pronoun. For example:

sie *s.*   <u>*sie*</u>

Nominative	**Accusative**
1. ich	_____
2. wir	_____
3. _____	euch
4. _____	Sie
5. du	_____
6. wer	_____
7. _____	sie *pl.*
8. er	_____
9. _____	es
10. _____	mich

 Wondering About This? Identical Nominative and Accusative Pronouns
Perhaps it seems strange that **sie** and **es** are both the nominative and the
accusative forms of those pronouns. It really causes no problem because their
meaning is determined by how they are used. For example:

Subject:	<u>Sie</u> ist meine Freundin.	*She is my girlfriend.*
	<u>Sie</u> haben meinen Wecker.	*You have my alarm clock.*
	Heute gehen <u>sie</u> nach Hause.	*Today they are going home.*
	Ist <u>es</u> ein Hemd?	*Is it a shirt?*

Direct object:	Er sieht <u>sie</u> im Garten.	He sees her in the garden.
	Ich besuche <u>Sie</u> im Sommer.	I visit you in the summer.
	Niemand kennt <u>sie</u>.	No one knows them.
	Verkaufst du <u>es</u>?	Are you selling it?

And don't forget that English speakers do the same thing with the pronoun *you*.

Subject:	*<u>You</u> are my best friend.*
Direct object:	*I will visit <u>You</u> next week.*

Step 3: Prepositions

Many prepositions are those words that describe the location of someone or something: *in the house, on the bed, between my parents, near him, under the table,* and so on. Others describe when something occurs: *before school, after the concert, during a lesson,* and so on. Nouns and pronouns that follow prepositions are in the accusative (objective) case. There is no effect on nouns, because they are identical in both cases. But pronouns use their accusative (objective) case forms after prepositions. For example:

Pronoun as Subject	**Pronoun After Preposition**
<u>He</u> is my brother.	*I rely <u>on him</u>.*
<u>You</u> are learning German.	*She studies <u>with you</u>.*
<u>I</u> live in Heidelberg.	*Mary got a postcard <u>from me</u>.*
<u>They</u> work in the bank.	*We give our money <u>to them</u>.*

German has some prepositions that are called *accusative prepositions*. Masculine nouns and pronouns have to use their accusative case forms after the accusative prepositions. They are:

bis	*until, up to*
durch	*through*
für	*for*
gegen	*against*
ohne	*without*
um	*around*
wider	*against (outdated)*

Let's look at some example sentences that contain accusative prepositions:

Der Zug fährt <u>durch den Tunnel</u>.	*The train goes through the tunnel.*
Ich arbeite für <u>meinen Onkel</u>.	*I work for my uncle.*
Wir haben nichts <u>gegen ihn</u>.	*We have nothing against him.*
Der Mann kommt <u>ohne sie</u>.	*The man comes without her.*

Say It Out Loud

Read each sentence out loud, paying attention to the nouns and pronouns that follow the prepositions.

Ich habe ein Geschenk für meinen Bruder.	*I have a gift for my brother.*
Wir haben ein Geschenk für ihn.	*We have a gift for him.*
Die Jungen gehen durch einen Garten.	*The boys go through a garden.*
Warum ist diese Dame gegen die Lehrerin?	*Why is this lady against the teacher?*
Warum bist du gegen mich?	*Why are you against me?*
Wer kommt um die Ecke?	*Who is coming around the corner?*
Die Kinder laufen um das Haus.	*The children run around the house.*
Ich bitte um ein Glas Milch.	*I ask for a glass of milk.*
Die Studentin kommt ohne Jacke.	*The student comes with a jacket.*
Haben sie etwas für uns?	*Do you have something for us?*
Ich habe nichts für euch.	*I have nothing for you.*
Niemand kommt durch den Park.	*No one is coming through the park.*
Wir singen ohne ihn.	*We sing without him.*

Exercise 6.4

Reword the sentence with the words or phrases provided in parentheses. For example:

Das ist ein Geschenk für _____.

(mein Bruder) *Das ist ein Geschenk für meinen Bruder.*

(Sie) *Das ist ein Geschenk für Sie.*

Der Amerikaner arbeitet für _____.

1. (ich) _____

2. (deine Schwester) _____

Warum kommen die Jungen ohne _____?

3. (du) _____

4. (der Sportler) _____

Niemand ist gegen _____.

5. (wir) _____

6. (unsereTochter) _____

Das Mädchen läuft durch _____.

7. (das Haus) _____

8. (die Straße) _____

Der Mann bittet um _____.

9. (der Wein) _____

10. (ein Geschenk) _____

Was hast du für _____?

11. (sie *s.*) _____

12. (diese Dame) _____

Herr Braun kommt ohne _____.

13. (sie *pl.*) _____

14. (seine Freundin) _____

Warum bitten Sie um _____?

15. (ein Bleistift) _____

Wondering About This? *bitten*

The verb **bitten** means *ask* or *request*. It is not used to ask a question; it *asks for something* or *requests something*. Look at these example sentences that illustrate this meaning:

Lars bittet um ein Glas Wasser.   *Lars requests a glass of water.*
Ich bitte um Hilfe.   *I ask for help.*

The verb **fragen** means *ask a question*. Compare the previous two examples with the following two:

Er fragt, wo Tina wohnt.   *He asks where Tina lives.*

Ich frage Hans, wie sie heißt.   *I ask Hans what her name is.*

The last two examples are the retelling of questions that someone has asked. For example:

Wo wohnt Tina?	*Where does Tina live?*
Hans, wie heißt sie?	*Hans, what is her name?*

Masculine Plurals

Sometimes English speakers find the German way of making a plural complicated. In truth, it is more complicated than in English. In the English language, nearly every noun is changed to the plural by adding -**s**: *boy–boys*, *house–houses*, and *radio–radios*. However, there are some irregularities such as *goose–geese*, *mouse–mice*, and *woman–women*.

German uses the -**s** ending only with a few words, most of which come from non-German sources. For example:

Singular/Plural	English
Auto/Autos	*autos, automobiles*
Kamera/Kameras	*cameras*
Laptop/Laptops	*laptops*
Sofa/Sofas	*sofas*

Most German nouns follow a few different patterns to form plurals.

There is a tendency for masculine nouns to form their plural by adding -**e**. If there is an umlaut vowel (**a, o, u**), it is sometimes added in the plural. For example:

Singular/Plural	English
der Bleistift/die Bleistifte	*pencils*
der Brief/die Briefe	*letters*
der Fluss/die Flüsse	*rivers*
der Schuh/die Schuhe	*shoes*
der Zug/die Züge	*trains*

There are important exceptions to this rule. For example, the noun **der Mann** changes to **die Männer** in the plural, and the noun **der Junge** changes to **die Jungen**. There are numerous exceptions in the formation of German plurals, which even cause a bit of woe for German children as they develop their language skills. Be patient. Take it step by step. It eventually all falls into place.

If a masculine noun ends in **-en**, **-el**, or **-er**, it requires no ending in the plural, but if there is an umlaut vowel (**a, o, u**), the umlaut is sometimes added to the noun. For example:

Singular/Plural	English
der Boden/die Böden	*the floors*
der Bruder/die Brüder	*the brothers*
der Lehrer/die Lehrer	*the teachers*
der Mantel/die Mäntel	*the coats*
der Onkel/die Onkel	*the uncles*
der Wagen/die Wagen	*the cars*

Wondering About This? Plural Definite Article

When any masculine, feminine, or neuter noun is changed to the plural, its definite article is always **die**. The article **die** identifies both feminine nouns and the plural of masculine, feminine, and neuter nouns. Its meaning remains *the* in the plural.

The definite article identifies someone or something *specific*. The indefinite article identifies someone or something *nonspecific* or *in general*. Consider the following two sentences and how they differ in meaning:

John sees <u>the</u> thief. (John sees a specific thief, one he has seen before.)

John sees <u>a</u> thief. (John sees someone who appears to be a thief.)

The same sentences in German have the same meaning: one is specific, and one is nonspecific:

Johann sieht <u>den</u> Dieb.

Johann sieht <u>einen</u> Dieb.

English and German do the same thing with definite and indefinite articles in the plural. The idea of *specific* and *nonspecific* or *in general* also occurs in the plural with definite and indefinite articles. But the plural indefinite article in both languages is *no article*. For example:

Johann sieht die Diebe.	*John sees the thieves.* (specific)
Johann sieht Diebe.	*John sees thieves.* (nonspecific)

Naturally, with nouns that follow numbers larger than **eins**, the plural noun is used: **drei Bleistifte** (*three pencils*), **sieben Männer** (*seven men*).

Say It Out Loud

Read each sentence out loud, paying attention to the plurals:

Die Männer aus Deutschland wohnen hier.	*The men from Germany live here.*
Wo wohnen die Amerikaner?	*Where do the Americans live?*
Wo wohnen die Jungen aus Frankreich?	*Where do the boys from France live?*
Meine Brüder kaufen einen Volkswagen.	*My brothers buy a Volkswagen.*
Was kaufen Ihre Freunde?	*What are your friends buying?*
Sie kaufen Bleistifte.	*They are buying pencils.*
Meine Freundin kauft Pullover.	*My girlfriend is buying sweaters.*
Wie viele Briefe hast du?	*How many letters do you have?*
Ich habe zehn Briefe.	*I have 10 letters.*
Wo sind die Züge?	*Where are the trains?*
Die Züge sind am Bahnhof.	*The trains are at the railroad station.*
Ich frage ihn, wie viele Bleistifte er hat.	*I ask him how many pencils he has.*
Er fragt mich, wie viele Stühle da sind.	*He asks me how many chairs are there.*
Fragen wir den Lehrer.	*Let's ask the teacher.*

Exercise 6.5

Reword each plural noun in the singular and each singular noun in the plural. Include the correct definite article. For example:

der Lehrer	*die Lehrer*
der Zug	die Züge

1. der Bruder _____

2. der Onkel _____

3. _____ die Jungen

4. _____ die Amerikaner

5. der Mantel _____

6. _____   die Briefe

7. der Bleistift   _____

8. der Wagen   _____

9. der Fluss   _____

10. _____   die Schuhe

11. der Mann   _____

12. _____   die Pullover

13. der Junge   _____

14. der Freund   _____

15. _____   die Diebe

Some Useful Phrases

The verb **kosten** means *cost* and is used like the English verb. When you ask the question **Wie viel kostet das?** (*How much does that cost?*), you are looking for a price expressed as money. If you are talking about American money, the German word is the same as English: **der Dollar**, a masculine noun. Its plural requires no ending. In the European Union, the euro is the most popular currency and in German is **der Euro**, a masculine noun. Let's look at some sentences that illustrate the use of **kosten**:

Wie viel kostet dieser Pullover?	*How much does this sweater cost?*
Er kostet zwanzig Dollar.	*It costs 20 dollars.*
Wie viel kosten diese Pullover?	*How much do these sweaters cost?*
Ich weiß es nicht. Sie sind teuer.	*I do not know. They are expensive.*
Wie viel kostet der Bleistift?	*How much does the pencil cost?*
Er kostet vier Euro.	*It costs 4 euros.*
Wie viel kosten Bleistifte?	*How much do pencils cost?*
Bleistifte sind nicht teuer.	*Pencils are not expensive.*
Ich weiß es nicht, aber Bleistifte sind billig.	*I do not know, but pencils are cheap.*

If the subject of **kosten** is singular, the verb is singular. If it is plural, the verb is plural:

Der Bleistift kost<u>et</u> vier Euro.	*The pencil costs 4 euros.*
Zwei Bleistifte kost<u>en</u> acht Euro.	*Two pencils cost 8 euros.*

Say It Out Loud

Read each sentence out loud, paying attention to the kind of article used with the plural nouns:

Wie viele Briefe schreibt sie?	*How many letters is she writing?*
Sie schreibt elf Briefe.	*She is writing 11 letters.*
Arbeiten Männer schneller?	*Do men work faster?*
Nein, Männer arbeiten nicht schneller.	*No, men do not work faster.*
Wie viel kosten diese Pullover?	*How much do these sweaters cost?*
Sie kosten sechzehn Euro.	*They cost 16 euros.*
Sind Autos billig oder teuer?	*Are cars cheap or expensive?*
Diese Autos sind teuer.	*These cars are expensive.*
Aber diese Autos sind billig.	*But these cars are cheap.*
Sind jene Stühle klein?	*Are those chairs small?*
Nein, jene Stühle sind groß.	*No, those chairs are big.*
Jungen sind jung, und Männer sind alt.	*Boys are young, and men are old.*

 **Let's Read**

Read the following text and determine the meaning of the lines on your own:

Monika und Erik sind heute in Heidelberg. Da besuchen sie einen Freund, Hans Bauer, und seine Familie. Hans hat vier Söhne und eine Tochter. Die Kinder sind sehr jung. Seine Frau heißt Marianne und arbeitet im Restaurant. Sie ist Kellnerin. Hans und Marianne haben zwei Wagen—einen Volkswagen und einen Mercedes. Sie haben kein Haus. Ein Haus in Heidelberg ist sehr teuer.

Review Quiz 6

Choose the letter of the word or phrase that best completes each sentence.

1. Kaufen Sie _____ Pullover?

   a. das

   b. einen

   c. mein

   d. bis

2. Ist das ein Geschenk für _____?

   a. er   c. mich

   b. wir   d. der Vater

3. Der Mann kommt _____ seine Frau.

   a. ohne   c. sie

   b. wohin   d. heute

4. Meine Cousine verkauft _____.

   a. es   c. du

   b. der Zug   d. wie viel

5. Er _____ seinen Freund im Garten.

   a. sieht   c. fährt

   b. laufen   d. kommen

6. Ich habe jetzt _____ Bleistifte.

   a. wie   c. rot

   b. durch   d. fünf

7. _____ besucht dein Bruder in der Schweiz?

   a. Was   c. Woher

   b. Wo   d. Wen

8. _____ Briefe hat sie?

   a. Wo   c. Wie viele

   b. Wer   d. Nicht heute

9. Der Hut _____ neunzehn Euro.

   a. sind   c. kostet

   b. mein   d. braucht

10. Diese Mäntel sind sehr _____.

   a. billig   c. wessen

   b. unsere   d. Fluss

New Vocabulary

arbeiten	*work*
bauen	*build*
besuchen	*visit*
Bier (*n.*)	*beer*
bitten (um)	*ask (for)*
brauchen	*need*
Brief (*m.*)	*letter*
Ecke (*f.*)	*corner*
etwas	*something*
Fluss (*m.*)	*river*
fotografieren	*photograph*
Geschenk (*n.*)	*gift, present*
Glas (*n.*)	*glass*
Jacke (*f.*)	*jacket*
kaufen	*buy*
kennen	*know*
kosten	*cost*
lehren	*teach*
lernen	*learn*
Milch (*f.*)	*milk*
nichts	*nothing*
niemand	*no one*
Postkarte (*f.*)	*postcard*
schreiben	*write*
Suppe (*f.*)	*soup*
Tee (*m.*)	*tea*
Tourist (*m.*)	*tourist*
Tunnel (*m.*)	*tunnel*
verkaufen	*sell*
verstehen	*understand*
Wein (*m.*)	*wine*
wen	*whom*
Wort (*n.*)	*word*
Zug (*m.*)	*train*

Mastery Check 1

This Mastery Check is provided to help you identify the areas of German covered in the last six chapters that you feel confident about or that you should review. Choose the letter of the word or phrase that best completes each sentence.

1. To pronounce **Üü**, purse your lips for the vowel sound **oo** but say _____.

   a. eh

   b. ee

   c. yoo

   d. uh

2. The first syllable of **sprechen** is pronounced _____.

   a. shpreh

   b. spree

   c. sper

   d. shrep

3. _____ dein Bruder in München?

   a. Wo

   b. Ist

   c. Heißt

   d. Heißen

4. Meine _____ ist Lehrerin.

   a. Schwester

   b. Frau Schäfer

   c. Buch

   d. Bruder

5. Ist Ihr _____ in der Schweiz?

   a. Onkel

   b. Küche

   c. dein

   d. in Amerika

6. Mein Auto ist _____.

   a. wo

   b. klein

   c. Straße

   d. heißen

7. _____ heißt sie?

   a. Wo

   b. Thomas

   c. Frau Benz

   d. Wie

8. Ist das Hemd blau? Nein, _____ ist gelb.

   a. sie

   b. es

   c. er

   d. Sie

9. Die Kinder _____ im Park.

    a. ist   c. bin

    b. seid   d. sind

10. Das ist mein Onkel. _____ ist alt.

    a. Er   c. Ihr

    b. Sie   d. Es

11. Wo _____ wir?

    a. sind   c. seid

    b. ist   d. bist

12. Meine Cousine wohnt _____ Schweiz.

    a. im   c. nach

    b. in der   d. zu Hause

13. Ich habe kein _____.

    a. CDs   c. Bier

    b. Kinder   d. Richterin

14. _____ du nach Frankreich?

    a. Wo wohnst   c. Kaufst

    b. Fliegst   d. Verkaufen

15. _____ ihr keine Zeit?

    a. Lernt   c. Bin

    b. Haben   d. Habt

16. Meine Mutter ist _____ zu Hause.

    a. nicht   c. kein

    b. nach   d. keine

17. Was gibt _____ Monika?

    a. er   c. sie *pl.*

    b. ihr   d. du

18. Im Winter wird es oft _____.

    a. heißt   c. kalt

    b. krank   d. woher

19. _____ gehen Sie heute, Frau Schäfer?

    a. Wie viel   c. Was

    b. Wen   d. Wohin

20. Acht plus drei ist _____.

    a. elf   c. vierzehn

    b. fünf   d. siebzehn

21. _____ wird wieder regnerisch.

    a. Sommer   c. Sie

    b. Es   d. Sie *s*.

22. Sie _____ ihre Freundin in Berlin.

    a. besucht   c. fährt

    b. laufen   d. kommen

23. Wir haben jetzt _____ Bleistifte.

    a. wie viel   c. blau

    b. durch   d. acht

24. _____ besuchen sie in Heidelberg?

    a. Was   c. Wen

    b. Wo   d. Woher

25. Diese Wagen sind sehr _____.

    a. unsere   c. wessen

    b. billig   d. zwanzig

7

Regular Past Tense and Interrogative Words

This chapter provides your first look at how German forms the past tense. In addition, new interrogative words will be introduced. You will also practice changing feminine nouns to the plural.

Some questions that will be answered are:

✓ What is the basic formation of the regular past tense?
✓ What conjugational endings are needed for the past tense?
✓ How are questions formed from different kinds of sentences?
✓ How do feminine nouns change to the plural?

The Past Tense

The past tense describes actions and events that are not taking place now but that took place at some point in time previous to the present. It can be something that occurred a thousand years ago or just a second or two ago, but it is stated with a verb in the past tense.

In English, the regular past tense is simple to form. The infinitive of a verb adds the suffix **-ed**. After that simple process, the verb then describes an action in the past:

Present Tense	Infinitive	Past Tense
I <u>work</u> at home.	work	I <u>worked</u> at home.
The boys <u>play</u> chess.	play	The boys <u>played</u> chess.
Jack <u>cooks</u> for his mother.	cook	Jack <u>cooked</u> for his mother.
She <u>kisses</u> the baby.	kiss	She <u>kissed</u> the baby.

Just as English has two present tense formations, it also has two past tense formations: a habitual or repeated action and an incomplete or ongoing action. Let's review these two formations in both tenses:

Habitual or Repeated Action	Incomplete or Ongoing Action
Present: *I work at home.*	*I am working at home.*
Past: *I worked at home.*	*I was working at home.*
Present: *She kisses the baby.*	*She is kissing the baby.*
Past: *She kissed the baby.*	*She was kissing the baby.*

It is important to remember that German has only one present tense formation, and the German past tense also has only one tense formation.

Step 1: The Past Tense Suffix *-te*

The German past tense of regular verbs is nearly as simple as the English past tense. The stem of the verb adds the suffix **-te**, and with that the meaning of the action of the verb is in the past tense. For example:

Infinitive	Stem	Past Tense	
spielen	spiel-	spielte	*played*
fragen	frag-	fragte	*asked*
machen	mach-	machte	*made, did*
sagen	sag-	sagte	*said*
besuchen	besuch-	besuchte	*visited*
suchen	such-	suchte	*looked for, sought*
kaufen	kauf-	kaufte	*bought*

 Each of these past tense verbs could also be translated in English with either the incomplete or ongoing meaning of the English verbs: *was playing, was asking, was making,* and so on.

Verbs like these are the basic past tense of the verb. But like German verbs in the present tense, past tense verbs also get conjugational endings that are similar (but not identical) to the present tense conjugational endings. Let's look at the full past tense conjugation of a few verbs:

	spielen		**sagen**		**lernen**	
ich	spielte	*I played*	sagte	*I said*	lernte	*I learned*
du	spieltest	*you played*	sagtest	*you said*	lerntest	*you learned*
er, sie, es	spielte	*he played*	sagte	*he said*	lernte	*he learned*

wir	spielten	*we played*	sagten	*we said*	lernten	*we learned*
ihr	spieltet	*you played*	sagtet	*you said*	lerntet	*you learned*
Sie	spielten	*you played*	sagten	*you said*	lernten	*you learned*
sie	spielten	*they played*	sagten	*they said*	lernten	*they learned*

If the subject of a sentence is a singular noun, it forms the past tense in the third person singular (**er, sie, es**). If it is plural, it forms the past tense in the third person plural (**sie** *pl.*). For example:

| der Mann spiel<u>te</u> | *the man played* |
| die Männer spiel<u>ten</u> | *the men played* |

Say It Out Loud

Read each sentence, paying attention to the formation and use of the past tense:

Viele Jungen spielten Fußball.	*Many boys played soccer.*
Viele Kinder lernten Deutsch.	*Many children learned German.*
Ich kaufte einen Volkswagen/VW (fow-vay).	*I bought a Volkswagen/VW.*
Wer kaufte diese Blumen?	*Who bought these flowers?*
Martin verkaufte sein Fahrrad.	*Martin sold his bicycle.*
Was verkauften deine Schwestern?	*What did your sisters sell?*
Der alte Mann sagte nichts.	*The old man said nothing.*
Was sagten sie?	*What did they say?*
Ich suchte eine Bibliothek.	*I was looking for a library.*
Was machtet ihr gestern?	*What did you do yesterday?*
Wir besuchten unsere Freundinnen.	*We visted our girlfriends.*
Wohin reiste die neue Diplomatin?	*Where did the young diplomat (f.) travel?*

Exercise 7.1

Reword each infinitive in the past tense with the subject provided in parentheses. For example:

lernen (du) *lerntest*

1. machen (er) _____

2. fragen (ich) _____

3. sagen (wir) _____

4. verkaufen (ihr) _____

5. kaufen (Sie) _____

6. suchen (die Dame) _____

7. hören (die Jungen) _____

8. besuchen (sie *s.*) _____

9. reisen (sie *pl.*) _____

10. wohnen (du) _____

If the stem of an infinitive ends in **-t** or **-d**, an extra **e** is added to the past tense suffix. For example:

	arbeiten *(work)*	**reden** *(talk)*
ich	arbeitete	redete
du	arbeitetest	redetest
er	arbeitete	redete
wir	arbeiteten	redeten
ihr	arbeitetet	redetet
Sie	arbeiteten	redeten
sie	arbeiteten	redeten

Exercise 7.2

Reword each present tense sentence in the past tense. For example:

Ich lerne Deutsch.
Ich lernte Deutsch.

1. Was macht Ihre Freundin?

_____

2. Wir arbeiten in Heidelberg.

_____

3. Thomas spielt gern Fußball.

_____

4. Wohnst du in München?

_____

5. Meine Eltern (*parents*) hören Radio.

_____

6. Die alte Dame redet kein Wort.

_____

7. Im Winter reist seine Familie nach Italien.

_____

8. Die Kinder lernen Mathematik.

_____

9. Suchen Sie den Bahnhof?

_____

10. Was bauen die Männer?

_____

Step 2: Adverbs for the Past Tense

Just as the adverbs **jetzt** (*now*) and **heute** (*today*) suggest that an action is happening in the present tense, there are adverbs that tell you that an action happened in the past tense. Some important ones are:

gestern	*yesterday*
vor einer Minute	*a minute ago*
vor zwei Minuten	*two minutes ago*
vor fünfzehn Minuten	*15 minutes ago*
vor einer Woche	*a week ago*
vor einem Monat	*a month ago*
vor drei Jahren	*three years ago*

These adverbs accompany past tense verbs and modify the action, telling when it took place. For example:

Gestern spielte Monika Fußball.	*Yesterday, Monika played soccer.*
Ich wohnte da vor sechs Jahren.	*I lived there six years ago.*
Wohin reiste sie vor einer Woche?	*Where did she travel a week ago?*

Now let's practice saying sentences in the past tense with adverbs.

Say It Out Loud

Read each sentence aloud, paying attention to the use of adverbs in the past tense.

Vor zwei Tagen kostete das Buch elf Euro.	*Two days ago the book cost 11 euros.*
Vor drei Jahren wohnten wir in Amerika.	*Three years ago we lived in America.*
Vor vier Jahren lehrte er in dieser Schule.	*Four years ago, he taught in this school.*
Vor einer Woche regnete es jeden Tag.	*A week ago it rained every day.*
Gestern fotografierte ich einen Filmstar.	*Yesterday I photographed a movie star.*
Gestern schneite es wieder.	*Yesterday it snowed again.*
Gestern blitzte und donnerte es.	*There were lightning and thunder yesterday.*
Gestern zeigte er Thomas sein Fahrrad.	*Yesterday he showed Thomas his bike.*
Wo wartetest du gestern?	*Where did you wait yesterday?*
Ich wartete an der Ecke.	*I waited on the corner.*
Wann besuchten Sie Ihre Tante?	*When did you visit your aunt?*
Ich besuchte sie vor zwei Monaten.	*I visited her two months ago.*

Exercise 7.3

Using the string of words provided, create a past tense sentence. For example:

gestern / er / kaufen / ein Hemd
Gestern kaufte er ein Hemd.

1. gestern / wir / warten / an der Ecke

   _____

2. gestern / sie *pl.* / zeigen / Frau Bauer / der Wagen

   _____

3. Eltern / reisen / nach Hamburg

   _____

4. vor einer Woche /es / regnen / jeden Tag

_____

5. vor drei Monaten / Thomas und Tina / wohnen / in Berlin

_____

Forming Questions

Let's review the basic ideas about forming questions. The primary idea is that the verb precedes the subject in questions. If an interrogative word begins the question, the verb still precedes the subject. For example:

Question:	Wohnten Sie zu Hause?	_Did you live at home?_
Interrogative:	Wo wohnten Sie vor zwei Jahren?	_Where did you live two years ago?_

Now it's time to add a few more interrogative words to your vocabulary. The following list contains the interrogative words you already know together with a few new ones:

wann	_when_
warum	_why_
was	_what_
wen	_whom_
wer	_who_
wie	_how_
wo	_where_
woher	_(from) where_
wohin	_where (to)_

Let's put these words in sentences to practice.

Say It Out Loud

Read each question aloud, paying attention to the interrogative words used.

Wann kommt der nächste Zug?	_When is the next train coming?_
Warum spielte er Tennis?	_Why did he play tennis?_
Er spielte Tennis, denn er ist Sportler.	_He played tennis because he's an athlete._
Was zeigte sie Hans?	_What did she show Hans?_
Wen fragten Sie?	_Whom did you ask?_
Wer antwortete?	_Who answered?_

Wie heißt die neue Studentin?	What is the new student's name?
Wo bauten sie die Bibliothek?	Where did they build the library?
Woher kommt der alte Herr?	Where does the old gentleman come from?
Wohin reiste seine Familie?	Where did his family travel?
Was möchten Sie heute, Frau Benz?	What would you like today, Ms. Benz?

Wondering About This? *warum* and *denn*

The interrogative word **warum** asks the question *why*. The answer to such a question requires the use of the conjunction *because* or *for*, which in German is **denn**. For example:

Warum ist Sonja zu Hause?	Why is Sonja at home?
Sie ist zu Hause, denn sie ist krank.	She is at home because she is sick.
Warum wohnten sie in Bonn?	Why did they live in Bonn?
Sie wohnten in Bonn, denn ihr Vater wohnte da.	They lived in Bonn because their father lived there.
Warum schneite es wieder?	Why did it snow again?
Es schneite wieder, denn es ist Winter.	It snowed again because it is winter.

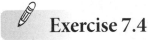

Exercise 7.4

Create an answer to each question with the information provided in parentheses. For example:

Warum lernt sie Deutsch? (Ihre Freunde sprechen Deutsch.)
Sie lernt Deutsch, denn ihre Freunde sprechen Deutsch.

1. Warum verkaufte er das Fahrrad? (Das Fahrrad ist alt.)

   _____

2. Warum fotografiert er das Mädchen? (Das Mädchen ist schön.)

   _____

3. Warum kosten die Blumen zwanzig Euro? (Die Blumen sind teuer.)

   _____

4. Warum reiste sie nach Paris? (Ihre Freunde wohnten in Frankreich.)

   _____

5. Warum versteht sie uns nicht? (Sie ist Amerikanerin.)

   _____

Wondering About This? *möchte*

The verb form **möchte** is popular in German. Such words are called *high-frequency* words, and **möchte** certainly fits that description. It means *would like* and can be followed by direct objects or other verbs. Using it will give you a lot of flexibility in your German. Let's look at the conjugational endings for this verb: **ich möchte, du möchtest, er möchte, wir möchten, ihr möchtet, Sie möchten**, and **sie möchten**. They are the past tense endings, but you will notice that the meaning of the verb is not exactly a past tense: *would like*. In fact, this verb is used to express something in either the present or the future. For example:

Möchtest du heute ein Geschenk?	*Would you like a gift today?*
Möchte sie nächste Woche ein Fahrrad?	*Would she like a bike next week?*

Let's look at how the verb is used with direct objects. Remember that German direct objects are in the accusative case:

Tina möchte eine neue Bluse.	*Tina would like a new blouse.*
Wir möchten Brot und Butter.	*We would like bread and butter.*
Möchten Sie einen Bleistift?	*Would you like a pencil?*

Now compare that with the same verb used with other verbs as infinitives. Notice that the infinitives are the final element in each sentence:

Tina möchte nach Berlin reisen.	*Tina would like to travel to Berlin.*
Wir möchten Kaffee und Tee trinken.	*We would like to drink coffee and tea.*
Möchtest du Radio hören?	*Would you like to listen to the radio?*

Tuck this important verb away for further use.

The interrogative used in a question depends upon the element in a sentence that it asks about. If it asks about a person, the interrogative is **wer** or **wen**. If it asks about a thing, it is **was**. If it asks about a moment in time, it is **wann**, and so on.

Let's look at a sentence and see how many questions can be made from it, by asking about different elements in the sentence:

Vor einem Jahr wohnte der Mann in Berlin.

Whole sentence:	Vor einem Jahr wohnte der Mann in Berlin?	*Did the man live in Berlin a year ago?*
When:	Wann wohnte der Mann in Berlin?	*When did the man live in Berlin?*
Who:	Wer wohnte vor einem Jahr in Berlin?	*Who lived in Berlin a year ago?*
Where:	Wo wohnte der Mann vor einem Jahr?	*Where did the man live a year ago?*

If a preposition is part of the question, the preposition precedes the interrogative. For example:

> für den Mann = für wen?
>
> gegen die Frau = gegen wen?

Exercise 7.5

Give a question with an interrogative word that asks about the underlined element in each sentence. For example:

> Er kennt das Mädchen aus Frankreich.
> *Wen kennt er?*

1. Gestern besuchte er seinen Onkel in Hamburg.

   _____

2. Im Winter fahren sie gern in die Alpen.

   _____

3. Es geht Frau Schneider gut.

   _____

4. Herr Bauer lehrte Deutsch hier.

   _____

5. Viele Studenten reisten nach Hause.

   _____

6. Die Touristen kommen aus Amerika.

   _____

7. Ihre Mutter ist heute zu Hause, denn sie ist sehr krank.

   _____

8. Martin fotografierte die junge Deutsche.

   _____

9. Wir möchten Brot und Bratwurst kaufen.

   _____

10. Unser Vater arbeitete für Frau Keller.

    _____

Step 3: Feminine Plurals

Most feminine nouns change to the plural by adding **-n** or **-en**. For example:

die Blume	die Blumen	*the flowers*
die Frau	die Frauen	*the women*
die Lampe	die Lampen	*the lamps*
die Schwester	die Schwestern	*the sisters*
die Tante	die Tanten	*the aunts*

Nouns that end in the suffix **-in** add the ending **-nen** in the plural: **die Freundin = die Freundinnen** and **die Amerikanerin = die Amerikanerinnen**. Two important exceptions to the use of **-en** to form the plural are **die Mutter = die Mütter** and **die Tochter = die Töchter**.

Just like masculine nouns, feminine nouns use the definite article **die** in the plural. If the noun is plural, the verb used with that noun must also be plural:

<u>Die Blumen sind</u> sehr schön.	*The flowers are very pretty.*
<u>Die Touristinnen warteten</u> an der Ecke.	*The tourists waited on the corner.*

Say It Out Loud

Read each sentence out loud, paying attention to the feminine plural nouns:

Diese Damen kommen aus England.	*These ladies come from England.*
Wo sind deine neuen Blusen?	*Where are your new blouses?*
Ich möchte zwei Postkarten schreiben.	*I would like to write two postcards.*
Meine Schwestern sind sehr jung.	*My sisters are very young.*
Wann kommen Ihre Töchter?	*When are your daughters coming?*
Zwei Wochen sind vierzehn Tage.	*Two weeks are 14 days.*
Thomas besuchte drei Freundinnen.	*Thomas visited three girlfriends.*
Diese Frauen wohnten in einer Wohnung.	*These women lived in an apartment.*
Diese Wohnungen sind sehr klein.	*These apartments are very little.*
Wo sind die Zeitungen?	*Where are the newspapers?*
Wie alt sind diese Uhren?	*How old are these clocks?*
Wohin laufen die Lehrerinnen?	*Where are the teachers running?*

Exercise 7.6

If the noun provided is singular, give its plural form. If it is plural, give its singular form.
For example:

die Lampe   *die Lampen*

Singular   **Plural**

1. die Touristin   _____

2. die Frau   _____

3. _____   die Blusen

4. die Schwester   _____

5. _____   die Tanten

6. _____   die Zeitungen

7. die Uhr   _____

8. _____   die Postkarten

9. die Straße   _____

10. die Mutter   _____

Some Useful Phrases

You have already encountered the impersonal pronoun **es**. There is another word that is used in a similar way. It does not refer to a specific person or thing but to a whole statement or idea. That word is **das** (*that*). It is frequently used followed by a verb (often **ist**) and a variety of adjectives or adverbs and is a response to something just stated. Look at the following statement. The phrases that follow it can be used to respond to it:

Heute schneit es wieder.   *It's snowing again today.*

Das stimmt.   *That's right.*

Das stimmt nicht.   *That's not right.*

Das macht nichts.   *That doesn't matter.*

Das geht.   *That will work. That's all right.*

Das ist egal.   *That doesn't matter.*

Das ist wahr.   *That's true.*

Das ist nicht wahr.   *That's not true.*

Remember that many professions and occupations that are described by a masculine noun can most often add the **-in** suffix to make it feminine. Its plural would, of course, be the ending **-nen**:

Masculine	Feminine	
der Arzt	die Ärztin	*doctor*
der Diplomat	die Diplomatin	*diplomat*
der Engländer	die Engländerin	*Englishwoman*
der Italiener	die Italienerin	*Italian*
der Mechaniker	die Mechanikerin	*mechanic*
der Polizist	die Polizistin	*police officer*
der Richter	die Richterin	*judge*
der Sänger	die Sängerin	*singer*
der Schaffner	die Schaffnerin	*conductor*
der Schüler	die Schülerin	*pupil*

The number of nouns that follow this pattern is very large.

Exercise 7.7

In the blank provided in each short dialogue, create a sentence that conforms to the topic of the dialogue. For example:

FRAU BRAU: Wie geht es Ihnen, Herr Benz?

HERR BENZ: Es geht mir gut. Wohin gehen Sie?

FRAU BENZ: *Ich gehe zum Park.*

1. MARTIN: Wo ist dein Bruder?

   MONIKA: _____

   MARTIN: Warum? Ist er krank?

2. MARTIN: Besuchtest du deinen Onkel?

   MONIKA: _____

   MARTIN: Wohnt sie jetzt in Heidelberg?

3. MARTIN: Ich habe drei Brüder und vier Schwestern.

   MONIKA: Meine Familie ist auch groß.

   MARTIN: _____

4. MARTIN: Warum lernst du Englisch?

   MONIKA: Ich möchte Englisch gut verstehen.

   MARTIN: _____

5. MARTIN: Heute regnet es wieder.

   MONIKA: Ja, und es ist auch sehr kalt.

   MARTIN: _____

Review Quiz 7

Choose the letter of the word or phrase that best completes each sentence.

1. Sie möchte eine neue Bluse _____.

   a. kaufen   c. suchte

   b. verkauft   d. hat

2. Gestern _____ die Kinder Fußball.

   a. machte   c. machen

   b. spielen   d. spielten

3. Meine Großmutter hat _____ in Berlin.

   a. zwei Wohnungen   c. warum

   b. ein Mechaniker   d. möchten

4. Vor einem Jahr _____ für meinen Onkel.

   a. besuchte   c. suchen sie

   b. arbeitete er   d. lernten

5. _____ ist das große Geschenk?

   a. Warum   c. Wann

   b. Wer   d. Für wen

6. Was _____ der alte Herr?

   a. fragen   c. besuchten

   b. sagte   d. antworte

7. Mein Bruder hat zwei _____.

   a. Freundinnen   c. wie viele

   b. Ärztin   d. keine Autos

8. _____ lernten die Kinder nichts.

    a. Sommer   c. Eine Woche

    b. Gestern   d. Das stimmt.

9. Diese Uhren _____ neu.

    a. ist   c. möchten

    b. macht   d. sind

10. Mein Bruder fährt nicht nach Bonn, _____ er hat kein Geld.

    a. wann   c. warum

    b. denn   d. dieser

New Vocabulary

an	*at, on*
antworten	*answer*
arbeiten	*work*
Blume (*f.*)	*flower*
das ist egal	*that doesn't matter*
das stimmt	*that's right*
denn	*because*
der Schaffner	*conductor*
der Schüler	*pupil*
Diplomat (*m.*)	*diplomat*
Ecke (*f.*)	*corner*
Eltern (*pl.*)	*parents*
Engländer (*m.*)	*Englishman*
Fahrrad (*n.*)	*bicycle, bike*
Filmstar (*m.*)	*movie star*
gestern	*yesterday*
Jahr (*n.*)	*year*
Mechaniker (*m.*)	*mechanic*
Minute (*f.*)	*minute*
möchten	*would like*
Monat (*m.*)	*month*
nächste	*next*

nichts	*nothing*
Polizist (*m.*)	*police officer*
reden	*talk*
sagen	*say*
Sänger (*m.*)	*singer*
suchen	*look for, seek*
vor einem Jahr	*a year ago*
vor einem Monat	*a month ago*
vor einem Tag	*a day ago*
vor einer Minute	*a minute ago*
vor einer Woche	*a week ago*
wahr	*true*
wann	*when*
warten	*wait*
warum	*why*
Woche (*f.*)	*week*
Wohnung (*f.*)	*apartment*
zeigen	*show*

8

Irregular Past Tense and Neuter Plurals

This chapter introduces the irregular past tense and its conjugations. In addition, you will become acquainted with more numbers, periods of time, and plural formations for neuter nouns.

Some questions that will be answered are:

✓ How is the irregular past tense different from the regular past tense?
✓ What are the conjugational endings for the irregular past tense?
✓ How are numbers greater than 20 used?
✓ How do neuter nouns change in the plural?

Irregular Past Tense

All European languages have irregularities in tense formation. English is no exception. In English, the irregular past tense differs from the regular past tense in a variety of ways. The primary difference is with the regular past tense suffix *-ed,* which is rarely used in the irregular past tense. In some instances, the irregular past tense is identical to the present tense. For example:

Present	Past
cut	*cut*
put	*put*
set	*set*

In general, the irregular past tense is formed not by a suffix but by a vowel shift or change. Let's look at a few examples:

Present	Past
come	*came*
do	*did*
run	*ran*
take	*took*

The most radical of the irregular past tense forms are the verbs *be* and *go*:

Present	Past
be	*was, were*
go	*went*

It is something of an advantage to be a speaker of English because its irregular past tense is similar to the German irregular past tense. Some of the vowel shifts are identical, and many irregular forms are therefore easy to remember.

Step 1: German Irregular Past Tense

The regular past tense in German requires the use of the suffix **-te** plus any necessary conjugational ending. For example:

Infinitive	Past Tense	
lernen	ich lernte	*I learned*
suchen	du suchtest	*you looked for*
brauchen	wir brauchten	*we needed*

The irregular past tense most often does not use the **-te** suffix. Instead, like English, there is most often a vowel shift of change. Let's look at some commonly used verbs that make a vowel shift similar to English:

Infinitive	Past Tense	English Infinitive/Past Tense
kommen	kam	*come/came*
singen	sang	*sing/sang*
trinken	trank	*drink/drank*
sehen	sah	*see/saw*

Naturally, not all German verbs follow the same pattern as English. Let's look at some other patterns:

Infinitive	Past Tense	English Infinitive/Past Tense
essen	aß	*eat/ate*
fahren	fuhr	*drive/drove*
finden	fand	*find/found*
fliegen	flog	*fly/flew*
gehen	ging	*go/went*
heißen	hieß	*call, be named/called, was named*
helfen	half	*help/helped*
laufen	lief	*run/ran*
lesen	las	*read/read*
schreiben	schrieb	*write/wrote*
sprechen	sprach	*speak/spoke*
tun	tat	*do/did*
verstehen	verstand	*understand/understood*

The German past tense verbs shown here are in their basic form. They still require conjugational endings similar to the ones you already know. The exceptions are the first and third persons singular (**ich** and **er, sie, es**), which require no conjugational endings. For example:

	essen		**lesen**		**schreiben**	
ich	aß	*I ate*	las	*I read*	schrieb	*I wrote*
du	aßt	*you ate*	last	*you read*	schriebst	*you wrote*
er	aß	*he ate*	las	*he read*	schrieb	*he wrote*
wir	aßen	*we ate*	lasen	*we read*	schrieben	*we wrote*
ihr	aßt	*you ate*	last	*you read*	schriebt	*you wrote*
Sie	aßen	*you ate*	lasen	*you read*	schrieben	*you wrote*
sie	aßen	*they ate*	lasen	*they read*	schrieben	*they wrote*

Exercise 8.1

Provide the conjugation of each of the verbs listed with the subjects provided.
For example:

lesen   **fahren**
ich las   fuhr
du last   fuhrst

	trinken	**verstehen**	**kommen**	**heißen**
1. ich	_____	_____	_____	_____
2. du	_____	_____	_____	_____
3. er	_____	_____	_____	_____
4. wir	_____	_____	_____	_____
5. ihr	_____	_____	_____	_____
6. Sie	_____	_____	_____	_____
7. sie *pl.*	_____	_____	_____	_____
8. Erik	_____	_____	_____	_____
9. wer	_____	_____	_____	_____
10. sie *s.*	_____	_____	_____	_____

When a past tense ends in **-s** or **-ß**, the second person singular (**du**) does not use the conjugational ending **-st** but only **-t**. For example:

lesen   ich las   du <u>last</u>
heißen   ich hieß   du <u>hießt</u>

Don't forget that conjugational endings add an **e** when the past tense stem ends in **-t** or **-d**. For example:

verstehen   ich verstand   du verstandest   ihr verstandet
bitten   ich bat   du batest   ihr batet

Say It Out Loud

Read each sentence out loud, paying attention to the conjugation of the irregular past tense verbs:

Ich fand zehn Euro auf der Straße.   *I found 10 euros on the street.*
Er sprach Russisch.   *He spoke Russian.*
Wir verstanden kein Wort.   *We did not understand a word.*

Die Kinder liefen durch den Garten.	*The children ran through the garden.*
Sie bat um ein Glas Wasser.	*She asked for a glass of water.*
Trank sie kein Bier oder Wein?	*Didn't she drink any beer or wine?*
Warum schrieben Sie diesen Brief?	*Why did you write this letter?*
Wer kam an die Tür?	*Who came to the door?*
Der Briefträger kam mit einer Postkarte.	*The letter carrier came with a postcard.*
Sangen die Kinder schön?	*Did the children sing nicely?*
Was tat er?	*What did he do?*
Er bekam einen Brief.	*He received a letter.*

Wondering About This? *bekam*

When the verb **kommen** adds the prefix **be-**, it becomes **bekommen**. Although **kommen** means *come,* **bekommen** means *receive* or *get.* Just as the past tense of **kommen** is **kam**, the past tense of **bekommen** is **bekam** (*received, got*). This use of prefixes is common in German as well as in English. Consider the following English words:

come	*have*	*sight*
become	*behave*	*insight*

Let's look at more examples in German:

stehen	*stand*	sprechen	*speak*	warten	*wait*
verstehen	*understand*	versprechen	*promise*	erwarten	*await, expect*

In nearly all cases, the past tense of a verb without a prefix is the same as the past tense of that verb with a prefix.

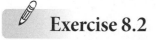

Exercise 8.2

Fill in the blank with the correct past tense of the verb in parentheses. For example:

(lesen) Die Kinder *lasen* das Buch.

1. (schreiben) Meine Mutter _____ vier Briefe.

2. (verstehen) Warum _____ Sie kein Wort?

3. (singen) Meine Schwestern _____ ein altes Lied (*song*).

4. (gehen) Niemand _____ zum Park.

5. (heißen) Das Kind _____ Angela.

6. (bitten) _____ du um eine Tasse (*cup*) Kaffee?

7. (trinken) _____ ihr keinen Wein?

8. (fahren) Gestern _____ ich in die Schweiz.

9. (fliegen) Der junge Pilot _____ nach Italien.

10. (bekommen) Warum _____ wir nur (*only*) eine Postkarte?

 There are a few more adverbial expressions that suggest that an action or event can take place in the past. They are:

am Vormittag	*in the morning*
am Mittag	*at noon*
am Nachmittag	*in the afternoon*
am Abend	*in the evening*
in der Nacht	*at night*

Say It Out Loud

Read each sentence out loud, paying attention to the adverbs that help describe when the past tense action took place:

Am Vormittag aßen wir in der Küche.	*In the morning we ate in the kitchen.*
Am Mittag ging er nach Hause.	*He went home at noon.*
Was tatet ihr am Nachmittag?	*What did you do in the afternoon?*
Am Abend lasen wir die Zeitung.	*In the evening we read the newspaper.*
In der Nacht kam ein Mann an die Tür.	*At night a man came to the door.*
Gestern flogen die Touristen nach Moskau.	*Yesterday the tourists flew to Moscow.*
Vor einer Woche fand er seinen Pass wieder.	*A week ago he found his passport again.*

 ## Step 2: Numbers, the Year, and Age

You have already learned the numbers from 1 to 20. Numbers greater than 20 do something special. The number is stated in the same way that it was in English in a former time: *4 and 20 blackbirds, 8 and 40 pounds.* Let's look at some numbers greater than 19:

20 zwanzig	30 dreißig
21 einundzwanzig	33 dreiunddreißig
22 zweiundzwanzig	40 vierzig

44 vierundvierzig	74 vierundsiebzig
50 fünfzig	80 achtzig
56 sechsundfünfzig	85 fünfundachtzig
59 neunundfünfzig	90 neunzig
60 sechzig	97 siebenundneunzig
61 einundsechzig	100 hundert
63 dreiundsechzig	1,000 tausend
70 siebzig	10,000 zehntausend

No matter how large a number is, it is written as one word; therefore, Germans tend to use numerals far more than words to express numbers. In order to be clear about how a number is structured, the following examples will not follow the German tendency and will express numbers as words.

Say It Out Loud

Read each sentence out loud, paying attention to how the numbers are formed.

Es kostete zweihundert Euro pro Monat.	*It cost 200 euros per month.*
Die Mäntel kosteten fünfundvierzig Euro.	*The coats cost 45 euros.*
Martin brauchte achthundert Dollar.	*Martin needed 800 dollars.*
Vierundneunzig minus fünf ist neunundachtzig.	*Ninety-four minus five is eighty-nine.*
Der Polizist ist vierundzwanzig Jahre alt.	*The police officer is 24 years old.*
Ich habe viertausend Euro in der Bank.	*I have 4,000 euros in the bank.*
Dreiunddreißig plus elf ist vierundvierzig.	*Thirty-three plus eleven is forty-four.*

The Year

A year is made up of 12 months, four weeks in each month, and seven days in each week. These are *high-frequency* elements of any language and play an important role in learning German.

German expresses years in an easy-to-understand way:

1855	achtzehnhundertfünfundfünfzig	*eighteen fifty-five*
1978	neunzehnhundertachtundsiebzig	*nineteen seventy-eight*
2019	zweitausendneunzehn	*two thousand nineteen, twenty nineteen*

Let's look at some example sentences that illustrate how years can be used.

Say It Out Loud

Read each sentence out loud, paying attention to how the years are expressed. Be careful pronouncing the years that are expressed as numerals.

Wann sind Sie geboren?	*When were you born?*
Ich bin im Jahre neunzehnhundert-neunundachtzig geboren.	*I was born in (the year) 1989.*
Ich bin im Jahre zweitausendeins geboren.	*I was born in (the year) 2001.*
Sie ist neunzehnhundertsiebzig geboren.	*She was born in 1970.*
Das Kind ist im Jahre 2009 geboren.	*The child was born in (the year) 2009.*
Die Zwillinge sind 1999 geboren.	*The twins were born in 1999.*
Er kam im Jahre 2012 nach Amerika.	*He came to America in (the year) 2012.*
Sie besuchte 2018 ihre Eltern in Bonn.	*In 2018 she visited her parents in Bonn.*

Wondering About This? *im Jahre*

German says *in a certain year* in two ways: with the phrase **im Jahre** and omitting the phrase **im Jahre**. In either case the English translation is the same. For example:

Sie ist im Jahre 1988 geboren.	*She was born in 1988.*
Sie ist 1988 geboren.	*She was born in 1988.*
Ich bin im Jahre 2002 geboren.	*I was born in 2002.*
Ich bin 2002 geboren.	*I was born in 2002.*

Be careful. Note that when **im Jahre** is omitted, there is no preposition **in** in the German sentence.

The Months

Remembering the German months is relatively simple because their names are similar to English:

Januar	*January*
Februar	*February*
März	*March*
April	*April*
Mai	*May*
Juni	*June*

Juli	*July*
August	*August*
September	*September*
Oktober	*October*
November	*November*
Dezember	*December*

When saying *in what month* something occurred, the preposition **im** precedes the month. For example:

Er ist im Oktober geboren.	*He was born in October.*
Erik besuchte Monika im Juli.	*Erik visited Monika in July.*
Im Dezember arbeitete ich in Berlin.	*In December I worked in Berlin.*

Just as **im** is used with the phrase **im Jahre** or with the months, it is also used when telling *in what season* something occurred:

Im Sommer wohnte sie in Heidelberg.	*In the summer she lived in Heidelberg.*
Im Herbst ist es oft kühl.	*In the fall, it is often cool.*
Im Winter schneit es.	*It snows in the winter.*
Im Frühling regnet es sehr oft.	*In the spring it rains very often.*

Days of the Week

The days of the week are:

Montag	*Monday*
Dienstag	*Tuesday*
Mittwoch	*Wednesday*
Donnerstag	*Thursday*
Freitag	*Friday*
Samstag/Sonnabend	*Saturday*
Sonntag	*Sunday*

When telling *on what day* something occurred, the preposition **am** precedes the day:

Am Montag ging ich zur Schule.	*On Monday I went to school.*
Was tut ihr am Mittwoch?	*What are you doing on Wednesday?*
Am Samstag kam Marianne nach Hause.	*Marianne came home on Saturday.*

In Chapter 7 you encountered the phrase **vor einem Jahr** (*a year ago*). Those words translated more literally to *a year before*. This expression like the years, months, and days describes a moment in time: **Vor einem Jahr wohnte ich in Spanien.** *A year ago I lived in Spain.* The noun **Jahr** can be replaced by other words that describe a moment in time. For example:

Vor einem Tag bekam ich seinen Brief.	*A day ago I received his letter.*
Vor einer Woche besuchten wir sie.	*A week ago we visited them.*
Vor einem Monat flog sie nach Polen.	*A month ago she flew to Poland.*

Say It Out Loud

Read each sentence out loud, paying attention to when the action takes place:

Im Jahre 1999 wohnten wir in Frankreich.	*In 1999 we lived in France.*
Bist du im Juni oder Juli geboren?	*Were you born in June or July?*
Mein Geburtstag ist im März.	*My birthday is in March.*
Ist Ihr Geburtstag im Februar?	*Is your birthday in February?*
Im August ist es sehr heiß.	*In August it is very hot.*
Ist es noch warm im Herbst?	*Is it still warm in the fall?*
Am Sonntag sind meine Eltern oft zu Hause.	*My parents are often at home on Sunday.*
Sein Geburtstag ist am Dienstag.	*His birthday is on Tuesday.*
Am Donnerstag flogen sie nach Spanien.	*On Thursday they flew to Spain.*
Wessen Geburtstag ist am Sonnabend?	*Whose birthday is on Saturday?*
Vor einem Monat bekam ich diese Postkarte.	*A month ago I received this postcard.*

 The noun **die Postkarte** means postcard. If you are talking about picture postcards that show images of places you visited, the noun you need is **die Ansichtskarte** (*picture postcard*).

Exercise 8.3

Reword each sentence with the word or phrase provided in parentheses. For example:

_____ arbeitete er in Berlin.

(September) *Im September arbeitete er in Berlin.*

(Winter) *Im Winter arbeitete er in Berlin.*

Ihr Geburtstag ist _____.

1. (Herbst) _____

2. (Dienstag) _____

3. (Januar) _____

Wo wohntet ihr _____?

4. (Oktober) _____

5. (Sommer) _____

6. (2010) _____

Mein Sohn ist _____ geboren.

7. (Montag) _____

8. (Dezember) _____

Ich besuchte meine Familie _____.

9. (Frühling) _____

10. (März) _____

Wondering About This? *im, am*

The words **im** and **am** are actually not prepositions but *contractions* of a preposition and a definite article. German often makes a contraction of these two elements. For example:

Preposition and Article	Contraction	
an dem	am	*on the, at the*
in das	ins	*into the*
in dem	im	*in the*
zu dem	zum	*to the*
zu der	zur	*to the*

For the time being, do not worry about the grammar associated with these contractions. This will be explained fully in a future chapter.

Using *fragen*

The verb **fragen** means *ask a question*. It is frequently used to introduce a question that was posed by someone. When this occurs in German, there is a different word order than when it occurs in English. Compare the English questions and statements that follow *ask*. Take note of the position of the verb.

> *Where <u>is</u> your brother today? She asks where your brother <u>is</u> today.*
>
> *Whom did you see there? I ask whom you <u>saw</u> there.*
>
> *Why must she tell lies? He asks why she <u>must</u> tell lies.*

Now look at similar questions in German and take note of the position of the verb:

Wo <u>arbeitet</u> Herr Bauer? Er fragt, wo Herr Bauer <u>arbeitet</u>.	*He asks where Mr. Bauer works.*
Wann <u>kommt</u> der nächste Zug? Ich frage, wann der nächste Zug <u>kommt</u>.	*I ask when the next train is coming.*
Wessen Freund <u>bekam</u> den Brief? Er fragt, wessen Freund den Brief <u>bekam</u>.	*He asks whose friend received the letter.*
Wie schnell <u>läuft</u> der Sportler? Sie fragen, wie schnell der Sportler <u>läuft</u>.	*They ask how fast the athlete runs.*

When a question is made into a statement after the verb **fragen**, the verb becomes the last element in the sentence.

Exercise 8.4

*Reword each question with the phrase **Er fragt.** For example:*

> Was kaufte die Frau? *Er fragt, was die Frau kaufte.*

1. Wer ist jetzt zwanzig Jahre alt? _____

2. Wessen Bruder wohnt in der Schweiz? _____

3. Wie heißen diese Mädchen? _____

4. Wen besuchten die Touristen in München? _____

5. Wie alt ist deine Tochter? _____

6. Wann möchten Sie nach Hause fahren? _____

7. Wohin liefen die Jungen? _____

8. Was kostet zweihundert Euro? _____

9. Woher kamen diese Männer? _____

10. Wann ist ihr Geburtstag? _____

Say It Out Loud

Read each sentence out loud, paying attention to how age is expressed:

Wie alt ist Ihre Frau?	*How old is your wife?*
Meine Frau ist einunddreißig Jahre alt.	*My wife is 31 years old.*
Wie alt ist die Burg?	*How old is the castle?*
Die Burg ist eintausendzwanzig Jahre alt.	*The castle is 1,020 years old.*
Wie alt ist das Baby?	*How old is the baby?*
Das Baby ist sechs Monate alt.	*The baby is six months old.*
Wie alt ist euer Haus?	*How old is your house?*
Unser Haus ist zwei Jahre alt.	*Our house is two years old.*

Neuter Plurals

Just like masculine and feminine plurals, neuter plurals follow some patterns, but these patterns are not always consistent, and irregularities sometimes occur. The simplest form of neuter plural is with nouns that end in the diminutive suffixes **-chen** and **-lein**:

Neuter	Plural	
das Mädchen	die Mädchen	*the girls*
kein Mädchen	keine Mädchen	*no girls*
ein Mädchen	Mädchen	*girls*
das Röslein	die Röslein	*the little roses*
dieses Röslein	diese Röslein	*these little roses*
ein Röslein	Röslein	*little roses*

As with masculine and feminine plurals, neuter plurals use the definite article **die**, and when the article suggests an indefinite meaning, no article is used. If **der**-words or **ein**-words modify plurals, they have an **-e** ending.

Neuter nouns that are of one syllable tend to form the plural with the ending **-er**. On less frequent occasions, nouns of more than one syllable use this ending as well. If the noun has an umlaut vowel (**a, o, u**), there is a tendency to add an umlaut in the plural. For example:

Neuter	Plural	
das Bild	die Bilder	the pictures
das Buch	die Bücher	the books
das Gesicht	die Gesichter	the faces
das Haus	die Häuser	the houses
das Kind	die Kinder	the children
das Land	die Länder	the lands, countries

You have already discovered that German plurals often break the rules. This is true of masculine, feminine, or neuter nouns. Some of the neuter plurals that break the rules are:

das Bett	die Betten	the beds
das Drama	die Dramen	the dramas
das Gebäude	die Gebäude	the buildings
das Hemd	die Hemden	the shirts
das Sweatshirt	die Sweatshirts	the sweatshirts
das Theater	die Theater	the theaters

 ## Exercise 8.5

Reword each sentence, changing the singular neuter subject to a plural subject. For example:

Das Kind ist drei Jahre alt.

Die Kinder sind drei Jahre alt.

1. Dieses Land ist sehr weit (*far*) von hier.

   _____

2. Das Mädchen lief sehr schnell.

   _____

3. Wo ist dein Haus?

   _____

4. Ist das Theater an der Ecke neu?

_____

5. Dieses Buch ist sehr alt.

_____

6. Mein Hemd ist rot und weiß.

_____

7. Das Kind spielt im Garten.

_____

8. Dieses Büchlein ist alt.

_____

9. Ihr Gesicht ist nicht schön.

_____

10. Ist dieses Lied alt?

_____

 **Let's Read**

Read the following dialogue and determine the meaning of the lines on your own:

WERNER: Guten Abend, Marianne. Wohin gehst du?

MARIANNE: Ich gehe zur Geburtstagsparty. Meine Großmutter ist achtzig.

WERNER: Wann hast du Geburtstag?

MARIANNE: Im Mai. Ich bin im Jahre 1998 geboren.

WERNER: Mein Geburtstag ist auch im Mai.

MARIANNE: Wann bist du geboren? 1998?

WERNER: Nein, ich bin 1991 geboren.

MARIANNE: Auf Wiedersehen, Werner.

WERNER: Tschüß.

✐ Review Quiz 8

Choose the letter of the word or phrase that best completes each sentence.

1. Er _____ eine Apfelsine und trank ein Glas Milch.

    a. trinkt   c. kaufst

    b. aß   d. verkauftest

2. Erik _____ um ein Glas Wasser.

    a. batet   c. möchtest

    b. bat   d. möchtet

3. _____ arbeitete ich in München.

    a. Ein Jahr   c. Vor einem Monat

    b. März   d. Sommer und Herbst

4. _____ Mädchen lasen die Zeitungen.

    a. Kein   c. Mein

    b. Dieses   d. Die

5. Am _____ ging ich ins Theater.

    a. Abend   c. Frühling

    b. Woche   d. vor einem Jahr

6. _____ du wieder nach Heidelberg?

    a. Fuhrst   c. Flogen

    b. Lief   d. Lauft

7. _____ Juni besuchten wir unsere Eltern.

    a. Vor einem   c. 2010

    b. Im   d. Im Jahre

8. Dieser Wagen kostete _____ Euro.

    a. wie viel   c. siebentausend

    b. ihr   d. eins

9. Seine _____ sind in der Küche.

    a. Lied   c. Boden

    b. Bücher   d. Landkarte

10. Unsere Tochter ist jetzt _____ alt.

    a. neunzehn Jahre   c. im Jahre 1999

    b. vor einem Jahr   d. das Jahr

New Vocabulary

Abend (*m.*)	*evening*
April	*April*
August	*August*
Baby (*n.*)	*baby*
bekommen	*receive, get*
Bett (*n.*)	*bed*
Bild (*n.*)	*picture*
Briefträger (*m.*)	*letter carrier*
Burg (*f.*)	*castle*
Dezember	*December*
Dienstag (*m.*)	*Tuesday*
Donnerstag (*m.*)	*Thursday*
Drama (*n.*)	*drama*
erwarten	*await, expect*
Februar	*February*
finden	*find*
fliegen	*fly*
Freitag (*m.*)	*Friday*
Frühling (*m.*)	*spring*
Gebäude (*n.*)	*building*
geboren	*born*
Geburtstag (*m.*)	*birthday*
Gesicht (*n.*)	*face*
helfen	*help*
Herbst (*m.*)	*fall, autumn*
Jahr (*n.*)	*year*
Januar	*January*
Juli	*July*
Juni	*June*
Lied (*n.*)	*song*
Mai	*May*
März	*March*
Mittag (*m.*)	*noon, midday*
Mittwoch (*m.*)	*Wednesday*

Monat (*m.*)	*month*
Montag (*m.*)	*Monday*
Nachmittag (*m.*)	*afternoon*
Nacht (*f.*)	*night*
November	*November*
Oktober	*October*
Russisch	*Russian*
Samstag/Sonnabend (*m.*)	*Saturday*
schön	*nice, pretty*
schreiben	*write*
September	*September*
Sommer (*m.*)	*summer*
Tasse (*f.*)	*cup*
Theater (*n.*)	*theater*
tun	*do*
Tür (*f.*)	*door*
versprechen	*promise*
verstehen	*understand*
vor	*before*
Vormittag (*m.*)	*morning*
Wasser (*n.*)	*water*
weit	*far*
Winter (*m.*)	*winter*
Woche (*f.*)	*week*

9

Dative Case and More Irregular Past Tense

In this chapter you will encounter the dative case and its use. Some important verbs and their various applications will also be introduced.

Some questions that will be answered are:

✓ How does the dative case differ from the nominative and accusative cases?
✓ What form do objects take in the dative case?
✓ How are **haben**, **sein**, and **werden** conjugated in the past tense?
✓ What are the conjugations of verbs like **wissen** and **kennen**?

Dative Case

There is no dative case in English. English uses the terms *subjective case* (nominative) and *object case* (accusative) to describe the two kinds of English declensions. In the objective case, *objects* are the nouns and primarily the pronouns that are affected by the case. For example:

Subjective: <u>The boys</u> are playing soccer.

   <u>They</u> are playing soccer.

Objective: We watch <u>the boys</u>. (direct object)

   We watch <u>them</u>. (direct object)

   We take pictures <u>of the boys</u>. (object of the preposition *of*)

   We take pictures <u>of them</u>. (object of the preposition *of*)

   We gave <u>the boys</u> their trophy. (indirect object)

   We gave <u>them</u> their trophy. (indirect object)

The objective case is used with direct objects, objects of prepositions, and indirect objects.

You have already learned how to identify the direct object: ask *whom* or *what* of the subject and verb. To identify the indirect object, ask *to whom* or *for whom* of the subject and verb. For example:

We gave *the boys their trophy.*	(To whom did we give *the boys* = indirect object the trophy?)
They sent *me another check.*	(To whom did they *me* = indirect object send another check?)
I bought Mary a gift.	(For whom did I buy a *Mary* = indirect object gift?)

It is important to be able to identify the indirect object in a sentence because German requires a special case with indirect objects: the dative case.

Step 1: Dative Case in German

Nouns

In the accusative case, only masculine nouns make a change from the nominative:

Nom.	der Mann, die Frau, das Kind, die Kinder
Acc.	<u>den</u> Mann, die Frau, das Kind, die Kinder

In the dative case all nouns make a change, and that change is identical with **der**-words or **ein**-words. Let's look at the dative endings for the three genders and the plural and with a variety of **der**-words and **ein**-words:

Masculine	Feminine	Neuter	Plural
dem Freund	der Freundin	dem Haus	den Lampen
einem Freund	keiner Freundin	diesem Haus	jenen Lampen
ihrem Freund	eurer Freundin	seinem Haus	meinen Lampen
unserem Freund	jeder Freundin	einem Haus	diesen Lampen

Something special takes place in the dative plural: The ending for **der**-words and **ein**-words is **-en**. But plural nouns also add an **-n** if their plural form does not end in one, for example, **diesen Kinder<u>n</u>, meinen Brüder<u>n</u>, keinen Filme<u>n</u>.**

Let's review the other two cases together with the new dative endings:

	Masculine	Feminine	Neuter	Plural
Nom.	der Stuhl	diese Zeitung	ein Buch	seine Bücher
Acc.	den Stuhl	diese Zeitung	ein Buch	seine Bücher
Dat.	dem Stuhl	dieser Zeitung	einem Buch	seinen Büchern

Now you have the new dative endings, but what do you do with them?

Indirect Objects

You now know how to identify an indirect object in English: ask *to whom* or *for whom* of the subject and verb. The same thing works in German: ask *wem* of the subject and verb. For example:

Ich sende dem Mann eine Ansichtskarte.	*I send the man a picture postcard.*	(Wem sende ich eine Ansichtskarte?)	dem Mann = *indirect object*
Wir kaufen unserer Tante eine Bluse.	*We buy our aunt a blouse.*	(Wem kaufen wir eine Bluse?)	unserer Tante = *indirect object*
Martin schenkt seinen Freunden Ansichtskarten.	*Martin gives (presents . . . with) his friends picture postcards.*	(Wem schenkt Martin Ansichtskarten?)	seinen Freunden = *indirect object*

Say It Out Loud

Read each sentence out loud while identifying the indirect object in each sentence:

Wir senden den Mädchen zwanzig Euro.	*We send the girls 20 euros.*
Was gibst du deiner Frau?	*What are you giving your wife?*
Thomas schenkte dem Lehrer einen Bleistift.	*Thomas gave the teacher a pencil.*
Kaufen Sie dem Kind Eis?	*Are you buying the child ice cream?*
Ich gebe der Kellnerin das Geld.	*I give the waitress the money.*
Sie bringt ihrem Bruder ein Glas Wasser.	*She brings her brother a glass of water.*
Geben sie den Sportlern neue Uniformen?	*Are they giving the athletes new uniforms?*

Exercise 9.1

Identify the indirect object in each sentence. For example:

Wir senden <u>dem Mann</u> eine Postkarte.

1. Ich kaufte meiner Frau drei Rosen.

2. Marianne bringt seiner Schwester einen Pullover.

3. Geben Sie Ihren Eltern genug (*enough*) Geld?

4. Ihr gebt dem Mann fünf Euro.

5. Vor einer Woche kauften sie den Jungen neue Sweatshirts.

6. Meine Mutter schenkte der Lehrerin Handschuhe (*gloves*).

7. Was sendet ihr dem Richter?

8. Herr Braun gibt seinem Sohn die Schlüssel (*keys*).

9. Sie schickt (*send*) ihren Freundinnen Ansichtskarten.

10. Bringst du dem Geburtstagskind (*birthday boy*) ein Geschenk?

Wondering About This? *senden, schicken*

Both **senden** and **schicken** mean *send* something to somebody. For the most part, they can be used interchangeably:

Ich sende der Frau eine Ansichtskarte.	*I send the woman a picture postcard.*
Ich schicke der Frau eine Ansichtskarte.	*I send the woman a picture postcard.*

However, **schicken** is also used in expressions in which people are sent somewhere. For example:

Wir schicken Hans nach Hause.	*We send Hans home.*

Exercise 9.2

Reword each sentence with the words provided in parentheses. For example:

Ich sende _____ einen Brief.

(mein Vater) *Ich sende meinem Vater einen Brief.*

Wir kauften _____ neue Handschuhe.

1. (eure Kinder) _____

2. (unser Sohn) _____

3. (die Dame) _____

Erik gibt _____ ein Geschenk.

4. (seine Freundin) _____

5. (das Geburtstagskind) _____

6. (sein Professor) _____

Was schickten Sie _____?

7. (Ihre Tochter) _____

8. (Ihre Eltern) _____

9. (Ihr Gast *guest*) _____

10. (das Mädchen) _____

Pronouns

Not only nouns have a dative declension, but pronouns also do. Let's compare the personal pronouns in the three cases:

Nominative	Accusative	Dative
ich	mich	mir
du	dich	dir
er	ihn	ihm
sie *s.*	sie	ihr
es	es	ihm

Nominative	Accusative	Dative
wir	uns	uns
ihr	euch	euch
Sie	Sie	Ihnen
sie *pl.*	sie	ihnen
wer	wen	wem

The dative pronouns are used as indirect objects just like nouns.

Say It Out Loud

Read each sentence out loud, paying attention to the use of the dative pronouns:

Was geben Sie Ihrem Sohn?	*What are you giving your son?*
Ich gebe ihm drei Geschenke.	*I am giving him three gifts.*
Marianne sendet mir eine SMS.	*Marianne sends me a text message.*
Wem sendet ihr diesen Brief?	*To whom are you sending this letter?*
Wir senden dir diesen Brief.	*We are sending you this letter.*
Karl kaufte ihr ein neues Kleid.	*Karl bought her a new dress.*
Warum schickten Sie uns keine Bücher?	*Why didn't you send us any books?*
Die Kellnerin bringt euch drei Glas Bier.	*The waitress brings you three glasses of beer.*
Ich möchte Ihnen ein paar Blumen schenken.	*I would like to give you a couple of flowers.*
Was möchtest du ihnen schicken?	*What would you like to send them?*

 ## Exercise 9.3

Reword each sentence with the pronouns provided in parentheses. For example:

Ich sende _____ einen Brief.

(er) *Ich sende ihm einen Brief.*

Was kaufen Sie _____?

1. (ich) _____

2. (er) _____

3. (sie *pl.*) _____

    Der Kellner bringt _____ eine Flasche (*bottle*) Wein.

4. (du) _____

5. (sie *s.*) _____

6. (ihr) _____

    Gibst du _____ genug Geld?

7. (wir) _____

8. (sie *pl.*) _____

9. (ich) _____

10. (er) _____

Prepositions

German has a short list of accusative case prepositions. There are also dative case prepositions. They are:

aus	*out, from*
außer	*except*
bei	*by, at, at the home of*
gegenüber	*across from, opposite*
mit	*with*
nach	*after*
seit	*since*
von	*from, of*
zu	*to, to a person's home*

Nouns and pronouns that follow these prepositions are in the dative case. For example:

Er kommt <u>aus der Schule</u>.	*He comes out of the school.*
Der Mann sprach <u>mit ihnen</u>.	*The man spoke with them.*
Was tut ihr <u>nach dem Konzert</u>?	*What are you doing after the concert?*
Thomas wohnt jetzt <u>bei mir</u>.	*Thomas now lives with me.*

Say It Out Loud

Read each sentence out loud, paying attention to the use of the dative prepositions:

Warum trinkst du aus der Flasche?	*Why are you drinking out of the bottle?*
Meine Cousine kommt aus Bremen.	*My cousin comes from Bremen.*
Niemand hilft mir außer dir.	*No one helps me except you.*
Wohnen Sie noch bei Ihren Eltern?	*Are you still living with your parents?*
Gegenüber dem Bahnhof steht das Rathaus.	*City hall is across from the railroad station.*
Der junge Sportler sitzt ihr gegenüber.	*The young athlete sits opposite her.*
Ich fahre mit dem Zug nach Österreich.	*I travel by train to Austria.*
Die Kinder möchten mit ihnen spielen.	*The children would like to play with them.*
Nach der Schule gingen wir ins Kino.	*After school we went to the movies.*
Der Tourist fragte nach ihm.	*The tourist asked about (after) him.*
Ich studiere seit Oktober in Hamburg.	*I've been studying in Hamburg since October.*
Er ist seit dem Unfall im Krankenhaus.	*He has been in the hospital since the accident.*
Eine hübsche Frau sitzt links von mir.	*A beautiful woman sits left of me.*
Sie gibt mir ein Stück von dem Kuchen.	*She gives me a piece of the cake.*
Mein Vater ging spät zur Arbeit.	*My father went to work late.*
Frau Benz fährt zum Arzt.	*Ms. Benz drives to the doctor.*

Wondering About This? *fragen nach, hilft mir*

The verb **fragen** is often accompanied by **nach** and means *ask about*. But the preposition *after* is also used for the translation, which is closer to the actual German meaning. The point being made here is that verbs are often accompanied by specific prepositions, such as **bitten um** (*ask for, request*).

This also occurs in English. You could pick prepositions at random to be used with a verb, but only certain ones are considered correct to achieve the desire meaning. For example:

I am interested in . . . (not *interested of* or *to* or *from*)

It belongs to . . . (not *belongs out* or *into* or *for*)

Only the combination of *interested* and *in* achieves the correct and desired meaning.

Some German verbs that are accompanied by specific prepositions are:

arbeiten bei	(*work at*)
fahren/fliegen mit	(*travel/fly by*)
reden von	(*talk about*)
sprechen von	(*speak about*)
wohnen bei	(*live at someone's home*)

You probably noticed that in one of the previous sentences, the dative pronoun **mir** followed the verb **hilft** (**Niemand hilft <u>mir</u> außer dir.**). This occurs because German has *dative verbs*. Two such high-frequency verbs are **helfen** (*help*) and **glauben** (*believe*). Let's look at some examples of these verbs in sentences:

Ich helfe meinem Vater im Garten.	*I help my father in the garden.*
Er möchte ihr helfen.	*He would like to help her.*
Wir glauben dem Dieb nicht.	*We do not believe the thief.*
Warum glaubst du ihnen?	*Why do you believe them?*

Exercise 9.4

Reword each sentence with the phrases provided in parentheses. For example:

Niemand arbeitet außer _____.
(dein Bruder) *Niemand arbeitet außer deinem Bruder.*

Seine Eltern arbeiten bei _____.

1. (eine Bank *bank*) _____

2. (diese Firma *company*) _____

3. (die Bahn *railroad*) _____

Meine Großmutter sprach oft von _____.

4. (ihr Mann) _____

5. (ihr) _____

6. (sie *pl.*) _____

Die Kinder liefen aus _____.

7. (das Haus) _____

8. (die Schule) _____

9. (das Kino) _____

   Fahren Sie oft mit _____.

10. (der Bus) _____

11. (dieser Zug) _____

12. (Ihr Auto) _____

   Heute Abend gehen wir zu _____.

13. (der Arzt) _____

14. (unsere Eltern) _____

15. (ein Freund) _____

 It is common to change three of the dative prepositions to contractions when they are followed by definite articles in the dative case. Those prepositions are **bei**, **von**, and **zu**. For example:

Preposition and Article	Contraction	
bei dem	beim	*by the, at the*
von dem	vom	*from the, of the*
zu dem	zum	*to the*
zu der	zur	*to the*

This means that sentence 13 in Exercise 9.4 would read: **Heute Abend gehen wir zum Arzt.**

Haben, sein, werden in the Past Tense

It has already been pointed out that **haben**, **sein**, and **werden** are important verbs because they have a variety of functions. They are irregular verbs in the present tense and also irregular in the past tense. Let's look at their past tense conjugation:

	haben		**sein**		**werden**	
ich	hatte	*I had*	war	*I was*	wurde	*I became, got*
du	hattest	*you had*	warst	*you were*	wurdest	*you became, got*
er	hatte	*he had*	war	*he was*	wurde	*he became, got*
wir	hatten	*we had*	waren	*we were*	wurden	*we became, got*
ihr	hattet	*you had*	wart	*you were*	wurdet	*you became, got*
Sie	hatten	*you had*	waren	*you were*	wurden	*you became, got*
sie *pl.*	hatten	*they had*	waren	*they were*	wurden	*you became, got*
wer	hatte	*who had*	war	*who was*	wurde	*who became, got*

Say It Out Loud

Read each sentence out loud, paying attention to the irregular past tense verbs:

Ich hatte leider keine Zeit.	*Unfortunately, I didn't have any time.*
Hattest du genug Geld?	*Did you have enough money?*
Er hatte die neue Studentin gern.	*He liked the new student.*
Vor einem Jahr hatten wir ein Haus in den Alpen.	*A year ago we had a house in the Alps.*
Sie war eine sehr gute Freundin von mir.	*She was a very good friend of mine.*
Wart ihr noch am Nachmittag in der Bank?	*Were you still in the bank in the afternoon?*
Am Montag war es kalt und regnerisch.	*It was cold and rainy on Monday.*
Wann wurden Sie Physiklehrer?	*When did you become a physics teacher?*
Wann wurden sie so groß?	*When did they get so big?*
Das Wetter wurde immer schlechter.	*The weather got worse and worse.*
Es war kalt, und das Wasser wurde zu Eis.	*It was cold, and the water turned into ice.*

Exercise 9.5

Reword each sentence in the past tense. For example:

Es wird sehr warm.

Es wurde sehr warm.

1. Angela ist eine alte Freundin von mir.

   _____

2. Hat er viele Geschwister (*brothers and sisters, siblings*)?

   _____

3. Im Winter wird es sehr kalt.

   _____

4. Ich bin leider wieder krank.

   _____

5. Sie hat zwei Schwestern und einen Bruder.

_____

6. Herr Schneider wird Zahnarzt.

_____

7. Bist du reich (*rich*)?

_____

8. Der reiche Herr wird arm (*poor*).

_____

9. Seid ihr im Esszimmer (*dining room*) oder im Wohnzimmer (*living room*)?

_____

10. Haben Sie keine Zeit, Frau Schäfer?

_____

Step 2: *Wissen* and *kennen*

These two verbs are also high-frequency verbs and are sometimes confused because they have a similar meaning. Both mean *know*. But **wissen** means *to know* in the sense of *having knowledge*. **Kennen** means *know* in the sense of *being acquainted* with someone or something.

Let's look at **wissen** first. In the present tense, it is an irregular verb, but unlike other irregular verbs, its irregular conjugations occur throughout the singular. For example:

ich weiß	*I know*	wir wissen	*we know*
du weißt	*you know*	ihr wisst	*you know*
er weiß	*he knows*	Sie wissen	*you know*
wer weiß	*who knows*	sie wissen	*they know*

The verb **kennen** is regular in the present tense:

ich kenne	*I know*	wir kennen	*we know*
du kennst	*you know*	ihr kennt	*you know*
er kennt	*he knows*	Sie kennen	*you know*
wer kennt	*who knows*	sie kennen	*they know*

Say It Out Loud

*Read each sentence out loud, paying attention to the different uses of **wissen** and **kennen**:*

Wissen Sie, wo der Bahnhof ist?	*Do you know where the railroad station is?*
Nein, ich weiß es leider nicht.	*No, unfortunately, I don't.*
Kennst du den Sportler auf dem Fußballfeld?	*Do you know the athlete on the soccer field?*
Ja, ich kenne ihn. Er ist ein Freund von mir.	*Yes, I know him. He's a friend of mine.*
Onkel Heinz weiß nicht, wann das Kind geboren ist.	*Uncle Heinz doesn't know when the child was born.*
Wisst ihr, wie die Frau krank wurde?	*Do you know how the woman became sick?*
Kennen Sie meine Gäste, Herr Bauer?	*Do you know my guests, Mr. Bauer?*
Ich möchte wissen, warum der Junge weint.	*I would like to know why the boy is crying.*
Niemand kennt den Mann an der Ecke.	*No one knows the man on the corner.*

In the past tense **wissen** and **kennen** are irregular but have an unusual formation. They have both a vowel change and the suffix **-te**.

wissen

ich wusste	*I knew*	wir wussten	*we knew*
du wusstest	*you knew*	ihr wusstet	*you knew*
er wusste	*he knew*	Sie wussten	*you knew*
wer wusste	*who knew*	sie wussten	*they knew*

kennen

ich kannte	*I knew*	wir kannten	*we knew*
du kannest	*you knew*	ihr kanntet	*you knew*
er kannte	*he knew*	Sie kannten	*you knew*
wer kannte	*who knew*	sie kannten	*they knew*

Say It Out Loud

Read each sentence out loud, paying attention to the past tense conjugations of **wissen** *and* **kennen**:

Er wusste nicht, wer seinen Volkswagen kaufte.	*He didn't know who bought his Volkswagen.*
Vor zehn Jahren kannte ich den Mann gut.	*Ten years ago I knew the man well.*
Wussten Sie, wie alt Frau Keller war?	*Did you know how old Ms. Keller was?*
Wer kannte diese arme Frau?	*Who knew this old woman?*
Wir wussten nicht, warum er das Geld stahl.	*We didn't know why he stole the money.*
Kannten deine Eltern diesen Filmstar?	*Did your parents know this movie star?*
Er ist tot? Ich wusste es nicht!	*He's dead? I didn't know that!*
Ich kannte die Stadt Bremen sehr gut.	*I knew the city of Bremen very well.*

 ## Exercise 9.6

Reword each verb in the present and past tenses with the subjects provided. For example:

kennen
ich	*kenne*	*kannte*
wir	*kennen*	*kannten*
	Present	**Past**

kennen

1. er　　　_____　_____

2. wir　　_____　_____

3. sie *s.*　_____　_____

4. die Jungen　_____　_____

5. Sie　　_____　_____

wissen

6. ich   _____   _____

7. ihr   _____   _____

8. du   _____   _____

9. sie *pl.*   _____   _____

10. wer   _____   _____

 Some Useful Phrases

When someone questions you, and you do not know what the answer is or do not wish to answer, German has a very helpful expression. For example:

Weißt du, warum er es stahl?   *Do you know why he stole it?*

Ich weiß von nichts.   *I don't know anything about it.*

The verb **kennen** is often combined with **lernen** to mean *get to know* or *become acquainted*. The verb **lernen** is conjugated, and the verb **kennen** remains an infinitive and stands at the end of the sentence. For example:

Gestern lernte ich seinen Bruder kennen.   *Yesterday I became acquainted with his brother.*

Tina lernt alle Gäste kennen.   *Tina gets to know all the guests.*

 # Review Quiz 9

Choose the letter of the word or phrase that best completes each sentence.

1. Karin _____ jetzt bei einer Freundin.
   a. kommt   c. wohnt
   b. kennt   d. wart

2. Was geben Sie _____ Mädchen?
   a. dem   c. diese
   b. der   d. einen

3. Niemand _____ dem alten Mann.
   a. hilft   c. war
   b. arbeitet   d. wurde

4. Ich möchte mit _____ Lehrerin sprechen.

   a. der   c. jenen

   b. diese   d. meinem

5. Herr Benz lernte meine Freundin _____.

   a. waren   c. wissen

   b. sein   d. kennen

6. Meine Mutter arbeitete bei einer _____.

   a. Zug   c. Theater

   b. Bank   d. Bahnhof

7. _____ schicken Sie diese Ansichtskarten?

   a. Wem   c. Sie *s.*

   b. Ihr   d. Nachmittag

8. Thomas schenkt _____ einen Pullover.

   a. mich   c. ein Geschenk

   b. ihr   d. das Geburtstagskind

9. Der Kellner bringt _____ ein Glas Wasser.

   a. die Frauen   c. Geschwister

   b. seine Schwester   d. unserem Gast

10. Ich _____ nicht, warum mein Vater so spät arbeitet.

   a. machte   c. weiß

   b. wurde   d. außer Ihnen

New Vocabulary

Ansichtskarte (*f.*)	*picture postcard*
arm	*poor*
Bahn (*f.*)	*railroad*
Bank (*f.*)	*bank*
bringen	*bring*
ein paar	*a couple*
Eis (*n.*)	*ice, ice cream*
Firma (*f.*)	*company, firm*
Flasche (*f.*)	*bottle*
Gast (*m.*)	*guest*
Geburtstagskind (*n.*)	*birthday boy*

genug	*enough*
Geschwister (*pl.*)	*brothers and sisters, sibling*
glauben	*believe*
Handschuh (*m.*)	*glove*
hübsch	*beautiful, handsome*
immer	*always*
kennen	*know (be acquainted)*
Kino (*n.*)	*movie theater*
Kleid (*n.*)	*dress*
Krankenhaus (*n.*)	*hospital*
Kuchen (*m.*)	*cake*
leider	*unfortunately*
links	*on the left*
noch	*still*
reich	*rich*
schenken	*give, present with*
schicken	*send*
schlechter	*worse*
Schlüssel (*m.*)	*key*
senden	*send*
sitzen	*sit*
SMS (*n.*)	*text message*
spät	*late*
Stück (*n.*)	*piece*
studieren	*study (at the university)*
Unfall (*m.*)	*accident*
Uniform (*f.*)	*uniform*
wissen	*know (have knowledge)*

10

Dative Expressions and Conjunctions
aber, oder, und, and *sondern*

This chapter continues the discussion of the dative case and its uses. The conjunctions **aber, oder, und,** and **sondern** will be introduced, and the conjugation of **können** and **müssen** will be discussed.

Some questions that will be answered are:

✓ What other verbs require a dative object?
✓ How are impersonal expressions used with the dative case?
✓ How do conjunctions act to combine sentences?
✓ How are the conjugations of **können** and **müssen** used?

The Dative Case

In Chapter 9 you discovered the declensional endings for the dative case and how they are used with indirect objects. Identifying an indirect object is the first step in applying the dative case. Let's review that process.

Ask **wem** of the subject and verb of a sentence. The answer to that question is the indirect object. For example:

Sie gibt dem Kind einen Apfel.	*She gives the child an apple.*
Wem gibt sie einen Apfel?	*To whom does she give an apple?*
dem Kind = *indirect object*	

A dative declension is also used after the dative prepositions (**aus, außer, bei, gegenüber, mit, nach, seit, von, zu**). For example:

Sonja sprach <u>mit</u> ihrem Professor.	*Sonja spoke with her professor.*
Ich bekam einen Brief <u>von</u> einem Freund.	*I received a letter from a friend.*

163

The dative case also follows *dative verbs*, such as **helfen** and **glauben**. In English, the object following such verbs is a direct object. This causes students of German to want to use the accusative case with the dative verbs, but the dative case is required:

Wir helfen der armen Frau.	*We help the poor woman.*
Warum glaubst du mir nicht?	*Why don't you believe me?*

Step 1: More Dative Verbs and Dative Expressions

Along with **helfen** and **glauben**, there is a short list of other high-frequency dative verbs. They are:

antworten	*answer, reply*
danken	*thank*
dienen	*serve*
folgen	*follow*
gehören	*belong to*
gratulieren	*congratulate*
imponieren	*impress*
passen	*fit*
passieren	*happen*
vertrauen	*trust*

Nouns and pronouns that are the objects of these verbs must be in the dative case. For example:

Ich möchte <u>Ihnen</u> danken.	*I would like to thank you.*
Wir gratulieren <u>den Gewinnern</u>.	*We congratulate the winners.*
Was ist <u>ihm</u> passiert?	*What happened to him?*
Thomas vertraut <u>dem Mann</u> nicht.	*Thomas doesn't trust the man.*

Say It Out Loud

Read each sentence out loud, paying attention to the use of the dative verbs:

Sie antwortet dem Lehrer auf seine Frage.	*She replies to the teacher's question.*
Das dient einer guten Sache.	*That serves a good cause.*
Ein kleiner Hund folgte mir nach Hause.	*A little dog followed me home.*
Diese Armbanduhr gehört einem Freund von mir.	*This wristwatch belongs to a friend of mine.*
Wie kann ich dem hübschen Mädchen imponieren?	*How can I impress the beautiful girl?*
Der braune Anzug passt dir gar nicht.	*The brown suit doesn't fit you at all.*
Wir möchten unserem Gastgeber danken.	*We would like to thank our host.*
Ich gratulierte ihr zum Geburtstag.	*I congratulated her on her birthday.*
Nichts passierte deiner Katze.	*Nothing happened to your cat.*
Wie kann man einem Dieb vertrauen?	*How can one (you) trust a thief?*

Wondering About This? *man*

The pronoun **man** looks like the English word, but it has nothing to do with the noun **der Mann**. **Man** simply means *one* or *you* and describes not a specific person but people in general. In English, *one* sounds quite formal. Most people use *you* in its place. But in German you cannot use **du**, **ihr**, or **Sie** to achieve the same meaning. You use **man**. For example:

Man kann im Wartesaal sitzen.	*One/You can sit in the waiting room.*
Warum braucht man so viel Geld?	*Why does one/do you need so much money?*
Man studiert oft in der Bibliothek.	*One often studies/You often study in the library.*

It is important not to try to use **du**, **ihr**, or **Sie** when the desired meaning is *people in general*.

Exercise 10.1

Fill in the blank with the word or phrase in parentheses as it would complete the sentence. For example:

Er wohnt bei _____.

(seine Tante) *seiner Tante*

(wir) *uns*

Ich möchte _____ für das Geschenk danken.

1. (Sie) _____

2. (sie *s.*) _____

3. (der Gastgeber) _____

   Die Jungen folgen _____ zum Park.

4. (der Hund) _____

5. (eine Katze) _____

6. (sie *pl.*) _____

   Wie kann man _____ imponieren?

7. (die Lehrerinnen) _____

8. (ihr) _____

   Ich vertraue _____ nicht.

9. (du) _____

10. (diese Männer) _____

Some Useful Phrases

There are some expressions that require the use of a dative pronoun, but in the case of third person pronouns, **ihm**, **ihr**, and **Ihnen** are not used. Instead a special pronoun called a *reflexive pronoun* is used: **sich**. Its basic meaning is *oneself.*

Three verbs that use this concept are **putzen** (*brush*, *polish*), **brechen** (*break*), and **waschen** (*wash*). Look at the following example sentences, in which the third person pronouns are replaced by **sich**. Be aware that **waschen** is irregular in the second and third person singular present tense: **ich wasche**, **du wäschst**, **er wäscht**, and so on.

putzen

Ich putze mir die Zähne.	*I brush my teeth.*
Du putzt dir die Zähne.	*You brush your teeth.*

| Er putzt <u>sich</u> die Zähne. | *He brushes his teeth.* |
| Sie putzt <u>sich</u> die Zähne. | *She brushes her teeth.* |

brechen

Man bricht <u>sich</u> den Arm.	*One breaks/You break one's/your arm.*
Sie brechen <u>sich</u> den Finger.	*You break your finger.*
Du brichst <u>dir</u> das Bein.	*You break your leg.*
Monika bricht <u>sich</u> den Zeh.	*Monika breaks her toe.*

waschen

Ich wasche mir das Gesicht.	*I wash my face.*
Sie wäscht sich die Haare.	*She washes her hair.*
Wir waschen uns die Hände.	*We wash our hands.*

Say It Out Loud

Read each sentence out loud, paying attention to the dative expressions used:

Was passierte ihm?	*What happened to him?*
Er brach sich die Hand.	*He broke his hand.*
Meine Söhne brachen sich beide Hände.	*My sons broke both hands.*
Was tun die Kinder im Badezimmer?	*What are the children doing in the bathroom?*
Martin wäscht sich das Gesicht.	*Martin washes his face.*
Angela putzt sich die Zähne.	*Angela brushes her teeth.*
Beim Fußball fällt er um und bricht sich den Arm.	*In soccer he falls down and breaks his arm.*
Möchten Sie sich die Hände waschen?	*Would you like to wash your hands?*
Nein, ich möchte mir die Nase putzen.	*No, I'd like to blow my nose.*

✎ Exercise 10.2

Reword each sentence with the new subjects provided in parentheses. For example:

Ich putze mir die Zähne.

(wir) *Wir putzen uns die Zähne*.

Ich putze mir die Nase (*blow my nose*).

1. (wir) _____

2. (Sie) _____

3. (das Kind) _____

Ich wasche mir das Gesicht (*face*).

4. (die Kinder) _____

5. (du) _____

6. (man) _____

7. (mein Sohn) _____

Karl bricht sich die Hände (*hands*).

8. (ihr) _____

9. (sie *pl.*) _____

10. (wer) _____

Conjunctions

Four high-frequency conjugations are **aber** (*but*), **oder** (*or*), **und** (*and*), and **sondern** (*but [rather]*). You have already encountered **denn** (*because*) and practiced using this conjunction to form sentences that answer **warum** questions. Let's review the use of **denn**.

When replying to the questions **warum**, the question can be restated and then followed by a clause introduced by **denn**. For example:

Warum steht er an der Ecke?	*Why is he standing on the corner?*
Er steht an der Ecke, denn er wartet auf den Bus.	*He's standing on the corner because he's waiting for the bus.*

The two sentences **Er steht an der Ecke** and **Er wartet auf den Bus** are combined by the conjunction **denn.** Let's take two more sentences and combine them with this conjunction:

Sie schläft auf der Couch.	*She is sleeping on the couch.*
Sie ist krank.	*She is sick.*
Sie schläft auf der Couch, denn sie ist krank.	

The four new conjunctions do the same thing: they combine two sentences into one. Let's practice some example sentences.

Say It Out Loud

Read each sentence out loud, paying attention to how each of the four conjunctions are used:

aber

Ich höre seine Stimme, aber ich verstehe ihn nicht.	*I hear his voice, but I don't understand him.*
Er fragte sie wieder, aber sie antwortete nicht.	*He asked her again, but she didn't answer.*
Tina telefonierte, aber niemand war zu Hause.	*Tina phoned, but no one was at home.*

oder

Wir können ins Kino gehen, oder wir können hier bleiben.	*We can go to the movies, or we can stay here.*
Möchtest du ins Café gehen, oder möchtest du etwas kochen?	*Would you like to go to a cafe, or would you like to cook something?*
Ist er ihr Mann, oder ist er ihr Bruder?	*Is he her husband, or is he her brother?*

und

Erik hört Radio und seine Frau arbeitet in der Küche.	*Erik listens to the radio, and his wife works in the kitchen.*
Sonja ist Krankenschwester und Tina ist Lehrerin.	*Sonja is a nurse, and Tina is a teacher.*
Ich war in der Stadt und ich besuchte meine Tante.	*I was in the city, and I visited my aunt.*

sondern

Wir gehen nicht ins Theater, sondern wir gehen nach Hause.

We're not going to the theater, but (rather) we are going home.

Er ist kein Pilot, sondern er ist Flugbegleiter.

He's not a pilot, but (rather) he is a flight attendant.

Das Haus ist nicht warm, sondern es ist kalt.

The house isn't warm, but rather it is cold.

Take note that the difference between **aber** and **sondern** is that a **sondern** clause is preceded by a negative sentence (**Das Haus ist <u>nicht</u> warm, sondern es ist kalt**).

Just like English, clauses combined by conjunctions that have the same subject in both clauses can omit the second subject. For example:

Ich war in der Stadt und besuchte meine Tante.

In this example, the subject **ich** in the second clause is understood and can be omitted.

In the case of **sondern**, more than just the subject can be omitted if the second clause has information that is understood. For example:

Er ist kein Pilot, sondern Flugbegleiter.

Das Haus ist nicht warm, sondern kalt.

Exercise 10.3

Combine each pair of sentences with the conjunction provided. For example:

und

Thomas ist im Garten. Tina ist im Wohnzimmer.

Thomas ist im Garten und Tina ist im Wohnzimmer.

und

1. Mein Bruder arbeitet bei einer Bank. Meine Schwester arbeitet für einen Arzt.

_____

2. Das Wetter war gut. Die Kinder spielten im Park.

_____

aber

3. Hans spricht Italienisch. Er versteht die Touristen nicht.

_____

4. Ich wartete an der Ecke. Kein Bus kam.

_____

5. Tina möchte ins Kino gehen. Sie hat nicht genug Geld.

_____

oder

6. Wart ihr in der Stadt? Besuchtet ihr Monika im Dorf (*village*)?

_____

7. Jeden Tag spielten die Kinder Tennis. Sie gingen ins Kino.

_____

sondern

8. Dein Freund ist nicht klug (*smart*). Er ist sehr dumm (*dumb, stupid*).

_____

9. Andreas spricht kein Englisch. Er kann Russisch und Spanisch.

_____

10. Nicht er tut es. Sie tut es.

_____

Step 2: *Können und müssen*

Two very helpful verbs are **können** (*can, be able to*) and **müssen** (*must, have to*). They are often combined with other verbs to describe someone's ability to carry out the action of the meaning of the other verb or someone's obligation to carry out the action of the other verb. The verbs **können** and **müssen** are conjugated, and the accompanying verb is in infinitive form and stands at the end of the sentence. For example:

Ich kann dem Mann helfen.　*I can help the man.* (ability)
Ich muss dem Mann helfen.　*I have to help the man.* (obligation)

Let's look at the present tense conjugation of these verbs because both are irregular in the present tense. They follow a pattern similar to **wissen**, which was introduced in Chapter 9. Compare **wissen** with **können** and **müssen**.

wissen

ich weiß	*I know*	wir wissen	*we know*
du weißt	*you know*	ihr wisst	*you know*
er weiß	*he knows*	Sie wissen	*you know*
wer weiß	*who knows*	sie wissen	*they know*

können

ich kann	*I can, am able to*	wir können	*we can, are able to*
du kannst	*you can, are able to*	ihr könnt	*you can, are able to*
er kann	*he can, is able to*	Sie können	*you can, are able to*
wer kann	*who can, is able to*	sie können	*they can, are able to*

müssen

ich muss	*I must, have to*	wir müssen	*we must, have to*
du musst	*you must, have to*	ihr müsst	*you must, have to*
er muss	*he must, has to*	Sie müssen	*you must, have to*
wer muss	*who must, has to*	sie müssen	*they must, have to*

Let's practice sentences that use these two verbs together with the infinitive of other verbs.

Say It Out Loud

*Read each sentence out loud, paying attention to the conjugation of **können** and **müssen** and the infinitive at the end of each sentence:*

Ich kann meine Bücher nicht finden.	*I can't find my books.*
Du musst sie im Keller suchen.	*You have to look for them in the basement.*
Müssen alle Jungen Tennis oder Fußball spielen?	*Do all the boys have to play tennis or soccer?*
Tennis, ja. Aber nur Erik muss Fußball spielen.	*Tennis, yes. But only Erik has to play soccer.*
Können die Mädchen hören, was wir sagen?	*Can the girls hear what we're saying?*

Hoffentlich können sie nichts hören.	*I hope (hopefully) they can't hear anything.*
Ich habe viel Hausarbeit. Ich muss heute Abend arbeiten.	*I have a lot of homework. I have to work (study) this evening.*
Könnt ihr morgen Nachmittag mit mir in die Stadt fahren?	*Can you go into the city with me tomorrow afternoon?*
Nein, morgen müssen wir zu Hause bleiben.	*No, tomorrow we have to stay home.*
Was müsst ihr tun?	*What do you have to do?*
Das ist ein Geheimnis. Es muss eine Überraschung sein.	*It's a secret. It has to be a surprise.*

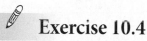

Exercise 10.4

*Reword the sentences with the verb (**können** or **müssen**) provided. For example:*

müssen

Ich arbeite im Garten.

Ich muss im Garten arbeiten.

können

1. Karin singt so schön.

   _____

2. Geben Sie mir zehn Euro?

   _____

3. Spielst du gut Schach (*chess*)?

   _____

4. Die Studentinnen schwimmen im Fluss (*swim in the river*).

   _____

5. Niemand versteht diese Leute (*people*).

   _____

müssen

6. Studiert man an einer Universität?

_____

7. Du sprichst ein bisschen lauter (*little louder*).

_____

8. Andreas kommt spät.

_____

9. Helft ihr diesen alten Leuten?

_____

10. Ich bringe dem kranken Mann ein Glas Wasser.

_____

Just like other verbs, **können** and **müssen** can be conjugated in the past tense. Notice that both verbs have an umlaut in the infinitive, but in the past tense, the umlaut is not used. For this reason, the verb is irregular. In addition, it uses the regular past tense suffix **-te**. Let's look at their past tense forms.

können

ich konnte	*I could, were able to*	wir konnten	*we could, were able to*
du konntest	*you could, were able to*	ihr konntet	*you could, were able to*
er konnte	*he could, was able to*	Sie konnten	*you could, were able to*
wer konnte	*who could, was able to*	sie konnten	*they could, were able to*

müssen

ich musste	*I had to*	wir mussten	*we had to*
du musstest	*you had to*	ihr musstet	*you had to*
er musste	*he had to*	Sie mussten	*you had to*
wer musste	*who had to*	sie mussten	*they had to*

Wondering About This? *kann, konnte and muss, musste*
Both **können** and **müssen** have two English meanings in the present tense. In the past tense, only **können** retains two meanings (**konnte** = *could, was/ were able to*). The verb *can* has a past tense form (*could*), and the verb phrase *be able to* is an alternative way of expressing the meaning of the verb. The verb *must* does not have a past tense form; therefore, when a sentence with the past tense verb **musste** is translated, it can only be translated with *had to*. Compare the following pairs of sentences.

Present:	Ich kann ihm helfen.	*I can help him. I am able to help him.* (two translations)
Past:	Ich konnte ihm helfen.	*I could help him. I was able to help him.* (two translations)
Present:	Ich muss ihm helfen.	*I must help him. I have to help him.* (two translations)
Past:	Ich musste ihm helfen.	*I had to help him.* (one translation)

Exercise 10.5

Reword each present tense sentence in the past tense. Reword each past tense sentence in the present tense. For example:

Ich kann ihm helfen.

Ich konnte ihm helfen. (present to past)

Ich musste ihm helfen.

Ich muss ihm helfen. (past to present)

1. Wir müssen am Montag nach Hause fahren.

   _____

2. Kann Erik Geige (*violin*) spielen?

   _____

3. Hans und Tina mussten vier Tage warten.

   _____

4. Hoffentlich kann der Mann euch helfen.

   _____

5. Musst du eine Woche in Russland bleiben?

   _____

6. Tina konnte uns dreißig Euro geben.

   _____

7. Warum mussten wir nach London reisen?

   _____

8. Müsst ihr den alten Volkswagen verkaufen?

   _____

9. Ich kann nur ein Jahr in Hamburg studieren.

_____

10. Können Sie ihnen ein paar Briefe schreiben?

_____

Some Useful Phrases

You have already discovered some impersonal expressions that use **es** as their subject. Two more such expressions begin with **es tut**. They are:

Es tut mir leid.	*I'm sorry.*
Es tut mir weh.	*It hurts me.*

Of course, the pronoun **mir** is only one example of a dative object that can be used in the expression. For example:

Es tut ihm leid.	He is sorry.
Es tut ihnen weh.	It hurts them.

The expression can also be used to ask a question. For example:

Tut es Ihnen leid?	Are you sorry?
Tut es dem Jungen weh?	Does it hurt the boy?

The last two expressions present a meaning that is nothing like the normal meaning of the verb **tun** (*do*). The two expressions are idiomatic—that is, they use the verb in an *idiom*, which is a combination of common words used to make a new meaning peculiar to a particular language. The idiomatic use of **tun** does not change the fact that its past tense is still **tat**, for example, **Es tat ihr leid.** (*She was sorry.*)

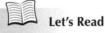

Let's Read

Read the following dialogue and determine the meaning of the lines on your own.

ANDREAS: Guten Morgen, Karin. Was tust du hier im Park?

KARIN: Ich warte auf Thomas. Wir gehen ins Kino.

ANDREAS: Wie schön. Wie heißt der Film?

KARIN: Ich weiß es nicht, aber Thomas sagt der Film ist gut.

ANDREAS: Ich gehe nicht oft ins Kino, sondern bleibe zu Hause und lese.

KARIN: Kannst du noch auf Englisch lesen?

ANDREAS: Ja, aber nicht schnell. Könnt ihr morgen zu mir kommen?

KARIN: Ich glaube, ja. Ich frage Thomas. Tschüß.

Review Quiz 10

Choose the letter of the word or phrase that best completes each sentence.

1. Ich dankte _____ Arzt für das Geschenk.
   - a. der
   - b. diese
   - c. diesen
   - d. dem

2. Eine kleine Katze _____ den Kindern nach Hause.
   - a. folgte
   - b. dienen
   - c. wartet
   - d. tut

3. Wir spielen nicht Basketball, _____ wir spielen Tennis oder Fußball.
   - a. sondern
   - b. oder
   - c. mussten
   - d. können

4. Das Mädchen _____ sich den Arm.
   - a. antwortet
   - b. konnte
   - c. bricht
   - d. möchte

5. Wir können hier warten, _____ wir können an der Ecke warten.
   - a. und
   - b. oder
   - c. müssen
   - d. taten

6. Es tut mir _____.
   - a. leid
   - b. tat
   - c. müssen
   - d. finden

7. Warum _____ ich zu Hause bleiben?
   - a. möchten
   - b. muss
   - c. hoffentlich
   - d. hier

8. Meine Eltern können Ihnen nicht _____.
   - a. tun
   - b. machen
   - c. hören
   - d. helfen

9. _____ tut dem alten Mann weh.
   - a. Du
   - b. Es
   - c. Eine Katze und ein Hund
   - d. Die Hände

10. Ich möchte mir die Zähne _____.
    - a. passieren
    - b. schlafen
    - c. putzen
    - d. können

New Vocabulary

aber	*but*
antworten	*answer, reply*
Anzug (*m.*)	*suit*
Arm (*m.*)	*arm*
Bein (*n.*)	*leg*
Bibliothek (*f.*)	*library*
bleiben	*remain, stay*
brechen	*break*
Couch (*f.*)	*couch*
danken	*thank*
dienen	*serve*
dumm	*dumb, stupid*
Finger (*m.*)	*finger*
Flugbegleiter (*m.*)	*flight attendant*
folgen	*follow*
Geheimnis (*n.*)	*secret*
gehören	*belong to*
Geige (*f.*)	*violin*
Geschwister (*n.*)	*brothers and sisters, siblings*
Gesicht (*n.*)	*face*
Gewinner (*m.*)	*winner*
gratulieren	*congratulate*
Haar (*n.*)	*hair*
Hand (*f.*)	*hand*
Hausarbeit (*f.*)	*homework*
imponieren	*impress*
klug	*smart*
können	*can, be able to*
Krankenschwester (*f.*)	*nurse*
leid tun	*be sorry*
man	*one, you*
müssen	*must, have to*

Nase (*f.*)	*nose*
oder	*or*
passen	*fit*
passieren	*happen*
putzen	*polish, brush teeth*
schlafen	*sleep*
sondern	*but rather*
Stadt (*f.*)	*city*
Überraschung (*f.*)	*surprise*
und	*and*
vertrauen	*trust*
waschen	*wash*
weh tun	*hurt, be sore*
Zahn (*m.*)	*tooth*
Zeh (*m.*)	*toe*

11

Regular Present Perfect Tense

This chapter will introduce you to the regular conjugations of the present perfect tense. In addition, you will learn to form ordinal numbers and use prefixes.

Some of the questions that will be answered are:

✓ How is the present perfect tense formed and used?
✓ How do **haben** and **sein** function in the present perfect tense?
✓ What are the formations and uses of ordinal numbers?
✓ How do prefixes affect verbs?

The Present Perfect Tense

This tense is named the *present perfect* because it uses the present tense conjugation of an auxiliary and a past participle. In English, the auxiliary of this tense is *have*. In the *regular* present perfect tense, past participles look like the regular past tense. They have the suffix *-ed*, for example, *helped*, *looked*, and *stopped*. The full conjugation of a verb in the regular present perfect tense looks like this:

	learn	*walk*
I	have learned	have walked
You	have learned	have walked
He	has learned	has walked
We	have learned	have walked
They	have learned	have walked
Who	has learned	has walked

181

This tense is used to describe an action that began in the past and ended in the present.

Remember that English often has more than one way to express a tense in order to differentiate between a habitual or completed action (*I have learned, You have walked*) and an ongoing or incomplete action. Look at the present perfect conjugation of an ongoing or incomplete action:

	learn	*walk*
I	have been learning	have been walking
You	have been learning	have been walking
He	has been learning	has been walking
We	have been learning	have been walking
They	have been learning	have been walking
Who	has been learning	has been walking

German has only one form of the present perfect tense. It can be translated into English in either of the English forms.

Step 1: *Haben* and Regular Past Participles

The verb **haben** is the auxiliary of the German present perfect tense. You are already familiar with its conjugation:

ich habe	*I have*
du hast	*you have*
er hat	*he has*
wir haben	*we have*
ihr habt	*you have*
Sie haben	*you have*
sie haben	*they have*
wer hat	*who has*

When **haben** is accompanied by a past participle, it forms the present perfect tense. German past participles are not formed like the past tense: **machen–machte, sagen–sagte, suchen–suchte,** and so on. Instead, the **-en** is removed from the infinitive to form the stem. Then the suffix **-t** and the prefix **ge-** are added. The process is simple. For example:

Infinitive	Stem	Past Participle	
machen	mach	gemacht	*made*
sagen	sag	gesagt	*said*
suchen	such	gesucht	*looked for, sought*
fragen	frag	gefragt	*asked*
lachen	lach	gelacht	*laughed*
spielen	spiel	gespielt	*played*

When **haben** accompanies one of these past participles, the present perfect tense is formed. In German, the past participle is the last element of a sentence. For example:

Ich habe ein Foto gemacht.	*I took a picture.*
Er hat nichts gesagt.	*He said nothing.*
Wir haben unseren Hund gesucht.	*We looked for our dog.*
Wer hat ihn gefragt?	*Who asked him?*
Die Jungen haben laut gelacht.	*The boys laughed loudly.*
Habt ihr wieder Schach gespielt?	*Did you play chess again?*

Wondering About This? *Ich habe ein Foto gemacht.*
Perhaps you noticed that the example sentences in German were all translated in English in the simple past tense. **Ich habe ein Foto gemacht** was not translated as *I have taken* a picture, but rather as *I took* a picture. There is a simple explanation for this.

There is a tendency in English to express actions performed in the past in the simple past tense. The tendency in German is to use the present perfect tense to express actions performed in the past. The main exception to this is narratives or anecdotes, which use the simple past tense. In ordinary German speech, the present perfect tense is preferred. For example:

Narrative	Ordinary Speech	Both Translated the Same
Ich machte ein Foto.	Ich habe ein Foto gemacht.	*I took a picture.*
Er spielte Tennis.	Er hat Tennis gespielt.	*He played tennis.*

If it seems appropriate, the English conjugation that expresses an ongoing or incomplete action can be used: *I was taking a picture. He was playing tennis.*

If a verb stem ends in **-t** or **-d**, an **e** is placed before the final **-t** in the participle, for example, **reden–red–gered<u>e</u>t** (*talked*).

Exercise 11.1

Reword each infinitive as a past participle. For example:

spielen *gespielt*

1. fragen _____

2. lachen _____

3. warten _____

4. stellen (*put, place*) _____

5. danken _____

6. antworten _____

7. schmecken (*taste*) _____

8. lernen _____

9. lehren (*teach*) _____

10. kaufen _____

11. hören _____

12. decken (*cover*) _____

13. baden (*bathe*) _____

14. glauben _____

15. kosten _____

Say It Out Loud

Read each sentence out loud, paying attention to the form and use of the present perfect tense:

Haben Sie ein Foto von der Familie gemacht?	*Did you take a picture of the family?*
Die Suppe hat sehr gut geschmeckt.	*The soup tasted very good.*
Haben die Kinder schon gebadet?	*Did the children already bathe (take a bath)?*
Ich habe den ganzen Abend Radio gehört.	*I listened to the radio the whole evening.*

Meine Brüder haben den Tisch gedeckt.	*My brothers set (covered) the table.*
Hast du die Vase auf das Klavier gestellt?	*Did you put the vase on the piano?*
Warum haben die Gäste gelacht?	*Why did the guests laugh?*
Mein Bruder hat Mathematik und Geographie gelernt.	*My brother learned math and geography.*
Wie viel haben diese Blumen gekostet?	*How much did these flowers cost?*
Ich habe dem Dieb gar nicht geglaubt.	*I didn't believe the thief at all.*
Was hast du den Polizisten geantwortet?	*What did you answer to the police officers?*
Sie haben mich nichts gefragt.	*They didn't ask me anything. (They asked me nothing.)*

Exercise 11.2

Reword each present tense sentence in the present perfect tense. For example:

Ich mache ein Foto.

Ich habe ein Foto gemacht.

1. Schmecken die Würstchen gut?

   _____

2. Ich bade spät am Abend.

   _____

3. Kaufen Sie einen alten BMW (bay-em-vay)?

   _____

4. Was antwortet Frau Schneider?

   _____

5. Tina und Hans decken den Tisch.

   _____

6. Meine Freunde lachen laut.

   _____

7. Wohin stellt sie die Lampe?

_____

8. Braucht man viel Geld?

_____

9. Der Professor redet mit uns.

_____

10. Was lehrt Frau Braun?

_____

 Some German verbs end in **-ieren**. They tend to be foreign words that have become a part of the German language. For example:

studieren	_study_
telefonieren	_telephone_
marschieren	_march_
organisieren	_organize_

When these verbs form a past participle, the prefix **ge-** is not used. Therefore, the present perfect tense of these verbs looks like this:

Ich habe studiert.	_I studied._
Wer hat mit ihr telefoniert?	_Who was on the phone with her?_

 ## Step 2: _Sein_ and the Present Perfect Tense

In an older form of English, the present perfect tense sometimes used the verb _be_ as its auxiliary. For example, in an earlier version of the Bible, there is a statement that says _The Lord is come._ In modern English we would say _The Lord has come._ This use of _be_ occurred when the verb in the sentence was a _verb of motion._ Verbs of motion are those that show a movement from one place to another. A few such verbs are _go, run, drive, walk, hurry,_ and _come._

In modern German, this concept of using **sein** (_be_) as the present perfect tense auxiliary with verbs of motion still holds true. Let's first review the conjugation of **sein** before using it in the present perfect tense.

ich bin	_I am_
du bist	_you are_
er ist	_he is_
wir sind	_we are_
ihr seid	_you are_

Sie sind	*you are*
sie sind	*they are*
man ist	*one is*

Four commonly used verbs of motion are **fahren** (*drive*), **kommen** (*come*), **marschieren** (*march*), and **reisen** (*travel*). Two of these verbs (**fahren** and **kommen**) form an irregular past participle by adding the suffix **-en** instead of **-t**: **gefahren** and **gekommen**. The auxiliary in the present perfect tense for these four verbs of motion is **sein**, and **sein** would have to be translated as *have* because English no longer uses *be* as the auxiliary for this tense. Because English speakers tend to translate this tense in the simple past perfect, there is really no problem. For example:

ich bin gefahren	*I have driven/drove*
du bist gefahren	*you have driven/drove*
er ist gefahren	*he has driven/drove*
wir sind gefahren	*we have driven/drove*
ihr seid gefahren	*you have driven/drove*
Sie sind gefahren	*you have driven/drove*
sie sind gefahren	*they have driven/drove*
man ist gefahren	*one has driven/drove*

Say It Out Loud

*Read each sentence out loud, paying attention to the use of **sein** as the present perfect tense auxiliary:*

Ich bin mit dem Bus nach Hause gefahren.	*I drove home on the bus.*
Seid ihr mit dem Auto gefahren?	*Did you go by car?*
Monika ist mit der Straßenbahn dorthin gefahren.	*Monika went there by streetcar.*
Der Zug ist durch einen Tunnel gekommen.	*The car came through a tunnel.*
Woher sind Sie gekommen, Herr Bauer?	*Where did you come from, Mr. Bauer?*
Sie sind gerade um die Ecke gekommen.	*They just came around the corner.*

Die müden Soldaten sind langsam marschiert.	*The tired soldiers marched slowly.*
Bist du auch in der Parade marschiert?	*Did you march in the parade, too?*
Der kleine Junge ist mit ihnen marschiert.	*The little boy marched with them.*
Erik ist gestern nach Holland gereist.	*Erik traveled to Holland yesterday.*
Vor einer Woche ist der Tourist dorthin gereist.	*The tourist traveled there a week ago.*
Ich bin nie ins Ausland gereist.	*I never traveled abroad.*

 ## Exercise 11.3

Reword each present tense sentence in the present perfect tense. Choose **haben** or **sein** correctly as the auxiliary for each one. For example:

Ich frage die Dame.

Ich habe die Dame gefragt.

1. Die Suppe schmeckt wunderbar (*wonderful*).

_____

2. Am Montag reisen wir nach Hause.

_____

3. Die Kinder marschieren zum Park.

_____

4. Der kranke Mann antwortet nicht.

_____

5. Karl fährt mit dem Zug.

_____

6. Wann kommst du ins Restaurant?

_____

7. Wer deckt den Tisch?

_____

8. Wohin reisen sie?

_____

9. Die Soldaten marschieren durch die Stadt (*city*).

_____

10. Im Sommer fahren wir nach Holland.

_____

Wondering About This? *Soldaten*

The noun **die Soldaten** is the plural of **der Soldat** (*soldier*). Normally, masculine nouns do not form their plural with an **-en** ending, but **Soldat** is treated differently because it is a masculine noun *that comes from a foreign source*. Such nouns add an **-en** to form not only the plural but also the accusative and dative singular. For example:

Nominative Singular		Accusative and Dative	Plural
der Diplomat	*diplomat*	den/dem Diplomaten	die Diplomaten
der Elefant	*elephant*	den/dem Elefanten	die Elefanten
der Soldat	*soldier*	den/dem Soldaten	die Soldaten
der Tourist	*tourist*	den/dem Touristen	die Touristen
der Komponist	*composer*	den/dem Komponisten	die Komponisten

Exercise 11.4

Reword each sentence in the missing tenses. For example:

Present: *Ich kaufe einen Mantel.*

Past: Ich kaufte einen Mantel.

Present perfect: *Ich habe einen Mantel gekauft.*

1. Present: Wir lernen Italienisch.

   Past: _____

   Present perfect: _____

2. Present: _____

   Past: Martin fuhr in die Stadt.

   Present perfect: _____

3. Present: Die Soldaten marschieren durch einen Tunnel.

Past: _____

Present perfect: _____

4. Present: _____

Past: _____

Present perfect: Wann ist Frau Becker nach Hause gekommen?

5. Present: Wie oft reist du in die Schweiz?

Past: _____

Present perfect: _____

Ordinal Numbers and Prefixes

In a sense, ordinal numbers and prefixes are not new to you. You have encountered a few in other chapters. This section will explain them more fully.

Step 3: Ordinal Numbers

You have already learned the cardinal numbers (**eins, zwei, zwanzig, hundert**, and so on). The ordinal numbers are those that show *in what order* something occurs: *first, tenth, thirtieth*.

Most English ordinal numbers end in the suffix *-th*. A few are irregular and form new words or change a letter. They are *first, second, third, fifth*, and *twelfth*. German ordinal numbers most often end in **-te** if less than 20 and **-ste** if 20 or greater. For example:

vierte	*fourth*
elfte	*eleventh*
neunzehnte	*nineteenth*
zwanzigste	*twentieth*
achtunddreißigste	*twenty-eighth*
hundertste	*hundredth*

A few numbers form their ordinal number in an irregular way. For example:

erste	*first*
dritte	*third*
siebte	*seventh*

Say It Out Loud

Read each sentence out loud, paying attention to the use of the ordinal numbers:

Der erste Junge in dieser Reihe ist Hans.	*The first boy in this row is Hans.*
Seine zweite Frau ist Amerikanerin.	*His second wife is an American.*
Dieser Zug hat keine dritte Klasse.	*This train has no third class.*
Das zehnte Haus links ist sehr alt.	*The tenth house on the left is very old.*
Heute ist der einundzwanzigste März.	*Today is the twenty-first of March.*
Am fünfundzwanzigsten feiern wir Weihnachten.	*On the twenty-fifth we celebrate Christmas.*
Meine Tochter ist am siebten Juni geboren.	*My daughter was born on the seventh of June.*
Der zwölfte Satz ist nicht richtig.	*The twelfth sentence is not correct.*
Beethovens neunte Sinfonie war seine Letzte.	*Beethoven's ninth symphony was his last.*

Wondering About This? *der einundzwanzigste März*

English uses ordinal numbers to express dates. German does, too. If you are simply stating the date, the ordinal ends in **-e**. If you use **am** or **im** with an ordinal, the ending changes to **-en**. For example:

der fünfte August	*the fifth of August*
am fünften August	*on the fifth of August*

This also occurs with phrases that do not express a date. For example:

der zweite Weltkrieg	*the Second World War*
im zweiten Weltkrieg	*in the Second World War*

Exercise 11.5

Using the number cues in parentheses, complete each sentence with the appropriate ordinal number. For example:

(acht) Heute ist der *achte* Mai.

1. (elf) Heute ist der _____ Juli.

2. (vierundzwanzig) Heute ist der _____ Oktober.

3. (eins) Heute ist der _____ Dezember.

4. (zwei) Gestern war der _____ Januar.

5. (dreißig) War gestern der _____ April?

6. (vier) Am _____ September ist er nach Hause gekommen.

7. (dreizehn) Am _____ August sind die Zwillinge geboren.

8. (drei) Am _____ Sonntag ist er nach Paris gefahren.

9. (eins) Im _____ Weltkrieg ist mein Großvater geboren.

10. (fünf) Im _____ Jahr habe ich in Heidelberg studiert.

Step 4: Inseparable Prefixes

Prefixes are as common in English as they are in German. In Chapter 8 you discovered that the basic use of the prefixes was not to change how the verb functioned but its meaning. For example:

warten	*wait*
erwarten	*await, expect*
sprechen	*speak*
suchen	*look for, seek*
versprechen	*promise*
besuchen	*visit*

In the present tense, the verbs **warten** and **besuchen** are regular. Those verbs with prefixes remain regular. For example:

ich erwarte	besuche
du erwartest	besuchst
er erwartet	besucht
wir erwarten	besuchen
ihr erwartet	besucht
Sie erwarten	besuchen
sie erwarten	besuchen
wer erwartet	besucht

Inseparable Prefixes

One group of prefixes is called *inseparable* because they do not change their position on the verb as the verb is conjugated. These prefixes are **be-**, **emp-**, **ent-**, **er-**, **ge-**, **ver-**, and **zer-**. Let's look at a few verbs and other words that use these prefixes:

antworten	*answer*	beantworten	*answer (a question)*
fehlen	*lack*	empfehlen	*recommend*
fern	*distant*	entfernen	*remove*
rot	*red*	erröten	*blush*
brauchen	*need*	gebrauchen	*use*
hungern	*starve*	verhungern	*starve to death*
stören	*disturb*	zerstören	*destroy*

Say It Out Loud

Read each sentence, paying attention to the use of the inseparable prefixes:

Niemand beantwortet ihre Frage.	*No one is answering her question.*
Mein Nachbar empfiehlt dieses Restaurant.	*My neighbor recommends this restaurant.*
Der Direktor entfernte Hans aus der Schule.	*The principal removed Hans from the school.*
Die Studentin errötet vor Scham.	*The student turns red in shame.*
Der Junge gebrauchte seinen Verstand.	*The boy used his common sense.*
Im Winter verhungerten viele Leute.	*Many people starved to death in winter.*
Warum zerstörten die Soldaten das Dorf?	*Why did the soldiers destroy the village?*
Am Dienstag bekam sie vier Briefe.	*On Tuesday she received four letters.*
Wem gehören diese Fahrräder?	*To whom do these bicycles belong?*

Wondering About This? *gehören*

The verb **gehören** is derived from **hören**, but the original meaning (*hear*) is lost when the prefix is added (*belong to*). The person to whom something belongs will be in the dative case when using this verb. For example:

Das Buch gehört <u>mir.</u>	*The book belongs to me.*
Gehören <u>euch</u> diese Mäntel?	*Do these coats belong to you?*
Diese Stiefeln <u>gehörten</u> einem Soldaten.	*These boots belonged to a soldier.*

No matter what tense the verb is in, the prefix remains static at the beginning of the verb. However, when the verb forms a participle, the inseparable prefix is used in place of **ge-**, for example, **er besucht**, **er besuchte**, and **er hat besucht**.

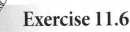

Exercise 11.6

Reword the present tense sentence in the past and present perfect. For example:

Present: Wir erwarten einen Gast.

Past: *Wir erwarteten einen Gast.*

Present perfect: *Wir haben einen Gast erwartet.*

1. Present: Wer beantwortet die Frage?

   Past: _____

   Present perfect: _____

2. Present: Die rote Bluse gehört ihr.

   Past: _____

   Present perfect: _____

3. Present: Mein Nachbar versucht es zu verstehen.

   Past: _____

   Present perfect: _____

4. Present: Tina errötet vor Scham.

   Past: _____

   Present perfect: _____

5. Present: Sie entfernen meinen Sohn aus der Schule.

   Past: _____

   Present perfect: _____

Exercise 11.7

In the blank provided in each short dialogue, write a sentence that conforms to the topic of the dialogue. For example:

FRAU BRAU: Wie geht es Ihnen, Herr Benz?

HERR BENZ: Es geht mir gut. Wohin gehen Sie?

FRAU BENZ: *Ich gehe zum Park.*

1. TINA: Ich bin vor zehn Minuten nach Hause gekommen.

   ERIK: Bist du mit dem Bus gefahren?

   TINA: _____

2. HERR BRAUN: _____

   HERR SCHNEIDER: Nein, ich habe sein drittes Buch gekauft.

   HERR BRAUN: Er schreibt sehr gut.

3. Marianne: Was tust du in Berlin?

   SONJA: _____

   MARIANNE: Möchtest du ein neues Auto kaufen?

Review Quiz 11

Choose the letter of the word or phrase that best completes each sentence.

1. Warum hast du mit dem Polizisten _____?

   a. gemacht   c. lachte

   b. geredet   d. lachten

2. Der Zug ist _____ einen Tunnel gekommen.

   a. von   c. durch

   b. außer   d. im

3. Seine _____ Sinfornie war die Neunte.

   a. drei   c. welche

   b. laut   d. letzte

4. Wer ist _____ Reihe?

   a. in der   c. aus dem

   b. von dem   d. zur

5. _____ Ihnen dieses Buch?

   a. Gehört   c. Verkaufte

   b. Erwartet   d. Empfehlen

6. Karin möchte _____ beantworten.

   a. dem Lehrer   c. viele Leute

   b. diese Frage   d. niemand

7. Wir haben _____ fotografiert.

   a. mit einem Dorf   c. der Tunnel

   b. einen Soldaten   d. Scham

8. Warum haben Sie diesen Studenten aus der Universität _____?

   a. entfernt   c. zerstört

   b. gestellt   d. bekam

9. Gestern _____ sie in die Stadt gefahren.

   a. sind   c. kamen

   b. kommt   d. hat

10. Unsere Tochter ist _____ Dezember geboren.

   a. am   c. in

   b. am dritten   d. vor sieben

New Vocabulary

Ausland (*n.*)	*foreign land*
baden	*bathe*
beantworten	*answer a question*
BMW (*m.*)	*BMW*
decken	*cover*
Dorf (*n.*)	*village*
Elefant (*m.*)	*elephant*
empfehlen	*recommend*
entfernen	*remove*
erröten vor	*blush*
fehlen	*lack*
feiern	*celebrate*
fern	*distant*

Foto (*n.*)	*photo, picture*
ganz	*whole, complete*
gebrauchen	*use*
gehören	*belong to*
Geographic (*f.*)	*geography*
gerade	*straight, just now*
hungern	*starve*
Klavier (*n.*)	*piano*
Komponist (*m.*)	*composer*
Kuchen (*m.*)	*cake*
lachen	*laugh*
langsam	*slow*
laut	*loud*
lehren	*teacher*
letzte	*last*
marschieren	*march*
Nachbar (*m.*)	*neighbor*
organisieren	*organize*
Parade (*f.*)	*parade*
Reihe (*f.*)	*row*
richtig	*right, correct*
Satz (*m.*)	*sentence*
Scham (*f.*)	*shame*
schmecken	*taste*
Sinfonie (*f.*)	*symphony*
Soldat (*m.*)	*soldier*
spät	*late*
spielen	*play*
stellen	*put, place*
stören	*disturb*
studieren	*study (at a university)*
telefonieren	*telephone*
Vase (*f.*)	*vase*

verhungern	*starve to death*
versuchen	*try*
vor	*before, in front of*
Weihnachten (*pl.*)	*Christmas*
Weltkrieg (*m.*)	*world war*
Würstchen (*n.*)	*sausage*
zerstören	*destroy*

12

Adjective Endings and Separable Prefixes

This chapter provides you with an explanation of adjective endings and when they are used. A further discussion of prefixes is also included. Important vocabulary for use when shopping will be presented.

Some questions that will be answered are:

✓ What are the different kinds of adjective endings?
✓ How do endings differ in the nominative and accusative cases?
✓ What role does gender play in determining an adjective ending?
✓ What are the separable prefixes, and how are they used?

Adjectives

Adjectives are words that modify or describe people and things. They tell what size, what color, what quality, and what condition things are in. There are two fundamental types of adjectives, which must be differentiated. They are *predicate adjectives* and *adjectives that accompany a noun*.

Predicate adjectives are the simplest to use. They follow a *linking verb* that points to the subject of the sentence. For example:

My brother is <u>smart</u>.

She was always <u>beautiful</u>.

The verb *be* is a frequently used linking verb and can be followed by a predicate adjective. Predicate adjectives do not accompany the noun they modify but are *linked* to the noun by the verb. Other linking verbs are *seem*, *become*, *get*, and *look*. For example:

> The sun seems very <u>bright</u> today.
>
> Our son is becoming <u>stronger</u> with every day.
>
> The sky was getting <u>dark.</u>
>
> *The man looks <u>old</u> in this strong light.*

If the adjective stands in front of the noun it modifies, it is not a predicate adjective but modifies a noun directly. Its meaning is not changed in this position, just its function. For example:

> *A <u>bright</u> sun shone over the desert landscape.*
>
> *A <u>stronger</u> wind blew against the windows.*
>
> *Those <u>dark</u> shadows are scary.*
>
> *The <u>old</u> man smiled cheerfully at us.*

Step 1: Adjective Endings

German also has predicate adjectives. They are simple to use because they require no endings. For example:

Der Wind ist heute Abend <u>stark</u>.	*The wind is strong this evening.*
Warum war ihre Stimme <u>schwach</u>?	*Why was her voice weak?*
Das Zimmer wurde ganz <u>still</u>.	*The room became quite quiet.*
Der Clown sieht <u>komisch</u> aus.	*The clown looks funny.*
Die Hexe sah <u>hässlich</u> aus.	*The witch looked ugly.*

Say It Out Loud

Read each sentence out loud, paying attention to the use and position of the predicate adjectives:

Ihre Haare sind braun.	*Her hair is brown.*
Ist diese Tinte schwarz oder blau?	*Is this ink black or blue?*
Man muss immer fleißig sein.	*You always have to be diligent.*
Der junge Sportler möchte muskulös werden.	*The young athlete would like to become muscular.*

Der Matrose sieht sehr froh aus.	*The sailor looks very happy.*
Diese Hose ist viel zu lang.	*The brown pants are much too long.*
Die Dame sah sehr blass aus.	*The sick lady looked very pale.*
Die kleine Küche war sehr hell und attraktiv.	*The little kitchen was very bright and attractive.*
Spät am Abend wurde der Himmel ganz dunkel.	*Late in the evening the sky got quite dark.*

Exercise 12.1

Complete each sentence with any appropriate predicate adjective. For example:

Mein Großvater ist sehr <u>*alt.*</u>

1. Ihre Kinder sind sehr _____.

2. Früh (*early*) am Morgen ist die Sonne _____.

3. In der Nacht war mein Schlafzimmer _____.

4. Nach ein paar Wochen wurde sie wieder _____.

5. Meine Nachbarn waren immer _____.

6. Warum bist du so _____?

7. Am Nachmittag ist der Himmel oft _____.

8. Ihre Söhne sehen _____ aus.

9. Seid ihr _____?

10. Man muss immer _____ sein.

Nominative Case Adjectives

When a German adjective stands in front of a noun and modifies it, it *must have an adjective ending*. You probably have noticed that various endings have been used so far. The following explanation should clear up any questions you might have.

First, the adjectives that accompany **der**-words need to be described. The **der**-words are **dieser, jener, jeder,** and **welcher.** When they modify a noun, the gender and number of the noun must be taken into consideration because gender is an important determiner in choosing an adjective ending.

If a **der**-word modifies a masculine noun, the masculine gender is shown in the **der**-word: **diese̱r**, **jene̱r**, **jede̱r**, and **welche̱r**. If the noun is feminine, the **der**-words become **diese̱**, **jene̱**, **jede̱**, and **welche̱**. If the noun is neuter, the **der**-words become **diese̱s**, **jene̱s**, **jede̱s**, and **welches**. The **der**-words used with plural nouns are **diese̱**, **jene̱**, **jede̱**, and **welche̱**.

When an adjective is added to a noun phrase introduced by a **der**-word, the adjective *always has an -e ending* in the nominative case *with singular nouns*. For example:

Masculine Nouns

der nette Junge	*the nice boy*
dieser warme Mantel	*this warm coat*
welcher alte Herr	*which old gentleman*

Feminine Nouns

die alte Frau	*the old woman*
jene große Schule	*that big school*
jede gelbe Bluse	*each yellow blouse*

Neuter Nouns

das kleine Haus	*the little house*
dieses billige Auto	*this cheap car*
jedes hübsche Mädchen	*each pretty girl*

Only plural nouns have a different adjective ending with **der**-words. It is always -**en**.

Plural Nouns

die starken Sportler	*the strong athletes*
diese kalten Tage	*these cold days*
jene hässlichen Hexen	*those ugly witches*

The adjective **dunkel** makes a minor spelling change when an ending is added. When it modifies a noun directly in the nominative case with a **der**-word, it is written as **der dunkle**, **die dunkle**, **das dunkle**, and **die dunklen** in the singular and plural, respectively. Adjectives that end in -**el** and -**er** follow this pattern, for example, **teuer** = **der teure Mantel**, **die teuren Mäntel.**

Say It Out Loud

Read each sentence out loud, paying attention to the adjectives and their endings:

Diese hübschen Frauen sind Italienerinnen.

These beautiful women are Italian.

Der muskulöse Sportler ist ein Freund von mir.

The muscular athlete is a friend of mine.

Jeder lange Satz war ein Problem für ihn.

Each long sentence was a problem for him.

Welches neue Klavier war sehr teuer?

Which new piano was very expensive?

Fährt die letzte Straßenbahn zum Rathaus?

Does the last streetcar go to city hall?

Jene reichen Leute kommen aus Kanada.

Those rich people come from Canada.

Der erste Zug fuhr nach Bonn ab.

The last train departed for Bonn.

Das kleine Schlafzimmer war ganz sauber.

The little bedroom was quite clean.

Welcher deutsche Komponist ist hier geboren?

What German composer was born here?

Exercise 12.2

Give the adjective in parentheses in the sentence with the correct adjective ending, if any. For example:

(klein) Der *kleine* Junge weinte.

1. (dunkel) Dieses _____ Wohnzimmer ist nicht schön.

2. (sauber) Das Badezimmer im Hotel ist _____.

3. (schön) Jener _____ Garten gehört meiner Tante.

4. (still) Der _____ See (*lake*) war warm und attraktiv.

5. (komisch) Diese _____ Clowns können gut singen und tanzen (*dance*).

6. (fleißig) Jede _____ Studentin bekommt gute Noten (*grades*).

7. (kalt) Die _____ Monate sind Dezember, Januar und Februar.

8. (krank) Die kleine Katze sieht _____ aus.

9. (schwach) Seid ihr _____ oder stark?

10. (hässlich) Was kocht (*cooks*) diese _____ Hexe?

Accusative Case Adjectives

When adjectives accompany **der**-words in the accusative case, they have the same endings as in the nominative case *except for those that modify masculine nouns*. Masculine singular nouns are modified by adjectives that end in -**en**. For example:

den netten Mann	*the nice man*	diesen teuren Wagen	*this expensive car*
jenen starken Jungen	*that strong boy*	den langen Satz	*the long sentence*

Remember that the accusative case is used when a noun or pronoun is a direct object or the object of an accusative preposition. You can review the accusative case in Chapter 6.

Say It Out Loud

Read each sentence out loud, paying attention to the masculine accusative case:

Ich habe den alten BMW verkauft.	*I sold the old BMW.*
Sie möchte diese schwarzen Handschuhe.	*She would like these black gloves.*
Wer hat diesen komischen Brief bekommen?	*Who received this funny letter?*
Er liebt jedes hübsche Mädchen.	*He loves every beautiful girl.*
Dieses Buch ist für den jungen Soldaten.	*This book is for the young soldier.*
Kannst du die langen Wörter verstehen?	*Can you understand the long words?*
Der Zug kam durch den kurzen Tunnel.	*The train came through the short tunnel.*

Warum ist er gegen diese spanische   *Why is he against this Spanish*
   Diplomatin?   *diplomat?*

Die Kinder liefen um die letzte Ecke. *The children ran around the last*
                                     corner.

Haben Sie jenen neuen Lehrer   *Did you become acquainted with*
   kennen gelernt?   *that new teacher?*

Exercise 12.3

Complete each sentence with the phrase in parentheses. Some answers require the nominative case, and others require the accusative case. For example:

(der junge Mann) Wir verstehen <u>den jungen Mann</u> nicht.

1. (die erste Frage) Kannst du _____ beantworten?

2. (diese schönen Damen) Woher kommen _____?

3. (der letzte Satz) Wer kann _____ lesen?

4. (jene langen Sätze) Ich konnte _____ nicht verstehen.

5. (welcher warme Mantel) _____ möchtest du kaufen?

6. (die fleißigen Schüler) _____ bekommen gute Noten.

7. (jeder amerikanische Gast) Das sind Geschenke für

   _____.

8. (das stille Klassenzimmer) Warum läuft sie durch _____?

9. (jene alte Bibliothek) Die Soldaten haben _____
   fotografiert.

10. (der deutsche Komponist) Niemand ist gegen _____.

11. (die sauberen Handschuhe) Wo sind _____?

12. (die neuen Bücher) Der Professor kam ohne _____.

13. (jedes dunkle Hotelzimmer) _____ muss zwei Lampen
   haben.

14. (jener muskulöse Sportler) Wann haben Sie _____
   kennen gelernt?

15. (der komische Mann) Arbeitet _____ als (*as*) Clown?

Wondering About This? *als Clown*

When describing a person's profession, including your own, the indefinite article is not used. This is why the phrase **als Clown** is not written as **als <u>ein</u> Clown**, as it is done in English. Here are some more examples:

Sie arbeitet als Lehrerin.	*She works as a teacher.*
Herr Schäfer ist Zahnarzt.	*Mr. Schaefer is a dentist.*
Mein Bruder wurde Rechtsanwalt.	*My brother became a lawyer.*
Wird ihre Tochter Schauspielerin?	*Is your daughter becoming an actress?*

When you speak about the person who has a specific profession, the definite article is used: **Kennen Sie <u>den</u> neuen Rechtsanwalt?** (*Do you know the new lawyer?*) <u>**Die**</u> **Komponistin spielt gut Klavier.** (*The composer plays the piano well.*)

Some Useful Phrases

When shopping, there are some important phrases to remember. You have already encountered the use of **kaufen** (*buy*) and **verkaufen** (*sell*) and the verb **kosten** (*cost*). Here are other verbs and accompanying vocabulary that you will find useful:

anprobieren (*try on*)

Ich möchte das blaue Kleid anprobieren.	*I would like to try on the blue dress.*
Hast du diesen Anzug anprobiert?	*Did you try on this suit?*

messen (*measure*)

Der Sportler misst 1,80 (ein Komma achtzig) Meter.	*The athlete is (measures) 1.80 meters tall.*
Man muss genau messen.	*You have to take exact measurements.*

einpacken (*pack up, wrap up*)

Können Sie diese Strümpfe einpacken?	*Can you wrap up these stockings?*
Er hat das Buch als Geschenk eingepackt.	*He wrapped the book up like a gift.*

bezahlen (*pay*)

Hans möchte mit einer Kreditkarte bezahlen.	*Hans would like to pay with a credit card.*
Sie können dort an der Kasse bezahlen.	*You can pay there at the cashier.*

Step 2: Separable Prefixes

You have already learned that English uses prefixes to change the meaning of verbs. You have also encountered the German inseparable prefixes. They belong to a short list of prefixes. But the *separable prefixes* are many. They can be adverbs, prepositions, or even other parts of speech. Some commonly used separable prefixes that come from prepositions are **aus-**, **bei-**, **vor-**, **ein-**, **hinter-**, **ab-**, and **zu-**. You will find them and other inseparable prefixes used not only with verbs but with other grammatical elements.

Here are some that are used with nouns:

der Ausgang	*exit*	der Eindruck	*impression*
der Weiterflug	*connecting flight*	die Landkarte	*map*

Do not be surprised when you see words that are not verbs with inseparable prefixes.

Here you will concentrate on verbs and prefixes. Two that you already know are **anprobieren** (*try on*) and **abfahren** (*depart*). Remember that regular verbs remain regular when conjugated with a prefix, as do irregular verbs. The most important thing to know about separable prefixes is that they *separate* from the infinitive when conjugated in the present tense. The prefix then stands at the end of the sentence. Let's look at **anprobieren** and **abfahren** in the present tense:

ich	probiere . . . an	*I try on*	fahre . . . ab	*I depart*
du	probierst . . . an	*you try on*	fährst . . . ab	*you depart*
er	probiert . . . an	*he tries on*	fährt . . . ab	*he departs*
wir	probieren . . . an	*we try on*	fahren . . . ab	*we depart*
ihr	probiert . . . an	*you try on*	fahrt . . . ab	*you depart*
Sie	probieren . . . an	*you try on*	fahren . . . ab	*you depart*
sie	probieren . . . an	*they try on*	fahren . . . ab	*they depart*

Here are a few sentences that contain these verbs:

Ich probiere dieses Hemd an.	*I try on this shirt.*
Probiert sie den schönen Rock an?	*Is she trying on the pretty skirt?*
Er fährt am Freitag nach Dresden ab.	*He departs for Dresden on Friday.*
Wann fahrt ihr zum Bahnhof ab?	*When are you departing for the railroad station?*

The same thing occurs in the past tense:

ich	probierte . . . an	*I tried on*	fuhr . . . ab	*I departed*
du	probiertest . . . an	*you tried on*	fuhrst . . . ab	*you departed*
er	probierte . . . an	*he tried on*	fuhr . . . ab	*he departed*
wir	probierten . . . an	*we tried on*	fuhren . . . ab	*we departed*
ihr	probiertet . . . an	*you tried on*	fuhrt . . . ab	*you departed*
Sie	probierten . . . an	*you tried on*	fuhren . . . ab	*you departed*
sie	probierten . . . an	*they tried on*	fuhren . . . ab	*they departed*

Let's look at a list of commonly used verbs that have separable prefixes:

ankommen	*arrive*
anrufen	*call up, phone*
aufmachen	*open*
aufstehen	*stand up, get up*
aussehen	*look like*
einladen	*invite*
einschlafen	*fall asleep*
mitkommen	*come along*
umsteigen	*transfer (on transportation)*
weglaufen	*run away*
zuhören	*listen*
zumachen	*close*
zurückgehen	*go back, return*

Say It Out Loud

Read each sentence out loud, paying attention to the use and position of the separable prefixes:

Die letzte Straßenbahn kommt in drei Minuten an.	*The last streetcar arrives in three minutes.*
Thomas rief mich nur einmal an.	*Thomas called me up only once.*
Ich machte alle Fenster auf.	*I opened all the windows.*
Monika muss die große Tür zumachen.	*Monika has to close the big door.*
Die Braut sieht sehr hübsch aus.	*The bride looks very beautiful.*
Herr Bauer lädt uns zum Essen ein.	*Mr. Bauer invites us to dinner.*
Die müden Sportlerinnen schlafen schnell ein.	*The tired athletes fall asleep fast.*
Der Rechtsanwalt kommt nicht mit.	*The lawyer is not coming along.*
Wir müssen an der Ecke umsteigen.	*We have to transfer at the corner.*
Warum lief der Hund weg?	*Why did the dog run away?*
Ich höre dem klugen Professor zu.	*I listen to the smart professor.*
Wer kann diesen schweren Koffer zumachen?	*Who can close this heavy suitcase?*
Nach dem Film ging er nach Hause zurück.	*After the movie he went back home.*

Wondering About This? *Monika muss die große Tür zumachen.*

In the sentence **Monika muss die große Tür zumachen**, the separable prefix *did not separate* from the verb. The explanation is simple. In that sentence, the verb **muss** is conjugated, and the verb **zumachen** is at the end of the sentence in infinitive form. In the present and past tenses of verbs with separable prefixes, the prefix separates. When an infinitive is required, the prefix does not separate. Let's look at more examples:

Ich möchte euch einladen.	*I would like to invite you.*	(The conjugated verb is **möchte**, and **einladen** is in the infinitive form.)
Er kann nicht einschlafen.	*He cannot fall asleep.*	(The conjugated verb is **kann**, and **einschlafen** is in the infinitive form.)
Wir müssen jetzt zurückgehen.	*We have to go back now.*	(The conjugated verb is **müssen**, and **zurückgehen** is in the infinitive form.)

Exercise 12.4

Conjugate each infinitive with the subjects provided in the present and past tenses. For example:

anprobieren

       ich <u>probiere an</u>   <u>probierte an</u>
       wir <u>probieren an</u>   <u>probierten an</u>

Present   **Past**

aussehen

1. ich _____   _____

2. du _____   _____

3. er _____   _____

zumachen

4. ihr _____   _____

5. Sie _____   _____

6. wer _____   _____

aufstehen

7. wir _____   _____

8. sie *s.* _____   _____

9. du _____   _____

weglaufen

10. sie pl. _____   _____

11. ich _____   _____

12. es _____   _____

zurückgehen

13. er _____   _____

14. ihr _____   _____

15. Tina _____   _____

Exercise 12.5

Reword each sentence by adding the auxiliary provided in parentheses. Keep the tense of the original sentence. For example:

Er probiert den Anzug an.

(müssen) *Er muss den Anzug anprobieren.*

Ich probierte das Hemd an.

(müssen) *Ich musste das Hemd anprobieren.*

1. Der Rechtsanwalt kommt sehr spät an.
   (müssen) _____

2. Wir laden ein paar Engländer ein.
   (können) _____

3. Kommst du auch mit?
   (können) _____

4. Erik machte den großen Koffer auf.
   (müssen) _____

5. Die Touristen aus Afrika steigen hier um.
   (können) _____

6. Ich höre der jungen Lehrerin zu.
   (müssen) _____

7. Wann gingen sie zurück?
   (müssen) _____

8. Das müde Kind schläft schnell ein.
   (können) _____

9. Steht ihr früh auf?
   (müssen) _____

10. Meine Freundin kam am Mittwoch an.
    (können) _____

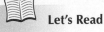

Let's Read

Read the following dialogue and determine the meaning of the lines on your own:

WERNER: Wo ist Erik? Es ist schon dunkel.

GABRIELE: Er musste spät abfahren. Seine Mutter ist krank.

WERNER: Das tut mir leid. Kommt Marianne auch mit?

GABRIELE: Ja, Tina lud sie auch ein.

WERNER: Wann hat Tina Geburtstag? Heute?

GABRIELE: Nein, am Sonnabend. Aber heute Abend feiern wir.

WERNER: Wie alt wird Tina? Einundzwanzig?

GABRIELE: Nein, dreiundzwanzig.

WERNER: Tina sieht immer sehr jung aus.

Review Quiz 12

Choose the letter of the word or phrase that best completes each sentence.

1. Ist das die _____ Diplomatin aus Frankreich?
   a. kluges
   b. schöner
   c. neue
   d. guten

2. Wir haben _____ Gast kennen gelernt.
   a. jeden amerikanischen
   b. die deutschen
   c. jene italienische
   d. der englischen

3. Monika hat für _____ Rechtsanwalt gearbeitet.
   a. den jungen
   b. die nette
   c. der jungen
   d. die netten

4. Mein kleiner Bruder möchte auch _____.
   a. mitkommen
   b. gegangen
   c. gehören
   d. wegliefen

5. Mein Freund ruft mich oft _____.

   a. mit

   b. hinter

   c. zurück

   d. an

6. Die Kinder _____ schnell ein.

   a. hören

   b. schlafen

   c. sehen

   d. machten

7. Ich muss meinen Nachbarn _____.

   a. aufmachen

   b. aufstehen

   c. einladen

   d. zumachen

8. Vor einer Woche _____ ich einen schönen Anzug an.

   a. probiere

   b. probierte

   c. rufen

   d. rief

9. Es ist kalt und wir machen alle Fenster _____.

   a. mit

   b. zu

   c. aus

   d. ab

10. Das Badezimmer ist nicht _____.

    a. schöne

    b. dunklen

    c. helles

    d. sauber

New Vocabulary

als	*as*
attraktiv	*attractive*
aufmachen	*open*
aufstehen	*stand up, get up*
Ausgang (*m.*)	*exit*
aussehen	*look like*
Badezimmer (*n.*)	*bathroom*
bezahlen	*pay*
Clown (*m.*)	*clown*
dunkel	*dark*
Eindruck (*m.*)	*impression*
einladen	*invite*
einpacken	*pack up, wrap up*

einschlafen	*fall asleep*
fleißig	*diligent*
froh	*happy*
früh	*early*
ganz	*completely, quite*
genau	*exactly*
Haar (*n.*)	*hair*
hässlich	*ugly*
hell	*bright, light*
Hexe (*f.*)	*witch*
Himmel (*m.*)	*sky, heaven*
Hose (*f.*)	*pants*
Hotel (*n.*)	*hotel*
Hotelzimmer (*n.*)	*hotel room*
immer	*always*
Kasse (*f.*)	*cashier*
Klassenzimmer (*n.*)	*classroom*
kochen	*cook*
komisch	*funny, comical*
Kreditkarte (*f.*)	*credit card*
lang	*long*
Matrose (*m.*)	*sailor*
messen	*measure*
mitkommen	*come along*
muskulös	*muscular*
Nachbar (*m.*)	*neighbor*
Note (*f.*)	*grade*
Problem (*n.*)	*problem*
Rathaus (*n.*)	*city hall*
Rechtsanwalt (*m.*)	*lawyer*
Satz (*m.*)	*sentence*
sauber	*clean*
Schauspielerin (*f.*)	*actress*

schwach	*weak*
See (*m.*)	*lake*
Sonne (*f.*)	*sun*
stark	*strong*
still	*quiet, still*
Stimme (*f.*)	*voice*
Strumpf (*m.*)	*stocking*
tanzen	*dance*
Tinte (*f.*)	*ink*
umsteigen	*transfer (on transportation)*
weglaufen	*run away*
Weiterflug (*m.*)	*connecting flight*
Wind (*m.*)	*wind*
Zimmer (*n.*)	*room*
zuhören	*listen*
zumachen	*close*
zurückgehen	*go back, return*

13

Irregular Present Perfect Tense and Prefixes

This chapter continues the discussion of the present perfect tense with irregular verbs. Both separable and inseparable prefixes will be used in the present perfect tense.

Some questions that will be answered are:

✓ How does the present perfect tense differ between regular and irregular verbs?
✓ How are **haben**, **sein**, and **werden** conjugated in the present perfect tense?
✓ How do prefixes function in the irregular perfect tense?

The Irregular Present Perfect Tense

Both English and German have irregularities in the present perfect tense. In English, there are three basic kinds of irregularities. One kind is the verb that is identical in the present tense and as a past participle in the present perfect tense. For example:

Present Tense	*Have* and Past Participle
burst	*it has burst*
cast	*they have cast*
cut	*I have cut*
hit	*we have hit*
put	*he has put*

Another form of irregular past participle is the change of a vowel or consonant and often simultaneously the stem of the verb. For example:

Present Tense	*Have* and Past Participle
begin	*it has begun*
hold	*you have held*
keep	*she has kept*
leave	*we have left*
make	*I have made*

The third basic kind of past participle sometimes makes a vowel or consonant change and adds the suffix -*en*. For example:

Present Tense	*Have* and Past Participle
break	*it has broken*
forget	*I have forgotten*
give	*they have given*
speak	*you have spoken*
take	*she has taken*

Remember that the present perfect tense is used in English to describe an event that began in the past and ended in the present. In German, this tense is the common way of expressing an event in the past but can be translated in English in the simple past tense:

er hat gekauft = *he has bought/he bought*

Step 1: German Irregular Past Participles

Two irregular past participles were provided in Chapter 11:

Wir sind in die Stadt <u>gefahren</u>.	*We drove into the city.*
Ist Erik <u>gekommen</u>?	*Did Erik come?*

It is easy to recognize that these two past participles are derived from the infinitives **fahren** and **kommen**. The primary difference is the suffix -**en**. This is true of other past participles. For example:

Infinitive	Past Participle	
laufen	gelaufen	*run*
fallen	gefallen	*fallen*
fangen	gefangen	*caught*

geben	gegeben	*given*
lesen	gelesen	*read*
heißen	geheißen	*called, named*
sehen	gesehen	*seen*
tragen	getragen	*carried, worn*

Just as with regular past participles, some verbs require **haben** as their auxiliary. Others require **sein**. If the verb has a *direct object*, it is transitive and uses **haben**. If it describes movement from one place to another, it is intransitive and uses **sein**. For example:

Transitive

| Sie hat den Ball gefangen. | *She caught the ball.* |
| Wer hat den Unfall gesehen? | *Who saw the accident?* |

Intransitive

| Er ist zum Park gelaufen. | *He ran to the park.* |
| Ich bin in den Schmutz gefallen. | *I fell into the dirt.* |

Say It Out Loud

Read each sentence out loud, paying attention to the auxiliary used and the past participle:

Warum hast du diesen Hut getragen?	*Why did you wear this hat?*
Wir sind ins Klassenzimmer gelaufen.	*We ran into the classroom.*
Niemand hat den russischen Matrosen gesehen.	*No one saw the Russian sailor.*
Der Soldat ist auf die Knie gefallen.	*The soldier fell to his knees.*
Ihre Tochter hat Angelika geheißen.	*Their daughter was named Angelika.*
Wer hat dir diese Gitarre gegeben?	*Who gave you this guitar?*
Sonja hat einen Igel gefangen.	*Sonja caught a hedgehog.*
Wer hat seinen letzten Roman gelesen?	*Who read his last novel?*

A large group of irregular past participles makes a vowel change and adds the suffix **-en**. For example:

Infinitive	**Past Participle**	
bleiben	geblieben	*stayed, remained*
brechen	gebrochen	*broken*
empfehlen	empfohlen	*recommended*

fliegen	geflogen	*flown*
gehen	gegangen	*gone*
helfen	geholfen	*helped*
nehmen	genommen	*taken*
schneiden	geschnitten	*cut*
schreiben	geschrieben	*written*
singen	gesungen	*sung*
stehen	gestanden	*stood*
stehlen	gestohlen	*stolen*
trinken	getrunken	*drunk*

Just like other verbs, this category of verbs contains both transitive and intransitive verbs, which use either **haben** or **sein** as their auxiliaries. For example:

Transitive

Wer hat das Fenster gebrochen?	*Who broke the window?*
Der Dieb hat meinen Ring gestohlen.	*The thief stole my ring.*

Intransitive

Er ist nach Amerika geflogen.	*He flew to America.*
Wir sind oft an den See gegangen.	*We often went to the lake.*

Say It Out Loud

Read each sentence out loud, paying attention to the auxiliary used and the past participle:

Wer hat seine Flasche Wein gestohlen?	*Who stole his bottle of wine?*
Wir sind den ganzen Tag am See geblieben.	*We stayed at the lake the whole day.*
Sie hat zehn Minuten vor dem Spiegel gestanden.	*She stood in front of the mirror for 10 minutes.*
Thomas hat sich den Arm gebrochen.	*Thomas broke his arm.*
Die Kinder haben sehr laut gesungen.	*The children sang very loudly.*
Tina hat dieses Lokal empfohlen.	*Tina recommended this pub.*
Haben Sie dem Matrosen schon geschrieben?	*Did you already write to the sailor?*

Ich bin mit einem Jumbo-Jet geflogen.	*I flew on a jumbo jet.*
Mutti hat ein paar Scheiben Brot geschnitten.	*Mom cut a couple slices of bread.*
Niemand ist heute Abend ins Kino gegangen.	*No one went to the movies this evening.*
Wer hat meinen Pass genommen?	*Who took my passport?*
Der Flugbegleiter hat uns mit den Koffern geholfen.	*The flight attendant helped us with the suitcases.*
Sie hat eine Tasse Tee getrunken.	*She drank a cup of tea.*

Wondering About This? *wir sind geblieben*

You may have noticed that the verb **bleiben** uses **sein** as its auxiliary. Yet **bleiben** is not a verb of motion. It does not show movement from one place to another. But it is in a special category of verbs that describe a *condition* that is out of the control of the doer of the action. You cannot carry out the command *stay*. This occurs only with the passage of time and has nothing to do with any movement a person makes. Although it may seem foreign to English speakers, it is the reason for the use of **sein** as the auxiliary:

Ich bin zwei Jahre in der Schweiz geblieben.	*I stayed in Switzerland two years.*
Bist du wieder zu Hause geblieben?	*Did you stay home again?*

You will encounter a few other verbs in this category later in the chapter. Some of their English counterparts are *be*, *become*, and *die*. Think about what those verbs mean and how their actions cannot be carried out.

Exercise 13.1

Give each infinitive with the subject provided in the present perfect tense. For example:

fahren	ich *bin gefahren*

1. schreiben   du _____

2. trinken   wir _____

3. geben   ich _____

4. lesen   wer _____

5. gehen   ihr _____

6. stehen   niemand _____

7. heißen   das Kind _____

8. fallen   er _____

9. stehlen   Erik _____

10. sehen   ich _____

11. tragen   sie *pl.* _____

12. brechen   der Sportler _____

13. laufen   du _____

14. fangen   Tina _____

15. singen   die Jungen _____

A small group of verbs has vowel changes in the irregular past participle but uses the suffix **-t**. For example:

Infinitive	Past Participle	
brennen	gebrannt	*burned*
bringen	gebracht	*brought*
denken	gedacht	*thought*
kennen	gekannt	*known, acquainted with*
nennen	genannt	*named*
rennen	gerannt	*run*
senden	gesandt	*sent*
wissen	gewusst	*known*

Except for **rennen**, these verbs are all transitive and use **haben** as their auxiliary. For example:

Felix ist um die Ecke gerannt.	*Felix ran around the corner.*
Ich habe es schon gewusst.	*I already knew it.*
Sie haben das Kind Werner genannt.	*They named the child Werner.*

 Two verbs that need to be highlighted are **essen** (*eat*) and **fressen** (*devour, eat like an animal*). First, **fressen** should not be used when talking about humans. The verb **essen** is unique because it forms its irregular past participle with an extra **g** in it. Let's look at these two verbs.

Infinitive	Past Participle	
essen	gegessen	*eaten*
fressen	gefressen	*eaten like an animal*
Haben Sie schon gegessen?	*Did you already eat?*	
Der Löwe hat schnell gefressen.	*The lion ate fast.*	

Use Appendix B to check for irregular past participles.

Exercise 13.2

Reword each present tense sentence in the present perfect tense. For example:

Er liest die Zeitung.

Er hat die Zeitung gelesen.

1. Wir bringen ihr ein paar Blumen.

   _____

2. Ich weiß es nicht.

   _____

3. Warum brennt ein Licht im Wohnzimmer?

   _____

4. Die Kinder essen langsam.

   _____

5. Wir kennen diesen Matrosen gut.

   _____

6. Wohin sendet ihr die Geschenke?

   _____

7. Sie denken an (*about*) ihre Eltern.

   _____

8. Die Mutter nennt ihren Sohn Johann.

   _____

9. Wer schreibt diesen Artikel?

   _____

10. Die Jungen rennen in die Bibliothek.

    _____

Step 2: *Haben, sein, werden, sterben*

Haben, sein, and **werden** can act as auxiliaries for other verbs. When they stand alone, they can form other tenses, including the present perfect tense. Although **haben** has an irregular past tense (**hatte**), its past participle is regular (**gehabt**). **Sein** and **werden** form irregular participles. Let's look at the present perfect conjugations of these important verbs:

	haben		**sein**		**werden**	
ich	habe gehabt	*I had*	bin gewesen	*was*	bin geworden	*became*
du	hast gehabt	*you had*	bist gewesen	*were*	bist geworden	*became*
er	hat gehabt	*he had*	ist gewesen	*was*	ist geworden	*became*
wir	haben gehabt	*we had*	sind gewesen	*were*	sind geworden	*became*
ihr	habt gehabt	*you had*	seid gewesen	*were*	seid geworden	*became*
Sie	haben gehabt	*you had*	sind gewesen	*were*	sind geworden	*became*
sie	haben gehabt	*they had*	sind gewesen	*were*	sind geworden	*became*

As a reminder, if these example verbs are translated literally, the translations would have been as follows: *I have had, I have been,* and *I have become,* and so on. The normal translation is in the simple past tense: *I had, I was,* and *I became.*

The verb **haben** is a transitive verb. It can be followed by a direct object, for example, **Ich habe einen Bruder gehabt**. *I had a brother.* Therefore, its auxiliary is **haben**. But **sein** and **werden** are intransitive and describe a condition or state of being out of the control of the doer of the action. Therefore, their auxiliary is **sein**, for example, **Er ist krank gewesen**. *He was sick.* **Meine Schwester ist Flugbegleiterin geworden**. *My sister became a flight attendant.*

Sterben

The verb **sterben** (*die*) is another verb that describes a condition or state of being out of the control of the doer of the action. It is intransitive and uses **sein** as its auxiliary. For example:

ich	bin gestorben	*I died*
du	bist gestorben	*you died*
er	ist gestorben	*he died*
wir	sind gestorben	*we died*
ihr	seid gestorben	*you died*
Sie	sind gestorben	*you died*
sie	sind gestorben	*they died*

This verb is irregular in the present and past tenses as well:

	Present		Past	
ich	sterbe	*die*	starb	*died*
du	stirbst		starbst	
er	stirbt		starb	
wir	sterben		starben	
ihr	sterbt		starbt	
Sie	sterben		starben	
sie	sterben		starben	

Say It Out Loud

Read each sentence out loud, paying attention to the auxiliary and past participle:

Wie lange bist du in Berlin gewesen?	*How long were you in Berlin?*
Der Rechtsanwalt hat keinen Pass gehabt.	*The lawyer had no passport.*
In welchem Jahr ist Mozart gestorben?	*In what year did Mozart die?*
Die Tage sind wieder regnerisch geworden.	*The days became rainy again.*
Ich bin nie im Ausland gewesen.	*I have never been in a foreign country.*
Er hat eine Wohnung in der Hauptstadt gehabt.	*He had an apartment in the capital city.*
Im Jahre 2011 ist sie Ärztin geworden.	*She became a doctor in 2011.*
Die alte Katze ist gestern Abend gestorben.	*The old cat died yesterday evening.*

Some Useful Phrases

The verb **haben** occurs in many phrases. You have already encountered **gern haben** (*like, be fond of someone*). Three more useful phrases are **Glück haben** (*have good luck, be lucky*), **Pech haben** (*have bad luck, be unlucky*), and **Lust haben** (*feel like doing something*). Like most phrases, these can be used in other tenses, including the present perfect tense. For example:

Present:	Monika hat ihn gern.	*Monika likes him.*
Past:	Monika hatte ihn gern.	*Monika liked him.*
Present perfect:	Monika hat ihn gern gehabt.	*Monika like/has liked him.*

Present:	Wir haben oft Glück.	*We often have luck.*
Past:	Wir hatten oft Glück.	*We often had luck.*
Present perfect:	Wir haben oft Glück gehabt.	*We often had/have had luck.*
Present:	Er hat wieder Pech.	*He has bad luck again.*
Past:	Er hatte wieder Pech.	*He had bad luck again.*
Present perfect:	Er hat wieder Pech gehabt.	*He had/has had bad luck again.*

With the word **Pech**, you can simply say: **Pech gehabt!** *Tough luck!*

Present:	Ich habe Lust, ins Kino zu gehen.	*I feel like going to the movies.*
Past:	Ich hatte Lust, ins Kino zu gehen.	*I felt like going to the movies.*
Present perfect:	Ich habe Lust gehabt, ins Kino zu gehen.	*I felt/have felt like going to the movies.*

Exercise 13.3

Give each infinitive in the past tense with the provided subject and in the present perfect tense with the other subject provided. For example:

singen   ich *sang*   du *hast gesungen*

		Past		**Present Perfect**
1.	sterben	er _____	wir _____
		sie *pl.* _____	ihr _____
2.	sein	ich _____	du _____
		Sie _____	wir _____
3.	kennen	er _____	sie *s.* _____
		du _____	wer _____
4.	haben	er _____	wir _____
		sie *pl.* _____	ich _____
5.	denken	ihr _____	er _____
		sie *s.* _____	du _____

Step 3: Prefixes

You have discovered how inseparable and separable prefixes work in the present and past tenses. Something similar happens in the present perfect tense. It is important to remember that no matter whether a verb has a regular or irregular conjugation, the prefixes function in the same way in both instances.

In the present and past tenses, inseparable prefixes remain fixed to the front of a verb in a conjugation. For example:

Present/Past	Present/Past
ich besuche/ich besuchte	wir erwarten/wir erwarteten
du verstehst/du verstandest	Sie bekommen/Sie bekamen

When the prefix is separable, the prefix in the present and past tenses is the last element in a sentence. For example:

Present/Past	Present/Past
du siehst . . . aus/du sahst . . . aus	er kommt . . . mit/er kam . . . mit
sie fährt . . . ab/sie fuhr . . . ab	ich lade . . . ein/ich lud . . . ein

In the present perfect tense, something similar happens. When the past participle of a verb is formed with an inseparable prefix, the inseparable prefix replaces the participial prefix **ge-**. For example:

bestellen	ich habe bestellt	*I ordered*
empfehlen	er hat empfohlen	*he recommended*
gefallen	es hat gefallen	*it pleased*
zerstören	sie haben zerstört	*they destroyed*

Wondering About This? *gefallen*

You have encountered two words that use the **fallen** as the main verb. The verb **fallen** (*fall*) itself and the verb with a prefix **gefallen** (*please*). Both become **gefallen** as past participles, but one used **sein** as its auxiliary and the other uses **haben**. For example:

Der Mann <u>ist</u> auf die Knie gefallen. *The man fell to his knees.*
Das Buch <u>hat</u> mir sehr gefallen. *I liked (was pleased by) the book very much.*

When a verb has a separable prefix, that prefix is separated from the rest of the participle by the suffix **ge-**. For example:

mitkommen	er ist mit<u>ge</u>kommen	*he came along*
aussehen	sie hat krank aus<u>ge</u>sehen	*she looked sick*
weglaufen	der Hund ist weg<u>ge</u>laufen	*the dog ran away*
zumachen	sie haben es zu<u>ge</u>macht	*they closed it*

When verbs *with any kind of prefix* are used with the auxiliaries **können**, **müssen**, and **möchte**, the prefixed verbs appear as infinitives. No changes are required:

Ich kann die Tür nicht <u>aufmachen</u>.	*I cannot open the door.*
Du musst ein Glas Bier <u>bestellen</u>.	*You have to order a glass of beer.*
Möchten Sie ins Restaurant <u>mitkommen</u>?	*Would you like to come along to the restaurant?*

Say It Out Loud

Read each sentence out loud, paying attention to the form the past participles take with prefixes:

Hoffentlich hat dir die Suppe gefallen.	*I hope (Hopefully) you liked the soup.*
Felix hat Würstchen mit Senf bestellt.	*Felix ordered sausages with mustard.*
Die Dame hat heute sehr hübsch ausgesehen.	*The lady looked very beautiful today.*
Um wie viel Uhr seid ihr abgefahren?	*What time did you depart?*
Wir sind um vier Uhr angekommen.	*We arrived at four o'clock.*
Der alte Mann ist um elf Uhr gestorben.	*The old man died at eleven o'clock.*
Tina hat einen schwarzen Pullover anprobiert.	*Tina tried on a black sweater.*
Haben Sie Ihren Pass vergessen?	*Did you forget your passport?*
Um wie viel Uhr ist dein Sohn aufgestanden?	*What time did your son get up?*
Die Touristen sind um zwanzig Uhr zurückgegangen.	*The tourists went back at 8 p.m.*
Haben sie die italienischen Diplomaten eingeladen?	*Did they invite the Italian diplomats?*
Die Party hat um achtzehn Uhr angefangen.	*The party began at 6 p.m.*
Das kleine Kind ist wieder in den Schmutz gefallen.	*The little child fell in the dirt again.*

Telling time in German is not a difficult matter. When the time is on the hour, simply use the correct number and the word **Uhr**. If you wish to say *at what time* something occurs, use the preposition **um**. For example:

Es ist neun Uhr.	*It is nine o'clock.*
Er kommt um ein Uhr.	*He is coming at one o'clock.*

On the half hour, use **halb** and the *hour that is coming up*. For example:

halb <u>drei</u>	*2:30*
halb <u>zehn</u>	*9:30*

With a *quarter after* the hour or a *quarter to* the hour, use **Viertel nach** and **Viertel vor**, respectively. For example:

Es ist schon Viertel nach vier.	*It is already a quarter after four.*
Sie kommt um Viertel vor sieben.	*She is coming at a quarter to seven.*

Like English, you can say various times by using the exact number of minutes after or before the hour. For example:

Es ist schon sechs Uhr zehn.	*It is already ten after six.*
Es fängt um zwanzig vor elf an.	*It starts at twenty to eleven.*

German often uses the *military* clock to be precise about hours after noon:

Sie machen um einundzwanzig Uhr zu.	*They close at 9 p.m.*
Es ist jetzt fünfzehn Uhr dreißig.	*It is now 3:30 p.m.*

Exercise 13.4

Reword each present tense sentence in the present perfect tense. Be careful when prefixes are used. For example:

Ich bestelle Brot mit Butter.

<u>*Ich habe Brot mit Butter bestellt.*</u>

1. Wir gehen um zehn Uhr zurück.

   _____

2. Lesen Sie die Zeitung?

   _____

3. Meine Tante verspricht mir diesen Ring.

   _____

4. Niemand kennt den russischen Matrosen.

   _____

5. Wer isst den Kuchen?

_____

6. Viele Mädchen kommen auf die Party mit.

_____

7. Erwarten sie Gäste?

_____

8. Wo steigen sie um?

_____

9. Mein alter Hund stirbt.

_____

10. Ich bin in den Alpen.

_____

11. Im April wird es oft regnerisch.

_____

12. Wisst ihr es schon?

_____

13. Der arme Mann hat wieder Pech.

_____

14. Um wie viel Uhr kommt der Zug an?

_____

15. Diese Jungen zerstören meinen Garten.

_____

 ## Review Quiz 13

Choose the letter of the word or phrase that best completes each sentence.

1. Er hat wieder keine Zeit _____.
   a. geworden   c. gehabt
   b. zumachen   d. bestellten

2. Das habe ich nie _____.
   a. gewusst   c. umgestiegen
   b. erwarten   d. vergass

3. Niemand _____ im Dorf geblieben.

   a. hat   c. wurde

   b. haben   d. ist

4. Wer kann dieses Fenster _____?

   a. aufmachen   c. zurückgegangen

   b. gewesen   d. zurückgehen

5. Um wie viel Uhr ist sie _____?

   a. gestorben   c. gewesen

   b. bestellt   d. wurde

6. _____ Sie dieses weiße Hemd anprobiert?

   a. Sind   c. Haben

   b. Sein   d. Gehabt

7. In der Küche hat ein Licht _____.

   a. gebrannt   c. stehlen

   b. lasen   d. ausgesehen

8. Die _____ hilft mir mit dem großen Koffer.

   a. Soldaten   c. Flugbegleiterin

   b. Polizist   d. Kellnerinnen

9. Der Matrose ist schnell um die Ecke _____.

   a. bekommen   c. gerannt

   b. empfohlen   d. weglaufen

10. Kommt der letzte Bus _____?

   a. die Ecke   c. halb elf

   b. um zwei Uhr   d. den Bahnhof

New Vocabulary

bleiben	*remain, stay*
brennen	*burn*
bringen	*bring*
denken	*think*
fangen	*catch*
Flasche (*f.*)	*bottle*
Flugbegleiter (*m.*)	*flight attendant*

fressen	eat (*like an animal*)
gefallen	please (*like*)
gehören	belong to
Glück haben	be lucky
halb	half
hoffentlich	hopefully
Jumbo-Jet (*m.*)	jumbo jet
Knie (*n.*)	knee
Koffer (*m.*)	suitcase
Lokal (*n.*)	pub, tavern
Lust haben	feel like (*doing something*)
Matrose (*m.*)	sailor
nennen	name
Party (*f.*)	party
Pass (*m.*)	passport
Pech haben	have bad luck
rennen	run
Ring (*m.*)	ring
Roman (*m.*)	novel
Scheibe (*f.*)	slice
Schmutz (*m.*)	dirt, filth
schneiden	catch
Senf (*m.*)	mustard
Spiegel (*m.*)	mirror
sterben	die
Suppe (*f.*)	soup
Tasse (*f.*)	cup
Tee (*m.*)	tea
um wie viel Uhr	at what time
Unfall (*m.*)	accident
vergessen	forget
versprechen	promise

Mastery Check 2

This Mastery Check is provided to help you identify the areas of German covered in the last seven chapters that you feel confident about or that you should review. Choose the letter of the word or phrase that best completes each sentence.

1. Ich möchte ein neues Hemd _____.
   a. habe
   b. verkauft
   c. suchte
   d. kaufen

2. Gestern _____ Hans Schach.
   a. machte
   b. spielen
   c. machen
   d. spielte

3. Vor einem Monat _____ für Frau Benz.
   a. besuchte
   b. arbeitete er
   c. suchen sie
   d. lernten

4. Am _____ gingen die Gäste nach Hause.
   a. Abend
   b. Woche
   c. Frühling
   d. vor einem Jahr

5. _____ du wieder nach Heidelberg?
   a. Läuft
   b. Lief
   c. Flogen
   d. Fuhrst

6. _____ Januar besuchten wir Karl und Monika.
   a. Vor einem
   b. Im
   c. 2010
   d. Im Jahre

7. Was gibst du _____ Mädchen?
   a. dem
   b. der
   c. diese
   d. einen

8. Meine Schwester _____ der alten Frau.
   a. hilft
   b. arbeitet
   c. war
   d. wurde

9. Ich möchte mit _____ Lehrerin sprechen.
   a. der
   b. diese
   c. jenen
   d. meinem

10. _____ schicken Sie diese Geschenke?

    a. Euch

    b. Wem

    c. Sie *s.*

    d. Nachmittag

11. Sie spielen nicht Tennis, _____ sie spielen Schach.

    a. sondern

    b. oder

    c. mussten

    d. können

12. Die Frau _____ sich den Arm.

    a. antwortet

    b. konnte

    c. bricht

    d. möchte

13. Wir können ins Kino gehen, _____ wir können ins Cafe gehen.

    a. und

    b. oder

    c. müssen

    d. taten

14. Er möchte sich die Zähne _____.

    a. passieren

    b. schlafen

    c. putzen

    d. können

15. War die neunte Sinfonie seine _____ Sinfornie?

    a. drei

    b. laut

    c. welche

    d. letzte

16. _____ dir dieser Bleistift?

    a. Gehört

    b. Erwartet

    c. Verkaufte

    d. Empfehlen

17. Ich kann _____ beantworten.

    a. der Lehrerin

    b. diese Frage

    c. viele Leute

    d. jenes Buch

18. Sein Bruder ist _____ Juli geboren.

    a. am

    b. am dritten

    c. in

    d. vor sieben

19. Er hat für _____ Arzt gearbeitet.

    a. den jungen

    b. die nette

    c. der jungen

    d. die netten

20. Herr Schäfer ruft uns oft _____.

    a. an

    b. hinter

    c. zurück

    d. mit

21. Marianne und Tina _____ schnell ein.
    a. hören   c. schlafen
    b. sehen   d. machten

22. Es ist heiß und wir machen alle Fenster _____.
    a. mit   c. auf
    b. vor   d. ab

23. Um wie viel Uhr ist dein Freund _____?
    a. gestorben   c. bestellt
    b. gewesen   d. wurde

24. _____ Sie den blauen Anzug anprobiert?
    a. Sind   c. Gehabt
    b. Sein   d. Haben

25. Im Keller hat ein Licht _____.
    a. gebrannt   c. lasen
    b. stehlen   d. ausgesehen

14

Genitive Case and Antonyms

This chapter provides an explanation of the genitive case declensions and its meaning and use. In addition, antonyms will be introduced as well as some special uses of the verb **gehen**.

Some questions that will be answered are:

✓ What are the ways that the genitive case is used?
✓ What are the genitive case prepositions?
✓ Which antonyms are high-frequency words?
✓ What purpose do antonyms have in building vocabulary?

Genitive Case

English has two major ways of showing possession with nouns. In one of the ways, the noun adds the suffix -s or -es and an apostrophe is placed before or after the suffix to identify singular and plural possessives. For example:

the man's car	the children's playroom
the lions' roar	the student's dorm
a magician's tricks	the houses' location

Phrases such as these identify to whom or to what something belongs or is associated.

The other method for making a possessive is to use the preposition *of* between the thing possessed and the possessor. For example:

the seller of the car	the father of the bride
the roar of the lions	the color of the drapes
the badge of the policeman	the new wife of Uncle Phil

This form of English possessive performs in a manner similar to the suffix –'s: ownership or a relationship is identified.

Step 1: German Possessives

There are some similarities between English and German possessive formation. The simplest one to recognize and understand is the use of the suffix -**s**. But in German an apostrophe is not used. This kind of possessive shows ownership and is used primarily with names. For example:

Erhardts Fahrrad	*Erhardt's bicycle*
Muttis Schinkenrezept	*Mom's ham recipe*
Angela Merkels Bericht	*Angela Merkel's report*
Mozarts letztes Werk	*Mozart's last work*
Gudruns neue Jeans	*Gudrun's new jeans*

In order to show ownership with other kinds of nouns, the genitive case is used. Let's look at its declension with both **der**-words and **ein**-words:

Masculine	des Mannes	*the man's*	eines Mannes	*a man's*
	dieses Lehrers	*this teacher's*	keines Lehrers	*no teacher's*
Feminine	der Tante	*the aunt's*	einer Tante	*an aunt's*
	jener Frau	*that woman's*	meiner Frau	*my wife's*
Neuter	des Kindes	*the child's*	eines Kindes	*a child's*
	welches Bootes	*what boat's*	Ihres Bootes	*your boat's*
Plural	der Jungen	*the boys'*	unserer Jungen	*our boys'*
	dieser Leute	*these people's*	keiner Leuter	*no people's*

Masculine nouns that end in -**e** or that come from a foreign source do not add the suffix -**s**. Instead, they add an -**n** or -**en** ending, for example, **der Junge** = **des Jungen**, **der Matrose** = **des Matrosen**, and **der Löwe** = **des Löwen**.

Wondering About This? *des Kindes*

The basic genitive ending for masculine and neuter nouns is -**s**. But with many nouns of one syllable or that are otherwise awkward to pronounce, the end -**es** can be used. For example:

des Kindes	*the child's*
des Buches	*the books'*
dieses Rathauses	*this city hall's*
meines Aufsatzes	*my essay's*

Say It Out Loud

Read each sentence out loud, paying attention to the use of the genitive case:

Der Klang der Musik ist furchtbar.	*The sound of the music is terrible.*
Wessen Bücher sind das?	*Whose books are those?*
Das sind die Bücher eines Freundes.	*Those are a friend's books.*
Wessen Wagen möchte er kaufen?	*Whose car would he like to buy?*
Er möchte den Wagen seines Onkels kaufen.	*He would like to buy his uncle's car.*
Wessen Aufsatz hat sie gelesen?	*Whose essay did she read?*
Sie hat Eriks Aufsatz gelesen.	*She read Erik's essay.*
Die Katzen der Mädchen waren alt.	*The girls' cats were old.*
Der Spiegel meines Großvaters ist zerbrochen.	*My grandfather's mirror is broken.*
Beethovens Oper heißt *Fidelio*.	*Beethoven's opera is called Fidelio.*
Der Regenschirm meiner Wirtin ist kaputt.	*My landlady's umbrella is broken.*
Die Tochter seiner Verwandten war in Rom.	*His relatives' daughter was in Rome.*

Exercise 14.1

Give the genitive case declension for each noun or phrase provided. For example:

der Mann <u>*des Mannes*</u>

1. diese Dame _____

2. Ihre Kinder _____

3. das Haus _____

4. jede Wirtin _____

5. Frau Bauer _____

6. ein Glas _____

7. Sonja ————————————————

8. keine Leute ——————————————

9. mein Fahrrad ——————————————

10. die Oper ——————————————

Since English also uses *of* to form possessives, many of these phrases can be translated with that preposition or with the suffix *-'s*. For example:

Ihrer Töchter	*your daughters'/of your daughters*
des Bootes	*the boat's/of the boat*
welches Aufsatzes	*which essay's/of which essay*

Adjective Endings

There are no new adjective endings in the genitive case. Adjectives with **der**-words and **ein**-words end in **-en** in all genders and the plural:

Masculine	des alt**en** Regenschirms	*the old umbrella's*
	dieses nett**en** Lehrers	*this nice teacher's*
Feminine	einer freundlich**en** Wirtin	*a kind landlady's*
	eurer ausländisch**en** Touristin	*your foreign tourist's*
Neuter	jenes hoh**en** Tors	*that high gate's*
	welches musikalisch**en** Werks	*which musical work's*
Plural	dieser reich**en** Verwandten	*these rich relatives'*
	keiner neu**en** Gäste	*no new guests'*

Say It Out Loud

Read each sentence out loud, paying attention to the genitive endings.

Der Sohn der jungen Ärztin hat in Bonn gewohnt.	*The young doctor's son lived in Bonn.*
Die Farbe dieser hübschen Kleider ist gelb.	*The color of these beautiful dresses is yellow.*
Wo ist das Hotel deiner ausländischen Gäste?	*Where is your foreign guests' hotel?*
Die Gesundheit ihres kleinen Kindes ist schlecht geworden.	*Her little child's health has gotten bad.*

Haben Sie den Aufsatz des klugen Studenten gelesen?	*Did you read the smart student's essay?*
Der Arzt hat ihre Temperatur gemessen.	*The doctor took her temperature.*
Der Chef meines besten Freundes ist in die Hauptstadt gefahren.	*My best friend's boss drove to the capital.*
Gudrun ist die Freundin dieses jungen Komponisten.	*Gudrun is this young composer's girlfriend.*
Die Wohnung meiner neuen Nachbarn ist klein.	*My new neighbors' apartment is small.*
Hans hat auf dem Boden des schmutzigen Zimmers geschlafen.	*Hans slept on the floor of the dirty room.*

Exercise 14.2

In the blank, give the correct form of the adjective provided in parentheses. For example:

(klein) Das ist das Bett seiner *kleinen* Katze.

1. (ausländisch) Die Wohnung meiner _____ Freunde ist sehr schön.

2. (hübsch) Ist das der Wagen des _____ Mannes in der Ecke?

3. (lang) Die Farbe dieses _____ Rocks ist dunkelblau.

4. (polnisch) Die Stimme jener _____ Sängerin ist furchtbar.

5. (alt) Ich habe den ersten Roman meiner _____ Wirtin gekauft.

6. (groß) Der Boden dieser _____ Zimmer ist schmutzig.

7. (musikalisch) Der Name dieses _____ Werks ist *Blauer Himmel.*

8. (reich) Der Regenschirm jener _____ Dame ist kaputt.

9. (kurz) Die Farbe seiner _____ Haare ist schwarz.

10. (freundlich) Die Hände der _____ Tänzerin sind sehr klein.

Step 2: Containers

Containers that express how much of something there is require a special look in German. The German language does something unique and quite different from English. In English, the container is stated and is followed by the preposition *of* and a noun. This is not a true possessive, but sentences such as these are quite common in both English and German and need to be examined. Look at these examples in English:

a box of tissue	*a bowl of nuts*
a piece of paper	*a bag of gold*
a slice of cake	*a glass of milk*

You will notice that the noun that follows *of* does not require the use of an article. That is where English and German are alike. German differs in that *it does not use the translation of "of" or any other preposition.*

First let's look at the names of containers in German:

das Glas	*glass*
das Stück	*piece*
der Korb	*basket*
der Sack	*bag, sack*
der Teller	*plate, soup bowl*
die Büchse	*tin, box*
die Dose	*can*
die Flasche	*bottle*
die Schachtel	*pack, packet*
die Schale	*bowl, dish*
die Scheibe	*slice*
die Tafel	*bar*
die Tasse	*cup*
die Tüte	*bag*

When nouns follow these containers, neither a preposition nor an article is required, for example, **ein Stück Brot** (*a piece of bread*), **ein Teller Suppe** (*a bowl of soup*), **eine Schachtel Zigaretten** (*a pack of cigarettes*), and **eine Tasse Kakao** (*a cup of cocoa*).

Say It Out Loud

Read each sentence out loud, paying attention to the use of the containers and the nouns that follow them.

Geben Sie mir bitte eine Flasche Rotwein!	*Please give me a bottle of red wine.*
Ich möchte lieber ein Glas Weißwein.	*I would prefer a glass of white wine.*
Er hat seinem Sohn eine Tafel Schokolade gekauft.	*He bought his son a bar of chocolate.*
Geben Sie ihr drei Scheiben Käse!	*Give her two slices of cheese.*
Ich habe zwei Teller Gulasch gegessen.	*I ate two plates of goulash.*
Hat er wirklich sechs Glas Bier getrunken?	*Did he really drink six glasses of beer?*
Er möchte lieber eine Dose Erbsen.	*He would prefer a can of peas.*
Zeigen Sie mir bitte einen großen Korb Äpfel!	*Please show me a big basket of apples.*
Eine Schale Apfelsinen ist auf dem Tisch.	*A bowl of oranges is on the table.*
Er hat eine ganze Tüte Chips gegessen.	*He ate a whole bag of chips.*
Bringen Sie mir bitte ein Glas Limonade!	*Bring me a glass of soda, please.*
Ich habe sechs Flaschen Cola bestellt.	*I ordered six bottles of cola.*

Some Useful Phrases for the Imperative

In the previous sentences, you used verb phrases that you may not have understood thoroughly. They are **Geben Sie** and **Zeigen Sie**. Notice that the verb precedes the subject **Sie**, but this is not a question.

When the verb precedes the pronoun **Sie**, the sentence is a command. When you use **Sie**, it is a command given to someone with whom you have a formal relationship. This is the *imperative* structure for many verbs. For example:

Bleiben Sie zu Hause!	*Stay at home.*
Kommen Sie bitte mit!	*Please come along.*
Warten Sie bitte an der Tür!	*Please wait at the door.*
Machen Sie die Fenster auf!	*Open the windows.*
Singen Sie ein bisschen lauter!	*Sing a little louder.*
Vergessen Sie nicht, wo ich wohne!	*Do not forget where I live.*

In Chapter 19, you will go into imperatives in detail.

Exercise 14.3

Fill in the blank with the cues provided in parentheses. For example:

(Glas Milch) Ich möchte *ein Glas Milch.*

1. (Tafel Schololade) Wo kann man _____ kaufen?

2. (Stück Kuchen) Geben Sie mir bitte _____!

3. (Scheibe Käse) Möchten Sie lieber _____ haben?

4. (Tasse Kaffee) Meine Großmutter trinkt nur _____.

5. (groß Flasche Limonade) Hast du schon _____ getrunken?

6. (Teller Gulasch) Wer hat _____ bestellt?

7. (Scheibe Brot mit Butter) Ich habe oft _____ gegessen.

8. (ganz Tüte Chips) Kann Erik wirklich _____ essen?

9. (zwei Dose Erbsen) Haben Sie _____?

10. (Korb Äpfel) Hat Herr Schäfer _____ verkauft?

Step 3: Genitive Prepositions

There are four high-frequency genitive prepositions: **anstatt** (or **statt**) (*instead of*), **trotz** (*despite, in spite of*), **während** (*during*), and **wegen** (*because of*). Notice that English translation of three of these prepositions uses the preposition *of*, which suggests the genitive case. Nouns that follow these prepositions will have a genitive case declension. For example:

Anstatt meines Bruders hat Hans mir geholfen.	*Instead of my brother, Hans helped me.*
Trotz des schlechten Wetters spielten wir Tennis.	*Despite the bad weather, we played tennis.*
Während des Krieges waren wir in Schweden.	*During the war, we were in Sweden.*
Wegen einer langen Krankheit blieb sie in Berlin.	*Because of a long illness, she stayed in Berlin.*

Say It Out Loud

Read each sentence out loud, paying attention to the use of the genitive prepositions:

Anstatt eines Briefs schickte er mir eine Postkarte.	*Instead of a letter, he sent me a postcard.*
Trotz der heißen Tage ging ich Jogging.	*Despite the hot days, I went jogging.*
Während des Frühlings hatte ich keinen Job.	*During the spring, I had no job.*
Wegen des Regens war die Apotheke geschlossen.	*Because of the rain, the drugstore was closed.*
Anstatt eines Ringes kaufte sie eine Halskette.	*Instead of a ring, she bought a necklace.*
Trotz meiner Bitten hat sie mich nicht angerufen.	*Despite my requests, she did not phone me.*
Während seiner Schulzeit wohnte er in Bonn.	*During his schooldays, he lived in Bonn.*
Sie konnte wegen des Schnees nicht mitkommen.	*She could not come along because of the snow.*

Exercise 14.4

Fill in the blank with any appropriate phrase that contains an adjective. For example:

Anstatt *seines jungen Freundes* hat Tina ihm geholfen.

1. Anstatt _____ kaufte ich einen blauen Anzug.

2. Trotz _____ musste ich nach Heidelberg fahren.

3. Während _____ wohnte ich bei meiner Tante.

4. Wegen _____ ist er im Krankenhaus geblieben.

5. Anstatt _____ besuchen uns unsere Verwandeten.

6. Trotz _____ spielten sie im Garten.

7. Während _____ ist Erik eingeschlafen.

8. Wir mussten wegen _____ mit dem Zug fahren.

Antonyms

Antonyms are pairs of words that are *opposites*. Some common antonym pairs are *good/bad*, *tall/short*, *big/little*, and *rich/poor*. Learning antonyms and other words that show a strong contrast is helpful in building a vocabulary. Until now, this book has presented at random words that have opposite meanings, but now we need to look at them more closely.

Step 4: Opposites in German

A few of the antonym pairs that you have already encountered are:

aufmachen/zumachen	*open/close*
gut/schlecht	*good/bad*
heiß/kalt	*hot/cold*
hier/da	*here/there*
schwarz/weiß	*black/white*

Here is a list of other useful antonym pairs:

alt/jung	*old/young*
alt/neu	*old/new*
arm/reich	*poor/rich*
das Leben/der Tod	*life/death*
der Junge/das Mädchen	*boy/girl*
der Krieg/der Frieden	*war/peace*
der Mann/die Frau	*man/woman*
der Tag/die Nacht	*day/night*
dick/dünn	*fat/skinny*
dunkel/hell	*dark/bright*
erste/letzte	*first/last*
faul/fleißig	*lazy/diligent*
gesund/krank	*healthy/sick*
hübsch/hässlich	*beautiful/ugly*
intelligent/dumm	*intelligent/stupid*
interessant/langweilig	*interesting/boring*
laut/leise	*loud/quiet*

leben/sterben	*live/die*
sauber/schmutzig	*clear/dirty*
schnell/langsam	*fast/slow*
wahr/falsch	*true/false*
weit/nah	*far/near*

The meaning of a sentence can be immediately changed by using the antonym of the word originally used. For example:

Dieser Roman ist sehr interessant.	*This book is very interesting.*
Dieser Roman ist sehr langweilig.	*This book is very boring.*
Was Tina sagte ist falsch.	*What Tina said is false.*
Was Tina sagte ist wahr.	*What Tina said is true.*
Der faule Schüler schläft ein.	*The lazy student falls asleep.*
Der fleißige Schüler schläft ein.	*The diligent student falls asleep.*
Der Krieg dauerte nur zwei Tage.	*The war lasted only two days.*
Der Frieden dauerte nur zwei Tage.	*The peace lasted only two days.*

Say It Out Loud

Read each pair of sentences out loud, paying attention to the difference in meaning of both:

Geben Sie mir ein großes Glas Limonade!	*Give me a large glass of soda.*
Geben Sie mir ein kleines Glas Limonade!	*Give me a little glass of soda.*
Der arme Mann wohnt in einem kleinen Haus.	*The poor man lives in a little house.*
Der reiche Mann wohnt in einem kleinen Haus.	*The rich man lives in a little house.*
Meine Tochter ist eine fleißige Schülerin.	*My daughter is a diligent student.*
Meine Tochter ist eine faule Schülerin.	*My daughter is a lazy student.*
Ist dieses Badetuch schmutzig?	*Is this bath towel dirty?*
Ist dieses Badetuch sauber?	*Is this bath towel clean?*
Deutschlands Hauptstadt ist nicht weit.	*Germany's capital is not far.*
Deutschlands Hauptstadt ist nicht nah.	*Germany's capital is not near.*

Beim kalten Wetter bleiben wir zu Hause.	In cold weather we stay home.
Beim heißen Wetter bleiben wir zu Hause.	In hot weather we stay home.
Der dicke Mann ist unser Kellner gewesen.	The fat man was our waiter.
Der dünne Mann ist unser Kellner gewesen.	The skinny man was our waiter.
Ein starker Mann hat uns nach dem Unfall geholfen.	A strong man helped us after the accident.
Ein schwacher Mann hat uns nach dem Unfall geholfen.	A weak man helped us after the accident.

Wondering About This? *schmutzig/schmutzigen*

Let's review endings on adjectives and adverbs. When an adjective is a predicate adjective, it requires no ending. When it modifies a noun directly, it does. For example:

| Der Boden ist wieder <u>schmutzig</u>. | The floor is dirty again. (predicate adjective) |
| Er schlief auf dem <u>schmutzigen</u> Boden. | He slept on the dirty floor. (modifies **Boden** directly) |

If the modifier is an adverb, it requires no ending. Remember that adverbs modify the action of a verb or another adverb. For example:

| Ich habe schnell gearbeitet. | I worked fast. (adverb modifies **gearbeitet**) |
| Sie gehen sehr langsam. | They walk very slowly. (adverb modifies adverb **langsam**) |

Exercise 14.5

Fill in the blank with the correct antonym of the word in parentheses. Make any needed changes and add any needed endings to the antonym. For example:

(weiß) Er hat das <u>schwarze</u> Hemd gekauft.

1. (groß) Ich möchte eine _____ Scheibe Käse.

2. (kurz) Bringen Sie mir bitte ein _____ Kleid!

3. (interessant) Ist der Roman _____ gewesen?

4. (leben) Der alte Mann ist gestern Abend _____ .

5. (laut) Warum hat er so _____ gesprochen?

6. (aufmachen) Mutti hat die Tür _____ .

7. (dunkel) Der Himmel ist sehr _____ geworden.

8. (schmutzig) Sie möchte lieber ein _____ Badezimmer.

9. (nah) Ist der Bahnhof _____ ?

10. (schnell) Die neue Wirtin ging _____ zum Park.

Gehen

The verb **gehen** is very versatile. It is used in idiomatic phrases such as **es geht mir gut** (*I am fine*), and it has a special use when combined with other verbs. That use is almost identical to how *go* can be used in English.

There are numerous English phrases that are introduced by *go* and are accompanied by a present participle. For example:

> *I go fishing every day.*
>
> *We want to go skiing next winter.*
>
> *Do you want to go hiking with us?*
>
> *She went swimming in Lake Michigan.*
>
> *No one wants to go camping with Bill.*

Step 5: *Gehen* and Infinitives

You are familiar with the irregular verb **gehen** (*go*). Like its English counterpart, **gehen** can be used to tell what activity someone is taking part in. The verb **gehen** is conjugated in an appropriate tense, and an infinitive is the last element in the sentence. For example:

Wir <u>gehen</u> am Abend <u>tanzen</u>.	*In the evening, we go dancing.*
Die Kinder <u>gingen</u> im Wald <u>wandern</u>.	*The children went hiking in the woods.*
Wie oft <u>seid</u> ihr <u>schwimmen</u> <u>gegangen</u>?	*How often did you go swimming?*

Say It Out Loud

*Read each sentence out loud, paying attention to **gehen** and its accompanying infinitive:*

Gehst du jeden Tag joggen?	*Do you go jogging every day?*
Meine Mutter ging heute einkaufen.	*My mother went shopping today.*
Unsere Eltern gehen gern spazieren.	*Our parents like to go strolling.*
Bist du in den Alpen klettern gegangen?	*Did you go climbing in the Alps?*
Im Winter gingen sie schlittschuhlaufen.	*In winter they went ice skating.*
Jede Woche gehen die Mädchen Tennis spielen.	*The girls go play tennis every week.*
Ich bin nie mit ihr tanzen gegangen.	*I never went dancing with her.*
Könnt ihr mit mir schwimmen gehen?	*Can you go swimming with me?*
Sie möchte am Freitag tauchen gehen.	*She wants to go diving on Friday.*
Früh am Morgen gingen sie im Park laufen.	*Early in the morning they went running in the park.*

Exercise 14.6

*Compose a brief sentence in the tense given with the infinitive provided in parentheses. Introduce each sentence with a form of **gehen**. For example:*

(*past*/schwimmen) <u>*Gestern ging ich schwimmen.*</u>

1. (*present*/joggen) _____

2. (*past*/wandern) _____

3. (*present perfect*/klettern) _____

4. (*present*/fischen *fish*) _____

5. (*past*/tauchen) _____

6. (*present perfect*/Fußball spielen) _____

7. (*present*/schlittschuhlaufen) _____

8. (*past*/einkaufen) _____

9. (*present perfect*/spazieren) _____

10. (*present*/segeln *sail*) _____

Let's Read

Read the following text, and determine its meaning on your own.

Im Oktober besuchte ich meine Verwandten in Hamburg. Sie hatten eine große Wohnung in der Schillerstraße nicht weit vom Bahnhof. Meine Cousine Angelika war auch da. Jeden Tag gingen wir in der Stadt spazieren. Hamburg is sehr interessant und groß. Die Stadt hat einen schönen See. Am See gingen wir jeden Tag schwimmen. Am Abend gingen wir ins Restaurant. Hamburg gefällt mir sehr!

Review Quiz 14

Choose the letter of the word or phrase that best completes each sentence.

1. Ist die Farbe _____ Haare braun?
   a. ihrer
   b. seine
   c. meines
   d. euer

2. Der Hund dieses _____ Kindes ist sehr alt.
   a. nett
   b. junge
   c. kleinen
   d. weinen

3. _____ des schlechten Wetters gingen wir spazieren.
   a. Am Abend
   b. Trotz
   c. Heute Abend
   d. Vor

4. Meine Verwandten sind nicht reich, sondern _____.
   a. in der Hauptstadt
   b. arm
   c. gesunde
   d. am Bahnhof

5. _____ neuer Aufsatz ist sehr interessant gewesen.
   a. Der Student
   b. Professor Schmidt
   c. Ein ausländischer Lehrer
   d. Eriks

6. Ist Werner sehr stark oder sehr _____?
   a. schwach
   b. netter
   c. gut
   d. schlechter

7. Ich gehe oft im Wald _____.
   a. gingen
   b. wandern

   c. nicht weit
   d. Sonntag

8. _____ hat nur ein paar Wochen gedauert.
   a. Die Verwandten
   b. Meine Wirtin

   c. Die Gesundheit
   d. Der Frieden

9. Können Sie gut _____?
   a. schlittschuhlaufen
   b. Tennis

   c. spielten Schach
   d. gegangen

10. Der neue Schüler ist wirklich sehr _____.
    a. faul
    b. kluge

    c. keine intelligente
    d. oft

New Vocabulary

anstatt	*instead of*
Apotheke (*f.*)	*drugstore*
arm	*poor*
Aufsatz (*m.*)	*essay*
ausländisch	*foreign*
Badetuch (*n.*)	*bath towel*
Bericht (*m.*)	*report*
bisschen	*a bit, a little*
Boden (*m.*)	*floor*
Büchse (*f.*)	*tin, box*
Chips (*pl.*)	*chips*
dauern	*last*
dick	*fat*
Dose (*f.*)	*can*
dumm	*dumb, stupid*
dünn	*skinny*
einkaufen	*shop*
Erbsen (*pl.*)	*peas*
falsch	*false*

faul	*lazy*
fischen	*fish*
freundlich	*kind*
Frieden (*m.*)	*peace*
Gesundheit (*f.*)	*health*
Gulasch (*m.*)	*goulash*
Haar (*n.*)	*hair*
Halskette (*f.*)	*necklace*
hell	*bright*
hoch	*high, tall*
interessant	*interesting*
Job (*m.*)	*job*
joggen	*jog*
Kakao (*m.*)	*cocoa*
Käse (*m.*)	*cheese*
Klang (*m.*)	*sound*
klettern	*climb*
Korb (*m.*)	*basket*
Krieg (*m.*)	*war*
langsam	*slow*
langweilig	*boring*
Leben (*n.*)	*life*
leben	*live*
leise	*quiet*
lieber	*rather, prefer*
Limonade (*f.*)	*soda, soft drink*
Löwe (*m.*)	*lion*
musikalisch	*musical*
nah	*near*
Pianist (*m.*)	*pianist*
Rathaus (*n.*)	*city hall*
Regenschirm (*m.*)	*umbrella*
Rotwein (*m.*)	*red wine*

Sack (*m.*)	*bag, sack*
Schachtel (*f.*)	*pack, packet*
Schale (*f.*)	*bowl, dish*
Scheibe (*f.*)	*slice*
Schinkenrezept (*n.*)	*ham recipe*
schlittschuhlaufen	*ice skate*
Schulzeit (*f.*)	*school days*
schwimmen	*swim*
segeln	*sail*
spazieren	*stroll*
Tafel (*f.*)	*bar*
tanzen	*dance*
tauchen	*dive*
Teller (*m.*)	*plate, soup bowl*
Temperatur (*f.*)	*temperature*
Tod (*m.*)	*death*
trotz	*despite, in spite of*
Tüte (*f.*)	*bag*
Verwandte (*m.*)	*relative*
wahr	*true*
während	*during*
wandern	*hike*
wegen	*because of*
Weißwein (*m.*)	*white wine*
weit	*far*
Werk (*n.*)	*work (of art)*
wirklich	*really*
Wirtin (*f.*)	*landlady*
zeigen	*show*
Zigarette (*f.*)	*cigarette*

15

Future Tense and Modal Auxiliaries

In this chapter you will encounter the final basic tense of the German language: the future tense. In addition, a special category of auxiliaries will be introduced as well as grammatical elements that can be used to define tenses.

Some questions that will be answered are:

✓ What forms can the future tense take?
✓ How does the verb **werden** function in the future tense?
✓ How are modal auxiliaries conjugated?
✓ How do sentences change in the various tenses?

The Future Tense

The future tense is used to describe events and actions that will take place in either the near future or the distant future. In English, this is done in two ways.

A present tense conjugation is used, but a future tense meaning is implied. This is sometimes done by adding an adverb or phrase that suggests a future meaning. For example:

> Tomorrow I fly to Mexico City.
>
> Are you still in town next week?
>
> On Monday the family is driving back to Pennsylvania.
>
> In two months, my new job finally begins.

The second method for forming the English future tense is to introduce a verb with the auxiliaries *will* or *shall*. *Will* is traditionally used by all the persons except the first person. *Shall* is meant to be used by the first person pronouns. For example:

I shall be in Toronto on Friday.	*We shall see you on Monday.*
You will have fun at the party.	*You will finally meet my fiancé.*
She will never see me again.	*Will they arrive here next month?*

Of course, most people today use *will* with all persons. The only time the first person tends to conform to the use of *shall* is in a question. If *will* is used, the question implies something else:

Shall I bring you another napkin? (asking a future tense question)

Yes, please. / No, thanks. (possible responses)

Will I bring you another napkin? (wondering whether I will bring this person another napkin)

No, I will not. / Yes, I will. (possible responses)

Shall we go to the movies tonight? (asking a future tense question)

Yes, let's. / No, let's not. (possible responses)

Will we go to the movies tonight? (wondering whether this date will actually take place)

No, we will not. / Yes, we will. (possible responses)

Step 1: German Future Tense

Because German and English are brother and sister languages, separated by several centuries to evolve individually, they have much in common and often use the same concepts in their languages. The future tense is one of them. German also has two ways to form the future tense, and they are identical to the English forms. One implies a future tense, and the other uses the auxiliary with an infinitive to form the future tense. For example:

Implying the Future

Morgen fahren wir in die Stadt.	*Tomorrow we are driving to the city.*
Hast du nächste Woche Zeit?	*Do you have time next week?*
Am Wochenende bleiben sie zu Hause.	*They are staying home on the weekend.*
Im Winter fliege ich ans Mittelmeer.	*In winter I am flying to the Mediterranean.*
Am Donnerstag kommt sie endlich an.	*On Thursday she finally arrives.*

Say It Out Loud

Read each sentence out loud, paying attention to how the future tense is implied:

Morgen haben die Zwillinge Geburtstag.	*The twins have their birthday tomorrow.*
Wann reisen Sie nach Südamerika? Im Oktober?	*When do you travel to South America? In October?*
Hoffentlich kann ich in München studieren.	*I hope I can study in Munich.*
Nächsten Monat kaufe ich einen neuen Sportwagen.	*Next month I'm buying a new sports car.*
Übermorgen gehen wir in den Bergen klettern.	*We are going climbing in the mountains the day after tomorrow.*
Nächstes Jahr feiern sie ihren zwanzigsten Hochzeitstag.	*Next year they celebrate their twentieth anniversary.*
Um Viertel nach neun startet der neue Jumbo-Jet.	*The new jumbo jet takes off at nine-fifteen.*
Du musst bis elf Uhr zu Hause sein.	*You have to be home by eleven o'clock.*
Bald kaufen wir ein Haus im Norden.	*We're buying a house in the north soon.*
Wohin laufen die Schüler nach der Schule?	*Where do the students run after school?*

Using *werden* to Form the Future

The verb **werden** is conjugated in the present tense when it is the auxiliary of the future tense. When it is accompanied by an infinitive *at the end of the sentence*, the future tense is formed, and the translation of **werden** is *shall* or *will*. Let's review the conjugation of **werden**:

ich werde	wir werden
du wirst	ihr werdet
er wird	Sie werden
sie wird	sie werden
es wird	

Future tense sentences will look like this:

Ich <u>werde</u> meine Verwandten in Bremen <u>besuchen.</u>	*I will visit my relatives in Bremen.*
Wirst du diesen Ausländern <u>helfen?</u>	*Will you help these foreigners?*
Was <u>wird</u> Felix im Keller <u>finden?</u>	*What will Felix find in the cellar?*
Wir <u>werden</u> hier im Garten bleiben.	*We will stay here in the garden.*
<u>Werdet</u> ihr im Hotel <u>übernachten?</u>	*Will you stay overnight in a hotel?*
Wann <u>werden</u> Sie <u>zurückkommen?</u>	*When will you come back?*
Nächste Woche <u>werden</u> sie nach Rom <u>ziehen.</u>	*Next week they will move to Rome.*

Say It Out Loud

Read each sentence out loud, paying attention to the combination of **werden** *and the infinitives:*

Übermorgen wird Angelika an die Uni gehen.	*Angelika will go to college the day after tomorrow.*
Heute werde ich hier bleiben und arbeiten.	*Today I will stay here and study.*
Wann wirst du wieder genug Zeit haben?	*When will you have enough time again?*
Werden Sie den Winter im Süden verbringen?	*Will you spend the winter in the south?*
Nein, ich werde hier im Westen bleiben.	*No, I will remain here in the west in winter.*
Meine Nichte wird das ganze Jahr im Osten verbringen.	*My niece will spend the whole year in the east.*
Vati wird im Einkaufszentrum einkaufen gehen.	*Dad will go shopping at the mall.*
Unser Flugzeug wird pünktlich um zwei landen.	*Our plane will land punctually at two.*
Wird der Rechtsanwalt es schon wissen?	*Will the lawyer already know it?*
Jemand wird kommen und uns retten.	*Someone will come and rescue us.*
Wo werdet ihr die Ferien verbringen?	*Where will you spend the holiday?*

Wondering About This? *arbeiten/studieren/lernen*
In an example sentence, the verb **arbeiten** was used and translated as *study*.
You cannot use **studieren** if you mean that someone is sitting at his or
her desk and absorbing academic material. **Studieren** means *to attend a
university*. **Arbeiten** means, of course, *to work* or *do labor* but is frequently
used where English prefers the verb *study*. And **lernen** is used with young
learners at educational levels before college.

Exercise 15.1

*Reword each present tense sentence twice. In the first sentence, imply the future
tense with the adverb provided in parentheses. In the second sentence, use* **werden** *to
form the future tense with the adverb provided in parentheses. For example:*

Ich fahre in die Schweiz.

(morgen) *Morgen fahre ich in die Schweiz.*

(am Montag) *Am Montag werde ich in die Schweiz fahren.*

1. Werner bleibt zu Hause und arbeitet.

   (übermorgen) _____

   (morgen) _____

2. Wir verbringen einen ganzen Tag in der Stadt.

   (übermorgen) _____

   (morgen) _____

3. Meine Familie zieht nach Schweden.

   (übermorgen) _____

   (morgen) _____

4. Stefan bekommt viele Geschenke zum Geburtstag.

   (übermorgen) _____

   (morgen) _____

5. Vati verkauft das alte Haus im Osten.

   (übermorgen) _____

   (morgen) _____

6. Das Flugzeug landet in Südafrika.

(übermorgen) _____

(morgen) _____

7. Er gibt seiner Frau einen teuren Ring.

(übermorgen) _____

(morgen) _____

8. Die Studenten stehen pünktlich auf.

(übermorgen) _____

(morgen) _____

9. Mein Großvater wird hundert Jahre alt.

(übermorgen) _____

(morgen) _____

10. Die Zwillinge haben Geburtstag.

(übermorgen) _____

(morgen) _____

11. Ich bin endlich im Norden in Russland.

(übermorgen) _____

(morgen) _____

12. Der Hund wartet vor dem Tor.

(übermorgen) _____

(morgen) _____

13. Sie fotografiert die Elefanten.

(übermorgen) _____

(morgen) _____

14. Jemand findet einen Sack Gold.

(übermorgen) _____

(morgen) _____

15. Der Direktor zeigt den Touristen die alten Bilder (*pictures*).

(übermorgen) _____

(morgen) _____

Some Useful Phrases

When the verb **bringen** has the prefix **ver-**, its meaning is changed from *bring* to *spend*. This verb *spend* refers only to time. The moments in time that are spent are *in the accusative case*. If you are spending money, use **ausgeben** (**geben** plus the prefix **aus**-). For example:

verbringen

Ich verbringe einen Tag in Berlin.	*I spend a day in Berlin.*
Wir verbrachten einen Monat da.	*We spend a month there.*
Wie viel Zeit hast du hier verbracht?	*How much time did you spend here?*
Sie wird eine Woche bei uns verbringen.	*She will spend a week at our house.*

ausgeben

Der Tourist gibt zu viel aus.	*The tourist spends too much.*
Er gab hundert Euro für den Ring aus.	*He spent a hundred euros for the ring.*
Haben Sie genug ausgegeben?	*Did you spend enough?*
Ich werde nur ein bisschen Geld ausgeben.	*I will only spend a little money.*

Notice that both verbs are irregular and retain their irregular conjugations despite the prefixes.

Exercise 15.2

Reword each present tense sentence in the other tenses (past, present perfect, and future). For example:

Er isst im Café.

Er aß im Café.

Er hat im Café gegessen.

Er wird im Café essen.

1. Die Soldaten marschieren durch das Dorf.

_____

_____

_____

2. Wir wohnen im Nordwesten.

_____

_____

_____

3. Wo verbringen Sie die Ferien?

_____

_____

_____

4. Sind eure Eltern gesund?

_____

_____

_____

5. Wie viel gibt er für die Jacke aus?

_____

_____

_____

6. Vati schneidet ein paar Scheiben Käse ab.

_____

_____

_____

7. Wir gehen oft im Wald wandern.

_____

_____

_____

8. Wann wirst du einundzwanzig Jahre alt?

_____

_____

_____

9. Spielt der Matrose Klavier?

_____

_____

_____

10. Zwei Flugzeuge starten um halb acht.

_____

_____

_____

Modal Auxiliaries

Both English and German have other kinds of auxiliaries that can function in more than one way. *Have*, for example, is both a transitive verb and the auxiliary of the present perfect tense: *I have 10 dollars. We have come home.*

There are also auxiliaries that show *to what degree of obligation*, *ability*, or *desire* an action is carried out. That statement will be clear to you when you look at the examples. Auxiliaries that do this are the *modal auxiliaries*. Some of the commonly used ones in English are *want*, *must*, and *can*. They combine with an infinitive and modify the meaning of the infinitive. For example:

> *I visit Mary.*
> *I <u>want</u> to visit Mary.* (desire to do this)
> *I <u>must</u> visit Mary.* (obligation to do this)
> *I <u>can</u> visit Mary.* (ability to do this)

Step 2: German Modal Auxiliaries

The German modal auxiliaries modify an accompanying infinitive by showing *to what degree of obligation*, *ability*, or *desire* an action is carried out. These auxiliaries are:

dürfen	*may, be allowed to*
können	*can, be able to*
mögen	*like, may, might*
müssen	*must, have to*
sollen	*should, be supposed to*
wollen	*want*

Consider the meaning of these modal auxiliaries and how each has a different degree of obligation, ability, and desire to carry out the action of the accompanying infinitive. First, let's look at the present tense conjugation of these verbs. Notice that their singular conjugation is somewhat different from their plural conjugation:

	dürfen	**können**	**mögen**
ich	darf	kann	mag
du	darfst	kannst	magst
er	darf	kann	mag
wir	dürfen	können	mögen
ihr	dürft	könnt	mögt
Sie	dürfen	können	mögen
sie	dürfen	können	mögen

	müssen	**sollen**	**wollen**
ich	muss	soll	will
du	musst	sollst	willst
er	muss	soll	will
wir	müssen	sollen	wollen
ihr	müsst	sollt	wollt
Sie	müssen	sollen	wollen
sie	müssen	sollen	wollen

Say It Out Loud

Read each sentence out loud, paying attention to the difference between the singular and plural conjugations of the modal auxiliaries:

Darf ich um diesen Tanz bitten?	*May I ask for this dance?*
Das dürfen die Kinder nicht tun.	*The children may not do that.*
Kannst du mir helfen?	*Can you help me?*
Wir können eine Woche hier verbringen.	*We can spend a week here.*
Die Frau mag mehr als vierzig sein.	*The woman may be more than 40.*
Wie viele Gäste mögen das sein?	*How many guests might there be?*
Hier muss man ruhig bleiben.	*You have to remain quiet here.*
Wir müssen nach Paris ziehen.	*We have to move to Paris.*

Du sollst sofort damit aufhören!   *You should stop that immediately.*

Sie sollen Ihr Geld zurückbekommen.   *You should get your money back.*

Niemand will mit ihm reisen.   *No one wants to travel with him.*

Die Jungen wollen Karten spielen.   *The boys want to play cards.*

Exercise 15.3

Reword each sentence using the modal auxiliary in parentheses. For example:

Meine Frau wartet an der Ecke.

(müssen) *Meine Frau muss an der Ecke warten.*

1. Schneidet er ein Stück Kuchen ab?

   (dürfen) _____

2. Ich verbringe den ganzen Monat im Süden.

   (können) _____

3. Der Tourist bekommt sein Geld zurück.

   (wollen) _____

4. Ihr Sohn ist wirklich sehr jung.

   (mögen) _____

5. Gibst du so viel Geld aus?

   (sollen) _____

6. Um wie viel Uhr landet der Jumbo-Jet?

   (müssen) _____

7. Heute ist der erste Mai.

   (mögen) _____

8. Viele Leute sprechen Deutsch.

   (können) _____

9. Probiert ihr diese Jeans an?

   (wollen) _____

10. Sitze (*sit*) ich in der dritten Reihe?

    (dürfen) _____

Although the modal auxiliaries are considered irregular verbs, their past tense is sometimes a combination of a regular and an irregular pattern. Let's look at the past tense of these verbs:

	dürfen		**können**		**mögen**	
ich	durfte	*was allowed to*	konnte	*could, was able to*	mochte	*liked, might*
du	durftest	*were able to*	konntest	*could, were able to*	mochtest	*liked, might*
er	durfte		konnte		mochte	
wir	durften		konnten		mochten	
ihr	durftet		konntet		mochtet	
Sie	durften		konnten		mochten	
sie	durften		konnten		mochten	

	müssen		**sollen**		**wollen**	
ich	musste	*had to*	sollte	*should, was supposed to*	wollte	*wanted to*
du	musstest		solltest		wolltest	
er	musste		sollte		wollte	
wir	mussten		sollten		wollten	
ihr	musstet		solltet		wolltet	
Sie	mussten		sollten		wollten	
sie	mussten		sollten		wollten	

Just like the present tense modal auxiliary, the past tense auxiliary is accompanied by an infinitive at the end of the sentence.

Say It Out Loud

Read each sentence out loud, paying attention to the past tense conjugation of the modal auxiliaries:

Dieser Schauspieler sollte die Hauptrolle spielen.	*This actor should play the lead role.*
Ich konnte kein Wort verstehen.	*I could not understand one word.*
Sie mochte keine roten Rosen.	*She did not like red roses.*
Wir mussten immer schneller fahren.	*We had to drive faster and faster.*
Du solltest dich schämen!	*You should be ashamed of yourself.*
Niemand wollte eine Stunde warten.	*No one wanted to wait an hour.*

Exercise 15.4

Reword each present tense sentence in the past tense. For example:

Ich will einen Pullover kaufen.
Ich wollte einen Pullover kaufen.

1. Sie darf den alten Hund nicht streicheln (*pet*).

   _____

2. Ich soll meinen Verwandten damit helfen.

   _____

3. Herr Schneider mag keinen Rotwein.

   _____

4. Muss deine Familie wirklich nach Amerika ziehen?

   _____

5. Der Verkäufer kann ihnen damit helfen.

   _____

6. Unsere Nichte will Flugbegleiterin werden.

   _____

7. Dürfen Sie in der Parade marschieren?

   _____

8. Wir können ein paar Tage in der Hauptstadt verbringen.

   _____

9. Müssen die Flugzeuge sofort landen?

   _____

10. Die Studentinnen wollen hier bleiben und arbeiten.

    _____

Review Quiz 15

Choose the letter of the word or phrase that best completes each sentence.

1. _____ zieht meine Familie nach Deutschland.

   a. Nächsten   c. Gestern

   b. Übermorgen   d. Wie oft

2. Morgen _____ sie dreiunddreißig Jahre alt.

   a. sein   c. kann

   b. wird   d. mag

3. Wir werden nur ein paar Tage am See _____.

   a. ausgegeben   c. verbringen

   b. ziehen   d. fotografiert

4. Darf _____ um diesen Tanz bitten?

   a. wir   c. diese Leute

   b. die Matrosen   d. ich

5. Gestern _____ die Studenten viel arbeiten.

   a. mussten   c. möchten

   b. dürfen   d. sollen

6. Was _____ du bestellen?

   a. wird   c. willst

   b. können   d. müsst

7. Die Touristen wollten sofort _____.

   a. starteten   c. immer schnell geflogen

   b. landen   d. mit dem Flugzeug

8. Warum habt ihr _____ ausgegeben?

   a. ein bisschen Zeit   c. in Nordamerika

   b. so viel Geld   d. damit

9. Werner will zweihundert Euro _____.

   a. ausgegeben   c. zurückbekommen

   b. verbringen   d. retten

10. Der alte Mann _____ mehr als neunzig Jahre alt sein.

    a. mag   c. musst

    b. könnt   d. sollen

New Vocabulary

ausgeben	*spend (money)*
Ausländer (*m.*)	*foreigner*
Berg (*m.*)	*mountain*
Bild (*n.*)	*picture*
damit	*with it, with that*
Einkaufszentrum (*n.*)	*shopping mall*
endlich	*finally*
Ferien (*pl.*)	*holiday*
genug	*enough*
Hochzeitstag (*m.*)	*wedding anniversary*
immer schneller	*faster and faster*
Karten (*pl.*)	*cards (game)*
landen	*land*
Mittelmeer (*n.*)	*Mediterranean*
nächste	*next*
Norden (*m.*)	*north*
Nordwesten (*m.*)	*northeast*
Osten (*m.*)	*east*
pünktlich	*punctually*
retten	*rescue, save*
schämen (sich)	*be ashamed (of oneself)*
sofort	*immediately*
Sportwagen (*m.*)	*sports car*
starten	*take off (aircraft)*
streicheln	*pet, stroke*
Stunde (*f.*)	*hour*
Südamerika	*South America*
Süden (*m.*)	*south*
übermorgen	*day after tomorrow*
übernachten	*stay overnight*

verbringen	*spend* (*time*)
Westen (*m.*)	*west*
wirklich	*really, actually*
Wochenende (*n.*)	*weekend*
Wort (*n.*)	*word*
ziehen	*move*
zurückbekommen	*get back*
Zwillinge (*pl.*)	*twins*

16

Dependent Clauses and Conjunctions

This chapter will introduce you to dependent clauses. Conjunctions that are in dependent clauses will also be explained.

Some questions that will be answered are:

✓ What is a dependent clause?
✓ How is the word order in a dependent clause different?
✓ What conjunctions are the signals for dependent clauses?

Dependent Clauses

Both English and German have independent and dependent clauses. Dependent clauses are sometimes called *subordinate clauses*. No matter what the name is, they are important parts of a sentence and are relatively easy to identify and understand.

English independent clauses are so named because they can stand independently and make sense. Two clauses are often linked together by a coordinating conjunction (*and*, *but*, *because*, *or*). For example:

Your writing is good, but your essay does not make a lot of sense.

Jack is working in the garage, and May is out shopping.

You get the scholarship because you are one of the brightest students I have ever had.

A dependent clause is introduced by a variety of conjunctions. A few of these are *if*, *when*, *after*, and *while*. Dependent clauses can stand at the beginning or the end of a sentence, but they cannot stand alone. For example:

If it starts to rain, we can run to that shelter.

We can run to that shelter if it starts to rain.

When you get home, you can take a warm bath.

You can take a warm bath when you get home.

After Jane arrives, we can make some dinner.

We can make some dinner after Jane arrives.

While the baby slept, I fixed the wobbly chair.

I fixed the wobbly chair while the baby slept.

Step 1: German Clauses

You have already learned about the major coordinating conjunctions in German. They are **aber, denn, oder, und,** and **sondern**. They combine two clauses that can stand alone as sentences. For example:

Er liest den Artikel.	*He reads the article.*
Er versteht kein Wort.	*He doesn't understand a word.*
Er liest den Artikel, aber er versteht kein Wort.	*He reads the article, but he doesn't understand a word.*
Willst du ins Kino gehen?	*Do you want to go to the movies?*
Willst du zu Hause bleiben?	*Do you want to stay home?*
Willst du ins Kino gehen, oder willst du zu Hause bleiben?	*Do you want to go to the movies, or do you want to stay home?*
Sie arbeitet nicht bei einer Bank.	*She doesn't work in a bank.*
Sie arbeitet als Flugbegleiterin.	*She works as a flight attendant.*
Sie arbeitet nicht bei einer Bank, sondern sie arbeitet als Flugbegleiterin.	*She doesn't work in a bank, but rather she works as a flight attendant.*

Say It Out Loud

Read each sentence out loud, paying attention to the use of the conjunctions:

Mein Vater ist Geschäftsmann, und mein Onkel ist Hausmakler.	*My father is a businessman, and my uncle is a real estate agent.*
Ich bleibe nicht in diesem Dorf, sondern reise bald ins Ausland.	*I am not staying in this village but traveling abroad soon.*

Der Winter kann sehr kalt sein, aber der Sommer ist warm und angenehm.	*The winter can be very cold, but the summer is warm and pleasant.*
Meine Tochter ist sehr begabt, denn sie kann vier Instrumente spielen.	*My daughter is very gifted because she can play four instruments.*
Haben sie eine Wohnung in dieser Straße, oder wohnen sie in der nächsten Straße?	*Do they have an apartment on this street, or do they live on the next street?*

It is important to note that the word order of the original sentences is not changed when they are combined by one of these conjunctions.

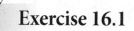

Exercise 16.1

Give any appropriate completion to each sentence. For example:

Der Hund schläft unter dem Tisch, und *die Katze schläft auf dem Klavier.*

1. Wir waren nicht reich, aber _____.

2. Musst du auf deine Freundin warten, oder _____?

3. _____, und meine Schwester ist schwimmen gegangen.

4. _____, denn das Wetter ist wieder angenehm.

5. Wir haben die Tür nicht zugemacht, sondern _____.

6. _____, aber es ist sehr regnerisch geworden.

7. _____, oder ich werde nach Oldenburg ziehen.

8. Ich wohnte im Studentenheim (*dorm*), und _____.

9. Max muss bis Samstag warten, denn _____.

10. Sie ist nicht mit dem Zug gefahren, sondern _____.

Some Useful Phrases

When making a statement for which you want confirmation, the accompanying word is **oder**. However, in this kind of usage its meaning is *right* or *don't you agree.*

For example:

Wir können Gulasch vorbereiten, oder?	*We can make goulash. Right?*
Der Hausmakler war ziemlich faul, oder?	*The real estate agent was rather lazy. Don't you agree?*
Sie spricht über einen deutschen Schriftsteller, oder?	*She is talking about a German writer. Right?*
Vorgestern ist dein Vater angekommen, oder?	*Your father arrived the day before yesterday. Right?*

Sometimes **nicht** or **nicht wahr** is used in place of **oder**:

Es ist schon halb sieben, nicht?	*It is already six-thirty. Right?*
Sie ist sehr alt geworden, nicht wahr?	*She has gotten very old. Don't you agree?*

Subordinating Conjunctions

Unlike the coordinating conjunctions that link together two main clauses, *subordinating conjunctions* link a main clause with a dependent clause. Remember that dependent clauses cannot stand alone and make complete sense.

A large group of conjunctions describes the *time* in which an action takes place. Some of the commonly used ones are:

als	*when (in the past tense)*
bevor/ehe	*before*
bis	*until, by the time*
nachdem	*after*
seit/seitdem	*since*
während	*while*
wenn	*when/whenever*

The clause that is introduced by a subordinating conjunction has the conjugated verb as the last element in the clause. For example:

Als ich in Berlin <u>war</u>, ging ich oft ins Theater.	*When I was in Berlin, I often went to the theater.*
Bis er nach Hause <u>kommt</u>, werde ich im Garten sitzen.	*Until he comes home, I will sit in the garden.*

Like English, in most cases, German can place the dependent clauses at the beginning or the end of the sentence. For example:

Ich ging oft ins Theater, als ich in Berlin war.

Ich werde im Garten sitzen, bis er nach Hause kommt.

If the main clause is the second clause, the conjugated verb will precede the subject in that clause. For example:

Als wir an der Uni waren, <u>lernte</u> ich Tina kennen.	*When we were at college, I met Tina.*

Say It Out Loud

Read each sentence out loud, paying attention to how the conjunctions are used:

Als die Touristen in Hamburg ankamen, besichtigten sie den alten Dom.	*When the tourists arrived in Hamburg, they viewed (went sightseeing) the old cathedral.*
Bevor sie Chefin wurde, arbeitete sie als Hausmaklerin.	*Before she became the boss, she worked as a real estate agent.*
Die Mutter sah ihre Söhne noch einmal an, ehe sie weggingen.	*The mother looked at her sons one more time before they left.*
Wir haben an der Ecke gewartet, bis er uns abgeholt hat.	*We waited on the corner until he picked us up.*
Nachdem die Mannschaft gewinnt, gehen sie ins Lokal.	*After the team wins, they go to a pub.*
Seit sie ihr Auto verkauft hat, fährt sie mit der Straßenbahn.	*Since she sold her car, she goes by streetcar.*
Hans wohnt allein, seitdem seine Mutter starb.	*Hans lives alone since his mother died.*
Während er in Amerika war, lernte er viele Filmstars kennen.	*While he lived in America, he got to know a lot of movie stars.*
Die Hausmaklerin bringt mir Obst, wenn sie vorbeikommt.	*The real estate agent brings me fruit when she stops by.*

Exercise 16.2

Combine each pair of sentences with the conjunction in parentheses. Place the conjunction at the beginning of the first clause. For example:

(als) Ich war Student. Ich wohnte im Studentenheim.

Als ich Student war, wohnte ich im Studentenheim.

1. (als) Er kam an. Er sah seine Frau auf dem Bahnsteig (*station platform*).

   _____

2. (bevor) Gudrun weinte. Er hat sie geküsst.

   _____

3. (bis) Es ist fünfzehn Uhr. Ich habe drei Briefe geschrieben.

   _____

4. (nachdem) Sie machte die Fenster zu. Es hörte auf zu regnen.

   _____

5. (seitdem) Ich kaufte dir eine Gitarre. Du spielst gar nicht mehr.

   _____

Follow the same directions but place the conjunction at the beginning of the second clause:

6. (während) Ich suchte sie im Studentenheim. Ich war an der Uni.

   _____

7. (wenn) Wir kaufen oft nichts. Wir gehen einkaufen.

   _____

8. (als) Wir haben eine fremde (*strange*) Stimme gehört. Wir haben ferngesehen (*watch TV*).

   _____

9. (ehe) Die Eltern müssen mehr verdienen (*earn*). Sie können eine Europareise machen.

   _____

10. (seit) Er fand viele alte Bilder. Sein Großvater starb.

    _____

Some conjunctions introduce a clause that describes *a cause* or *a reason*. Some of these are:

da	*since*
damit	*so that*
falls	*in case*
obwohl	*although*
weil	*because*

A few conjunctions describe *the means* by which something is carried out and *the similarity* of things. These conjunctions are:

indem	*by (means)*
soviel	*as far as*
so . . . wie	*as . . . as*

These conjunctions function in the same way as those already introduced.

Say It Out Loud

Read each sentence out loud, paying attention to how the conjunctions are used:

Da der Mann betrunken war, konnte er nicht fahren.	*Since the man was drunk, he could not drive.*
Wir müssen schneller gehen, damit wir nicht spät ankommen.	*We have to go faster so that we do not arrive late.*
Falls Max genug Geld hat, wird er auch mitkommen.	*If Max has enough money, he will also come along.*
Obwohl der Arzt alles getan hat, ist der Mann gestorben.	*Although the doctor did everything, the man died.*
Er musste noch eine Stunde warten, weil er den Bus verpasste.	*He had to wait another hour because he missed the bus.*
Sie hat genug Geld verdient, indem sie Überstunden machte.	*She earned enough money by working overtime.*
Soviel wir wussten, war der Verbrecher noch im Gefängnis.	*As far as we knew, the criminal was still in prison.*
Sein Artikel ist nicht so gut, wie sein Aufsatz.	*His article is not as good as his essay.*

Wondering About This? *so . . . wie*

When you use **so . . . wie**, the verb in the second clause can be omitted if it is understood. The previous example sentence could have read: **Sein Artikel ist nicht so gut, wie sein Aufsatz <u>ist</u>**. Also note that there is usually a modifier that follows **so** before the clause introduced by **wie** is said. **Er ist nicht so <u>klug</u>, wie seine Frau.** *He is not as smart as his wife.*

Exercise 16.3

Combine each pair of sentences with the conjunction in parentheses. Place the conjunction in any appropriate position. For example:

(als) Ich war Student. Ich wohnte zu Hause.

Als ich Student war, wohnte ich zu Hause.

1. (da) Die Frau ist sehr müde. Sie fährt sofort ins Hotel.

   _____

2. (damit) Ich lerne jeden Abend. Ich bekomme gute Noten.

   _____

3. (falls) Mein Kollege (*colleague, fellow worker*) kommt vorbei. Er hat Zeit.

   _____

4. (obwohl) Der Ring ist sehr schön. Er ist wirklich zu teuer.

   _____

5. (weil) Gudrun muss eine Brille tragen (*wear glasses*). Sie kann nicht gut sehen.

   _____

6. (indem) Wir haben ihnen geholfen. Wir gaben ihnen €100 (hundert Euro).

   _____

7. (soviel) Sie weiß. Es geht ihren Verwandten noch gut.

   _____

8. (so . . . wie) Seine Romane sind nicht schlecht. Seine Gedichte (*poems*) sind schlecht.

   _____

9. (weil) Der Student ist vor seinen Büchern eingeschlafen. Er ist sehr müde.

_____

10. (so . . . wie) Der Harz (*Hartz Mountains*) ist nicht hoch. Die Alpen sind hoch.

_____

Step 2: *Dass* and *ob*

Two conjunctions that require special attention are **dass** (*that*) and **ob** (*whether/if*). They are somewhat different from the other subordinating conjunctions because they tend to be used to introduce a second clause and not the first clause.

The conjunction **dass** is used frequently to tell what someone has stated (*said, written, whispered, informed,* and so on). For example:

er sagt, dass	*he says that*
sie berichtet dass	*she reports that*
wir schreiben, dass	*we write that*

The conjunction **ob** tells what someone asks or what someone does not know. This conjunction is translated as *whether*. Many use *if* colloquially in its place. Let's look at some example phrases:

Sie fragen, ob	*you ask whether*
wisst ihr, ob	*do you know whether*
ich weiß nicht, ob	*I don't know whether*

Say It Out Loud

Read each sentence out loud, paying attention to the use of the conjunctions **dass** *and* **ob**:

Der Reporter sagt, dass die Polizei den Verbrecher verhaftet hat.	*The reporter said that the police arrested the criminal.*
Niemand wusste, ob das Kind schon geboren ist.	*No one knows whether the child has been born yet.*
In der Zeitung steht, dass die Kanzlerin nach Moskau fliegt.	*In the paper it said that the chancellor is flying to Moscow.*

Der Hausmakler fragt, ob wir eine große Wohnung suchen.	*The real estate agent asks whether we are looking for a large apartment.*
Sagt sie, dass sie schon mehr als €250 (zweihundertfünfzig Euro) verdient hat?	*Is she saying that she has already earned more than 250 euros?*
Wissen Sie, ob Wagner diese Oper komponiert hat?	*Do you know whether Wagner composed this opera?*
Max berichtet, dass Goethe ein Denkmal in Weimar hat.	*Max reports that Goethe has a monument in Weimar.*

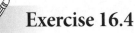 **Exercise 16.4**

Complete each sentence with any appropriate clause. For example:

Martin fragt, ob *der neue Film heute spielt.*

1. Meine Kollegen fragen mich, ob _____.

2. Seine Cousine sagt, dass _____.

3. Weißt du, ob _____?

4. Der Schüler antwortet, dass _____.

5. Ich lese, dass _____.

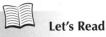 **Let's Read**

Read the following text and determine its meaning on your own:

Als meine Familie in den Alpen wohnte, gingen wir oft skilaufen. Meine Schwester war sehr begabt und konnte sehr gut skilaufen. Aber ich ging lieber schlittschuhlaufen. Nicht weit von unserer Berghütte war ein See, wo ich schlittschuhlaufen ging. Mein Bruder war an der Universität in Zürich und kam nur dreimal im Jahr nach Hause. Er war guter Student und auch guter Sportler. Auf dem Fußballfeld war er einer der Besten.

Review Quiz 16

Choose the letter of the word or phrase that best completes each sentence.

1. Ich habe meinen Bruder nicht besucht, _____ ich bin joggen gegangen.

   a. als

   b. sondern

   c. weil

   d. wie

2. Wir müssen im Hotel bleiben, _____ es so kalt und regnerisch geworden ist.

   a. aber

   b. weil

   c. dass

   d. ob

3. Tina trägt eine Brille, aber _____.

   a. es wird dunkel werden

   b. wegen der heißen Sonne

   c. sie kann sehr gut sehen

   d. ihr wollt den Roman nicht lesen

4. Als _____, bin ich oft in die Bibliothek gegangen.

   a. ich studiere in Heidelberg

   b. ein Student hat mich eingeladen

   c. ich besichtigte die Universität

   d. ich eine Woche in Bonn verbrachte

5. Das Kind wäscht sich die Hände, _____.

   a. damit es gesund bleibt

   b. soviel wir es wussten

   c. ob der Boden schmutzig ist

   d. denn sie sind sauber

6. Unser Chef war nicht so nett, _____.

   a. und er hat mir viel geholfen

   b. wie unser Direktor

   c. dass wir Geschenke hatten

   d. wenn er ist in einer Fabrik

7. Ich werde warten, _____ der Zug kommt.

   a. bis

   b. als

   c. oder

   d. seitdem

8. _____ ich die Suppe vorbereitete, ging ich einkaufen.

   a. Ob

   b. Denn

   c. Wenn

   d. Nachdem

9. Sie stand an der Tür, _____ sie machte die Tür nicht auf.

    a. weil   c. sondern

    b. dass   d. aber

10. _____, ob Herr Bauer hier wohnt?

    a. Niemand fragt   c. Der Reporter berichtet

    b. Wissen Sie   d. Meine Chefin antwortet

New Vocabulary

angenehm	*pleasant*
Bahnsteig (*m.*)	*station platform*
bald	*soon*
begabt	*gifted*
besichtigen	*view, go sightseeing*
Brille (*f.*)	*glasses, spectacles*
Chef (*m.*)	*boss*
Chefin (*f.*)	*boss*
Dom (*m.*)	*cathedral*
fernsehen	*watch television*
fremd	*strange*
Gebirge (*n.*)	*mountain range*
Gedicht (*n.*)	*poem*
Gefängnis (*n.*)	*prison*
Geschäftsmann (*m.*)	*businessman*
Hausmakler (*m.*)	*real estate agent*
Kollege (*m.*)	*colleague*
Obst (*n.*)	*fruit*
Studentenheim (*m.*)	*dormitory*
tragen	*wear, carry*
Überstunden (*pl.*)	*overtime*
Verbrecher (*m.*)	*criminal*
verdienen	*earn*
verpassen	*miss (transportation)*
vorbeikommen	*come by, drop by*
vorbereiten	*prepare, make (food)*

17

Dative-Accusative Prepositions

In this chapter you will discover prepositions that can be used with two different cases. You will also have a look at geography from a German point of view. Some questions that will be answered are:

✓ What prepositions can be used with both the dative and accusative cases?
✓ What is the difference in meaning with each case?
✓ What German geographical information is important to know?

Prepositions with More Than One Function

Although English and German are not the same when it comes to using the same preposition with different cases, English is similar on a small scale. A few English prepositions are a compound of two prepositions and have a counterpart that consists of only one in the compound. A commonly used pair is *into* and *in*.

Into is used specifically to show a motion from outside a place to its interior. *In* can be used in the same way in modern English, but it also provides the meaning of *location*. For example:

We ran into the house. (We went from outside to inside the house.)

I dropped a coin into the slot. (The coin went from outside the machine to inside the machine.)

The boys hid in the closet. (The boys were located in the closet.)

There was a necklace lying in the drawer. (The necklace was located in the drawer.)

Something similar occurs with *onto* and *on*; *upon* does something even more unique—it can show both motion and location. For example:

> *He dropped paint onto the floor.* (The paint moved from his brush and landed on the floor.)
>
> *The girls sat on the floor.* (The girls were located on the floor.)
>
> *The young prince was placed upon the throne.* (The prince was moved from where he stood to his seat on the throne.)
>
> *He sat upon his bed and cried.* (He was located on his bed when he cried.)

This concept of a preposition having two functions is carried much further in the German language.

Step 1: Dative Case

You have already learned about the dative case in Chapter 9. Let's briefly review the endings of this case.

Masculine	Feminine	Neuter	Plural
dem -en Mann	der -en Frau	dem -en Kind	den -en Kindern
keinem -en Mann	keiner -en Frau	keinem -en Kind	keinen -en Kindern

All adjectives that accompany **der**-words and **ein**-words in this case end in **-en**.

Pronouns also have a dative declension:

Nom.	ich	du	er	sie	es	wir	ihr	Sie	sie	wer
Dat.	mir	dir	ihm	ihr	ihm	uns	euch	Ihnen	ihnen	wem

These declensions are used with indirect objects. For example:

Ich gab <u>dem jungen Mann</u> einen Bleistift.   *I gave the young man a pencil.*

They are used after dative prepositions. For example:

Er tanzte mit <u>ihr</u>.   *He danced with her.*

They are also used for objects of dative verbs. For example:

Wir helfen <u>diesen alten Leuten</u>.   *We help these old people.*

A new use for the dative case is with a list of prepositions that can require a dative declension or an accusative declension. These prepositions are:

an	*at*
auf	*on*
hinter	*behind*
in	*in*
neben	*next to*
über	*over, above*
unter	*under*
vor	*before, in front of*
zwischen	*between*

When these prepositions are used with a verb that describes location, the dative case declension is required with this list of prepositions.

Say It Out Loud

Read each sentence out loud, paying attention to the use of the prepositions:

Jemand steht an der Tür und klopft.	*Someone is standing at the door and knocking.*
Die Katzen schlafen auf dem Klavier.	*The cats sleep on the piano.*
Der Junge verbirgt sich hinter der Garage.	*The boy hides behind the garage.*
Ich finde es in einer schmutzigen Schublade.	*I find it in a dirty drawer.*
Er hat neben mir gesessen.	*He sat next to me.*
Über der Stadt fliegen Düsenjäger.	*Fighter jets are flying over the city.*
Das Baby schläft unter einer warmen Decke.	*The baby sleeps under a warm blanket.*
Warten Sie bitte vor jenem Fernsehturm!	*Please wait in front of that TV tower.*
Unser Haus ist zwischen zwei großen weißen Häusern.	*Our house is between two big, white houses.*

When these prepositions are used with pronouns, the pronouns have to be in the dative case, for example, **Er hat neben mir gesessen.** *He sat near me.* But the pronouns that do this refer *only to people.* For example:

Das Kind verbirgt sich hinter mir.	*The child hides behind me.*
Warum stehst du zwischen uns?	*Why are you standing between us?*
Ein schwarzer Vogel fliegt über ihr.	*A black bird flies above her.*
Ich stand vor ihm und weinte.	*I stood in front of him and cried.*

Exercise 17.1

Reword each word or phrase in parentheses as it would appear in the sentence. For example:

Ich sende _____ eine Ansichtskarte.

(der kleine Junge) *dem kleinen Jungen*

1. Wir haben es unter _____ gefunden.

   (ihre neue Decke) _____

   (seine Bücher) _____

   (ein brauner Korb) _____

2. Über _____ sind zwei Düsenjäger geflogen.

   (unsere neue Schule) _____

   (das große Einkaufszentrum) _____

   (wir) _____

3. Vor _____ stehen viele neue Arbeiter.

   (der hohe Fernsehturm) _____

   (die schmutzigen Fenster) _____

   (ich) _____

4. Sie haben ein Haus an _____.

   (ein langer Fluss) _____

   (dieser See) _____

   (das Ende der Straße) _____

5. Warum sitzten sie auf _____?

(der hohe Baum *tree*) _____

(die Straße) _____

(das Dach *roof*) _____

6. Der Pilot hat neben _____ gesessen und geschlafen.

(der junge Chef) _____

(seine Freundin) _____

(ihr) _____

7. Die Kinder verbergen sich unter _____.

(eine dicke Decke) _____

(diese kleinen Betten) _____

(die Bettcouch *studio couch*) _____

8. Der betrunkene Mann liegt (*is lying*) zwischen _____.

(der Arzt und die Krankenschwester) _____

(die Stühle) _____

(wir) _____

9. Wir mussten in _____ warten.

(ein kleines Zimmer) _____

(sein Wartesaal *waiting room*) _____

(die dunkle Garage) _____

10. Hinter _____ hat eine ausländische Familie gewohnt.

(die neue Bibliothek) _____

(ein kleiner Berg) _____

(sie *s.*) _____

Step 2: Inanimate Pronouns

German has a concept that still exists in English but on a limited scale. Prepositions that refer to inanimate objects form a prepositional phrase with *there*. For example:

Modern English	**Older English**
to it	*thereto*
upon it	*thereupon*
with it	*therewith*

Of course, today some of these older expressions are used in other ways, but the form of this kind of phrase remains German.

In German, if the pronoun refers to an inanimate object, it does not form the usual prepositional phrase. Instead, the preposition follows **da-** or **dar-**. Take note that **da** means *there*. **Da-** is used with prepositions that begin with a consonant; **dar-** is used with prepositions that begin with a vowel, for example, **davor** (*in front of it*), **dahinter** (*behind it*), **da<u>r</u>in** (*in it*), **da<u>r</u>auf** (*on it*). This kind of prepositional phrase does not take gender or number into consideration. For example:

Masc.	auf dem Stuhl (*on the chair*)	= darauf
Fem.	auf der Straße (*on the street*)	= darauf
Neut.	auf dem Dach (*on the roof*)	= darauf
Pl.	auf den Büchern (*on the books*)	= darauf

This form of prepositional phrase with inanimate pronouns is used with nearly *all prepositions*. For example:

mit dem Bus = damit *dative*
zu einer Schule = dazu *dative*
durch einen Tunnel = dadurch *accusative*
um die Ecke = darum *accusative*

Say It Out Loud

Read each sentence out loud, paying attention to the use of the inanimate pronouns:

Der Hund hat sehr oft darunter geschlafen.	The dog slept under it very often.
Warum stehen die Arbeiter davor?	Why are the workers standing in front of it?
Seht ihr die Flugzeuge darüber?	Do you see the airplanes above it?
Der Geschäftsmann stand daran und klopfte.	The businessman stood there (at it) and knocked.
Der Bäcker (baker) sitzt darauf und denkt.	The baker sits on it and thinks.
Dahinter baut man einen großen Dom.	Someone is building a large cathedral behind it.
Ich habe €200 (zweihundert Euro) darin.	I have 200 euros in it.
Was liegt auf dem Boden daneben?	What is lying on the floor next to it?
Diese Firma wird ein Gebäude dazwischen bauen.	This company will build a building between them.

Exercise 17.2

Reword each prepositional phrase with the noun changed to a pronoun. For example:

hinter dem Mann *hinter ihm*

hinter der Tür *dahinter*

1. vor meinem Chef _____

2. in der Küche _____

3. am Tor _____

4. zwischen deinen Eltern _____

5. über dem Dom _____

6. auf dem Dach _____

7. vor Ihrem Freund _____

8. unter einer warmen Decke _____

9. neben ihren Nachbarn _____

10. vor dem Rathaus _____

Step 3: Accusative Case

In Chapter 6 you learned about the accusative case. Let's briefly review the endings of this case:

Masculine	Feminine	Neuter	Plural
den -en Mann	die -e Frau	das -e Kind	die -en Kinder
keinen -en Mann	keine -e Frau	kein -e Kind	keine -en Kinder

Pronouns also have an accusative declension:

Nom.	ich	du	er	sie	es	wir	ihr	Sie	sie	wer
Acc.	mich	dich	ihn	sie	es	uns	euch	Sie	sie	wen

If the prepositions **an, auf, hinter, in, neben, über, unter, vor,** and **zwischen** are accompanied by a verb of motion, these prepositions require the accusative case. For example:

Verb of Motion

Er <u>ging</u> an die Tür.   *He went to the door.*

Die Kinder <u>laufen</u> hinter einen Baum.   *The children run behind a tree.*

Heute <u>fahren</u> sie in die Stadt.   *They are driving to the city today.*

The accusative case is used in another instance with these prepositions. The accusative is needed when there is no verb of motion but when the idea of location is not the desired meaning. For example:

Ich warte auf den Mann.	*I am waiting for the man.*
Ich warte auf den Bus.	*I am waiting for the bus.*

The accusative case is used here because the dative case would suggest that *I am waiting on top of the man or the bus.* I am not located there. Therefore, the accusative is the correct case.

Here is a short list of verbs that use the dative-accusative prepositions in the accusative case, because the idea of location is not the desired meaning:

denken an	*think about*
sich freuen auf	*look forward to*
sich verlieben in	*fall in love with*
bitten um	*ask for*
sich freuen über	*be glad about*
warnen vor	*warn against/about*

Say It Out Loud

Read each sentence out loud, paying attention to the case used with the prepositions:

Ich habe oft an meine Eltern gedacht.	*I often thought about my parents.*
Ich freue mich sehr auf deine Party.	*I am looking forward to your party very much.*
Der hübsche Soldat verliebte sich in meine Schwester.	*The handsome soldier fell in love with my sister.*
Darf ich um den nächsten Tanz bitten?	*May I have (ask for) the next dance?*
Das Geburtstagskind freute sich über mein Geschenk.	*The birthday boy was happy with my gift.*
Ich muss dich vor diesen Hausmakler warnen.	*I have to warn you about this real estate agent.*
Wir freuen uns schon sehr darauf.	*We are already looking forward to it very much.*
Sie hat unhöflich darum gebeten.	*She asked for it rudely.*

Freust du dich darüber?	*Are you glad about it?*
Wie kann man diese Leute davor warnen?	*How can you warn these people about it?*

Wondering About This? *sehr*
The adverb **sehr** means *very*. However, it is frequently used where in English we would say *very much*. For example:

Ich danke Ihnen sehr.	*I thank you very much.*
Er freut sich sehr darauf.	*He is looking forward to it very much.*
Sie hat Martin sehr gern.	*She likes Martin very much.*
Wir waren sehr dagegen.	*We were very much against it.*

Don't forget that some verbs have reflexive pronoun objects (**sich verlieben in**, **sich freuen auf**). The reflexive pronoun changes according to the subject of the sentence. For example:

ich freue mich	wir freuen uns
du freust dich	ihr freut euch
er freut sich	Sie freuen sich
sie freut sich	sie freuen sich
der Mann freut sich	die Männer freuen sich

When you encounter new verbs accompanied by a dative-accusative preposition, choose the accusative case when it is apparent that the desired meaning is not location, for example, **glauben an** (*believe in*). This is not location; therefore, **Ich glaube an meinen Freund.** *I believe in my friend.*

Exercise 17.3

Reword each word or phrase in parentheses as it would appear in the sentence. If a pronoun is accompanied by an.*, it is animate. If accompanied by* inan.*, it is inanimate. For example:*

Ich warte auf _____.

(der kleine Junge) *den kleinen Jungen*

(es *inan.*) *darauf*

1. Sie sind unter _____ gelaufen.

(eine alte Brücke *bridge*) _____

(der große Baum) _____

(es *inan.*) _____

2. Hat er sich in _____ verliebt?

(deine Töchter) _____

(diese hübsche Ausländerin) _____

(sie *s. an.*) _____

3. Wie kann man an _____ glauben?

(dieser Verbrecher) _____

(seine unehrlichen [*dishonest*] Verwandten) _____

(Sie) _____

4. Wir haben uns sehr auf _____ gefreut.

(Ihre Geburtstagsparty) _____

(seine nächste Rede) _____

(es *inan.*) _____

5. Er bat mich um _____.

(ein Stück Kuchen) _____

(eine heiße Tasse Tee) _____

(es *inan.*) _____

6. Du sollst dich nicht in _____ verlieben.

(dieser fremde Mann) _____

(ein italienischer Matrose) _____

(er *an.*) _____

7. Niemand freut sich über _____.

(seine Probleme) _____

(dieser lange Krieg) _____

(es *inan.*) _____

8. Mein Nachbar warnte uns vor _____.

(der starke Wind) _____

(die fremde Frau an der Ecke) _____

(sie *s. an.*) _____

9. Der Reporter wird über _____ schreiben.

(das Gewitter *storm*) _____

(ein furchtbarer Unfall *terrible accident*) _____

(wir) _____

10. Warum denkst du so oft an _____?

(dieses Problem) _____

(die neue Chefin) _____

(ich) _____

Geography

When looking at geography in English or German, there is a great similarity in both languages because there are numerous cognates that describe places and landscapes. This is very useful for developing new vocabulary quickly. Whether you are talking about continents, countries, cities, or mountain ranges, German will not seem too foreign to you.

Step 4: *Die Welt* (The World)

The world is made up of many countries on the seven continents. Let's look at some sentences that tell us where places are located. Notice how many continents and countries are used without any article.

Say It Out Loud

Read each sentence out loud, paying attention to the names of the continents and countries.

Thailand, Japan, und die Philippinen sind in Asien.	*Thailand, Japan, and the Philippines are in Asia.*
Sind Südafrika und Simbabwe in Afrika?	*Are South Africa and Zimbabwe in Africa?*
Tasmanien ist eine Insel an der Küste Australiens.	*Tasmania is an island off the coast of Australia.*
Schottland und Dänemark sind europäische Länder.	*Scotland and Denmark are European countries.*
In der Antarktis findet man kleine Siedlungen aber keine Städte.	*In Antarctica you will find little settlements but no cities.*
Venezuela und Argentinien befinden sich in Südamerika.	*Venezuela and Argentina are located in South America.*
Kanada und die Vereinigten Staaten von Amerika sind nordamerikanische Länder.	*Canada and the United States of America are North American countries.*

Countries and Languages

Use the following list to see how the names of countries and the modifiers that go with them differ from English:

Country	Adjective	Language	Citizen: Male/Female
Brasilien	brasilianisch	Portugesisch	Brasilianer/-in
China	chinesisch	Chinesisch	Chinese/-in
Deutschland	deutsch	Deutsch	Deutscher/-e
England	englisch	Englisch	Engländer/-in
Frankreich	französisch	Französisch	Franzose/Französin
Iran	iranisch	Farsi	Iraner/-in
Italien	italienisch	Italienisch	Italiener/-in
Japan	japanisch	Japanisch	Japaner/-in
Kanada	kanadisch	English Französisch	Kanadier/-in
Mexiko	mexikanisch	Spanisch	Mexikaner/-in
Österreich	österreichisch	Deutsch	Österreicher/-in
Russland	russisch	Russisch	Russe/-in
die Schweiz	schweizerisch	Deutsch Französisch Italienisch	Schweizer/-in
Spanien	spanisch	Spanisch	Spanier/-in
die USA (oo ess ah)	amerikanisch	Englisch	Amerikaner/-in

Landscape

Various features make up the landscape of the continents. Some of the most commonly talked about are:

das Gebirge	*mountain range*
das Meer	*sea*
das Tal	*valley*
der Berg	*mountain*
der Fluss	*river*
der Gletscher	*glacier*

der Ozean	*ocean*
der Regenwald	*rain forest*
der See	*lake*
der Sueskanal	*Suez Canal*
der Wasserfall	*waterfall*
die Ebene	*plain*
die Wüste	*desert*

 Exercise 17.4

Choose the word or phrase that best completes each sentence. For example:

Berlin ist in _____.
Amerika   <u>Europa</u>   Asien   Südafrika

1. Der Rhein ist ein _____ in Deutschland.
   See   Fluss   Gebirge   Berg

2. In Panama befindet sich ein _____.
   Alpen   Tal   Kanal   Brücke

3. Das Mittelmeer ist ein _____.
   Wasserfall   Gletscher   Ebene   Meer

4. Der _____ befindet sich in Südamerika.
   Mississippi   Nil   Harzgebirge   Amazonas

5. Eine _____ hat oft keinen Regen.
   Gletscher   Tal   Ozean   Wüste

6. Marseilles ist eine Stadt in _____.
   Frankreich   Schottland   Asien   Paris

7. Die Hauptstadt Russlands ist _____.
   Warschau   Prag   Moskau   Kiew

8. Im _____ kann es sehr kalt sein.
   Süden   Wüste   Norden   Sueskanal

9. Die _____ ist ein Fluss zwischen Deutschland und Polen.
   Gletscher   Oder   See   Regenwald

10. Spanien ist ein Nachbar von _____.
    Schweden   Österreich   Dänemark   Frankreich

11. In Alaska kann man _____ sehen.
    Wüsten   Gletscher   Brücken   Südwesten

12. Die Schweiz ist ein Nachbar von _____.
    Liechtenstein   Kanada   Mexiko   Portugalien

13. Der Atlantik ist zwischen Amerika und _____.
    Asien   Luxemburg   Europa   Westen

14. Kamele können in der _____ leben.
    Wasserfall   Wüste   Alpen   Ozean

15. Ein großer _____ befindet sich in Brasilien.
    Ebene   Regenwald   Tal   Berg

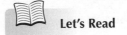

Let's Read

Read the following text and determine its meaning on your own:

Ich bin in Deutschland geboren, wo ich als Kind lebte. Als ich zehn Jahre alt
war, zog meine Familie nach Amerika und kam nach San Diego. Da wohnten
wir fünfundzwanzig Jahre. Jetzt habe ich eine Frau, zwei Kinder und ein Haus
in der Stadt. Meine Familie ist gesund und froh, und meine Kinder sind
intelligent und sehr fleißige Schüler. Das Leben ist gut! Alles ist perfekt.

Review Quiz 17

Choose the letter of the word or phrase that best completes each sentence.

1. Warum sitzt dein Sohn unter _____?
   a. dem Tisch   c. diese Decken
   b. den Tisch   d. dieser Decken

2. Hast du nie _____ mich gedacht?
   a. an   c. vor
   b. auf   d. ins

3. Zwei Vögel fliegen _____ dem alten Baum.
   a. an   c. im
   b. über   d. zwischen

4. Sie müssen _____ im Wartesaal warten.
   a. vor uns   c. über ihnen
   b. hinter sie   d. auf ihn

5. Er wollte einen Artikel über _____ schreiben.

   a. ihrem Hochzeitstag   c. diesen Ausländern

   b. mein Leben   d. seinem Tod

6. Der Amazonas befindet sich in _____.

   a. Dänemark   c. Brasilien

   b. Simbabwe   d. den Atlantik

7. Ich habe meine Strümpfe unter _____ gefunden.

   a. der alten Decke   c. den alten Hund

   b. ein Badetuch   d. dem Schlafzimmer

8. Ein paar Düsenjäger flogen über _____.

   a. im großen Einkaufszentrum   c. Regenwald und Flüsse

   b. unserer Stadt   d. das kleine Buch

9. Viele Leute standen _____ dem Rathaus.

   a. mit   c. am

   b. vor   d. auf ihn

10. Wo ist der Bus? Ich warte schon solange _____.

   a. an sie   c. vor ihn

   b. darauf   d. hinter

New Vocabulary

Atlantik (*m.*)	*Atlantic*
Bäcker (*m.*)	*baker*
bauen	*build*
Baum (*m.*)	*tree*
sich befinden	*be located*
behalten	*keep*
Bettcouch (*f.*)	*studio couch*
Dach (*n.*)	*roof*
Decke (*f.*)	*blanket*
Dom (*m.*)	*cathedral*
Düsenjäger (*m.*)	*jet fighter*
Ebene (*f.*)	*plain*
Ende (*n.*)	*end*
europäisch	*European*

Firma (f.)	company
sich freuen auf	look forward to
sich freuen über	be glad about
furchtbar	terrible
Gebäude (n.)	building
Geschäftsmann	businessman
Gewitter (n.)	storm
Gletscher (m.)	glacier
Kamel (m.)	camel
Kanal (m.)	canal
klopfen	knock
liegen	lie
Meer (n.)	sea
Mittelmeer (n.)	Mediterranean Sea
Ozean (m.)	ocean
Regenwald (m.)	rain forest
Schublade (f.)	drawer
Siedlung (f.)	settlement
Tal (n.)	valley
unehrlich	dishonest
unhöflich	impolite
sich verbergen	hide
Vereinigten Staaten von Amerika (pl.)	United States of America
sich verlieben in	fall in love with
Vogel (m.)	bird
warnen	warn
Wartesaal (m.)	waiting room
Wasserfall (m.)	waterfall
Welt (f.)	world
Wind (m.)	wind
Wüste (f.)	desert

18

Comparative and Superlative

This chapter will introduce you to the comparative and superlative forms of adverbs and adjectives. An explanation of their declension as adjectives will also be provided and practiced.

Some questions that will be answered are:

✓ How are the comparative and superlative different from the positive form of adverbs and adjectives?
✓ How is the comparative formed and used?
✓ How is the superlative formed and used?

Comparative

The basic form of an adverb or adjective is called the *positive form*. That form is the one you have been using until now. In English they look like this:

Adverb	Adjectives
early	*early*
interestingly	*interesting*
quickly	*quick*
slowly	*slow*

These adverbs and adjectives make a statement about the verbs and nouns they modify. For example:

She moved <u>quickly</u> across the room. (This tells at what speed she moved.)
He has a <u>quick</u> mind. (This tells that he has a clever mind.)

The comparative makes a *comparison* between two people or things. The English comparative is formed in two ways: add the suffix *-er* or precede the adverb or adjective with the adverb *more*. Most adjectives use the suffix *-er*. For example:

Positive	Comparative
big	bigger
kind	kinder
tall	taller

If the adjective is a long word or comes from a foreign source such as Latin, the adjective is preceded by *more*. For example:

Positive	Comparative
interesting	more interesting
serious	more serious
benevolent	more benevolent

A few adverbs that are identical to their adjectival equivalent form their comparative in the same way as the adjectival form:

Positive Adjective	Positive Adverb	Comparative
early	early	earlier
fast	fast	faster

Other adverbs are preceded by *more*. This is also the form for long words or words of a foreign origin:

Positive	Comparative
carefully	more carefully
quickly	more quickly
slowly	more slowly
benevolently	more benevolently
interestingly	more interestingly
seriously	more seriously

Step 1: German Comparative Adverbs and Adjectives

To form the comparative of a German adverb or adjective, the suffix **-er** is added to the positive form of the adverb or adjective. For example:

Positive	Comparative	
einsam	einsamer	*lonelier*
intelligent	intelligenter	*more intelligent*
langsam	langsamer	*slower*
leicht	leichter	*easier, lighter*
schnell	schneller	*faster*
schwer	schwerer	*harder, heavier*

In German, there is no distinction between the formation of the comparative of adverbs or the comparative of adjectives.

A few adverbs and adjectives of one syllable often add an umlaut to an umlaut vowel. For example:

Positive	Comparative	
alt	älter	*older*
arm	ärmer	*poorer*
dumm	dümmer	*dumber, more stupid*
jung	jünger	*younger*
klug	klüger	*smarter*
krank	kränker	*sicker*
kurz	kürzer	*shorter*
lang	länger	*longer*
schwach	schwächer	*weaker*
stark	stärker	*stronger*
warm	wärmer	*warmer*

When comparing two people or things, the pair of words is separated by **als** (*than*). For example:

Martin läuft schneller <u>als</u> Hans.	*Martin runs faster than Hans.*
Der alte Mann geht langsamer <u>als</u> ich.	*The old man goes more slowly than me.*

Wondering About This? *langsamer als ich*

In German, the conjunction **als** is followed by the nominative subject of a sentence that is understood but not uttered. For example:

Der alte Mann geht langsamer als <u>ich gehe</u>.   *The old man goes more*
                                                         slowly than <u>I go</u>.

Then why was the translation of **als ich** in the original example given as *than me*? English can translate such sentences in two ways. If you assume that *I* is the subject of a sentence that is understood but not uttered, the translation is *than I*. If you assume that *than* is being used as a preposition, the translation is *than me*. Either way is correct.

The comparative of an adverb never has an ending. The comparative of an adjective that is a predicate adjective never has an ending. For example:

Adverb:	Er wartet <u>länger</u> als Thomas.	*He waits longer than Thomas.*
Adjective:	Meine Schwester ist <u>intelligenter</u> als ich.	*My sister is more intelligent than me.*

Say It Out Loud

Read each sentence out loud, paying attention to the comparative adverbs and adjectives:

Herr Bauer tanzt schlechter als seine Frau.	*Mr. Bauer dances worse than his wife.*
Der Junge hat langsamer gelesen als das Mädchen.	*The boy read more slowly than the girl.*
Der Dom ist viel größer als die Kirche.	*The cathedral is much larger than the church.*
Diese Rosen riechen schöner als jene.	*These roses smell prettier than those.*
Eine Reise nach Berlin ist billiger als eine Reise nach Paris.	*A trip to Berlin is cheaper than a trip to Paris.*
Der Schauspieler war hübscher als der Sänger.	*The actor was more handsome than the singer.*
Ist dieser Tisch kürzer als der braune Tisch?	*Is this table shorter than the brown table?*

Im Wohnzimmer ist es viel wärmer als im Keller.	*It is a lot warmer in the living room than in the cellar.*
Sein Artikel darüber war langweiliger als sein Roman.	*His article about it was more boring than his novel.*

Declined Adjectives

Predicate adjectives require no declensional endings. When an adjective modifies a noun directly, it must have an ending that reflects the number, gender, and case of the noun. This is also true of a comparative adjective. For example:

Masculine

Nom.	der jüngere Mann	*the younger man*	ein jüngerer Mann	*a younger man*
Acc.	den jüngeren Mann		einen jüngeren Mann	
Dat.	dem jüngeren Mann		einem jüngeren Mann	
Gen.	des jüngeren Mannes		eines jüngeren Mannes	

Feminine

Nom.	die ältere Frau	*the older woman*	eine ältere Frau	*an older woman*
Acc.	die ältere Frau		eine ältere Frau	
Dat.	der älteren Frau		einer älteren Frau	
Gen.	der älteren Frau		einer älteren Frau	

Neuter

Nom.	dieses nettere Kind	*this nicer child*	kein netteres Kind	*no nicer child*
Acc.	dieses nettere Kind		kein netteres Kind	
Dat.	diesem netteren Kind		keinem netteren Kind	
Gen.	dieses netteren Kindes		keines netteren Kindes	

Plural

Nom.	jene kleineren Katzen	*those smaller cats*
Acc.	jene kleineren Katzen	
Dat.	jenen kleineren Katzen	
Gen.	jener kleineren Katzen	

Nom.	seine kleineren Katzen	*his smaller cats*
Acc.	seine kleineren Katzen	
Dat.	seinen kleineren Katzen	
Gen.	seiner kleineren Katzen	

Exercise 18.1

Change the adjective provided in parentheses to the comparative. Then reword the phrase with that comparative adjective. For example:

(alt) Eine *ältere* Dame wohnt hier.

1. (groß) Wir haben einen _____ Wagen gekauft.

2. (schön) Das _____ Mädchen ist meine Cousine.

3. (dumm) Ein _____ Schüler ist oft nicht fleißig.

4. (reich) Diese _____ Leute haben eine Wohnung in London.

5. (stark) Ein _____ Mann kann den schweren Koffer tragen.

6. (komisch) Sie hat einen _____ Satz geschrieben.

7. (schnell) Wir möchten mit dem _____ Zug fahren.

8. (schlecht) Ich habe einen _____ Roman gelesen.

9. (lang) Sie haben eine Waldhütte an einem _____ Fluss.

10. (hell) Die _____ Lampen kosten €60.

Step 2: Irregular Comparatives

English has some comparatives that have an irregular formation. For example:

Positive	Comparative
bad	*worse*
far	*farther/further*
good	*better*
little (amount)	*less*
many	*more*
much	*more*

They are used like other comparatives; they just have an irregular formation. German also has a few irregular comparatives. Let's take a look at them:

Positive	Comparative	
bald	eher	*sooner*
gut	besser	*better*
hoch	höher	*higher, taller*
viel	mehr	*more*

Say It Out Loud

Read each sentence out loud, paying attention to the irregular comparatives.

Ich bin eher da gewesen als der Bauer.	*I was there sooner than the farmer.*
Renate kann besser singen als Angelika.	*Renate can sing better than Angelika.*
Ist der Fernsehturm höher als dieser Wolkenkratzer?	*Is the TV tower taller than this skyscraper?*
Ich brauchte viel mehr als €25.	*I needed more than 25 euros.*
Eher will ich sterben als mit diesem Mann zusammenwohnen.	*I'd sooner die than live with that man.*
Ich möchte eine bessere Gitarre kaufen.	*I would like to buy a better guitar.*
Das Dach meines Haus ist höher als das Dach Ihres Hauses.	*My house's roof is higher than your house's roof.*

Exercise 18.2

Using the string of words provided, compose a sentence with a comparative adjective or adverb. For example:

Tina / laufen / schnell / Hans

Tina läuft schneller als Hans.

1. ihr / sein / einsam / ich

   _____

2. der Kellner / arbeiten / langsam / die Kellnerin

   _____

3. meine Tochter / schreiben / gut / mein Sohn

_____

4. diese Straße / sein / lang / Schillerstraße

_____

5. der Professor / reden / laut / sein Kollege

_____

6. der Düsenjäger / fliegen / hoch / der Jumbo-Jet

_____

7. der Bus / ankommen / spät / der Zug

_____

8. wir / abfahren / bald / unsere Eltern

_____

9. im Januar / sein / das Wetter / kalt / im September

_____

10. Thailand / sein / weit / Österreich

_____

Superlative

The English superlative describes the highest or most extreme quality of a person or thing. An adjective adds the suffix -*est* to form the superlative. Adverbs tend to follow the adverb *most*. For example:

Adverb	Adjective
most brightly	*brightest*
fastest	*fastest*
most quickly	*quickest*
most slowly	*slowest*

If the adverb or adjective is a long word from a foreign source, both adverbs and adjectives follow the adverb *most*:

Adverb	Adjective
most benevolently	*most benevolent*
most interestingly	*most interesting*
most notably	*most notable*

A superlative predicate adjective can appear in two forms. One form is to use the superlative adjective like any other predicate adjective. For example:

Positive: *Jack is <u>busy</u> in the spring.*

Superlative: *Jack is <u>busiest</u> in spring.*

Another form uses the same superlative adjective but precedes it with the article *the*:

Positive: *Jack is <u>busy</u> in the spring.*

Superlative: *Jack is <u>the busiest</u> in the spring.*

Step 3: German Superlative Adverbs and Adjectives

To form the superlative of a German adverb or adjective, the suffix **-ste** is added to the positive form of the adverb or adjective. If the adverb or adjective ends in **-d, -t, -s, -z, -sch**, or **-ß** or is otherwise difficult to pronounce, the suffix becomes **-este**. For example:

Positive	**Superlative**	
einsam	einsamste	*loneliest*
hübsch	hübscheste	*most handsome*
interessant	interessanteste	*most interesting*
klein	kleinste	*smallest*
kurz	kürzeste	*shortest*
lang	längste	*longest*
langweilig	langweiligste	*most boring*
schön	schönste	*prettiest*
weit	weiteste	*farthest*

Just like in the comparative, words of one syllable tend to add an umlaut to an umlaut vowel in the superlative (**lang, längste, kurz, kürzeste**).

Adverbs in the superlative form a short prepositional phrase with **am** and the adjective ending **-n**. For example:

Sie läuft am schnellsten.	*She runs the fastest.*
Die Kinder sprechen am lautesten.	*The children speak the loudest.*

Wondering About This? *the fastest*
The German superlative adverb can be translated in two ways: with the article *the* or without the article *the*. For example:

Martin lernt am langsamsten.	*Martin learns the slowest/slowest.*
Sie singt am schönsten.	*She sings the prettiest/prettiest.*

Superlative predicate adjectives also form a short prepositional phrase with **am** and the adjective ending **-n**. For example:

Am Abend wurde es am dunkelsten.	*In the evening it became the darkest.*
Du warst am klügsten in der Klasse.	*You were the smartest in the class.*
Ist dieser Fluss am längsten?	*Is this river the longest?*

Say It Out Loud

Read each sentence out loud, paying attention to the superlative adverbs and adjectives:

In der Küche ist es immer am wärmsten.	*It is always the warmest in the kitchen.*
Warum lachen diese Mädchen am lautesten?	*Why do these girls laugh the loudest?*
Die älteren Schüler sind am intelligentesten.	*The older students are the most intelligent.*
Zwei Gäste kamen am spätesten.	*Two guests came the latest.*
Meine Brüder kommen immer am frühesten.	*My brothers always come the earliest.*
Diese Schlipse waren am teuersten.	*These ties were the most expensive.*
Im Sommer ist es am heißesten geworden.	*In the summer it became the hottest.*

Step 4: Irregular Superlatives

Just as in the comparative, there are irregularities in the superlative. For example:

Positive	Superlative	
bald	am ehesten	*soonest*
groß	am größten	*biggest*
gut	am besten	*best*
hoch	am höchsten	*highest, tallest*
nah	am nächsten	*nearest, next*
viel	am meisten	*most*

Exercise 18.3

In the blank provided, give the superlative form of each adverb and adjective. For example:

(laut) *am lautesten*

1. (schmutzig) _____
2. (gut) _____
3. (schlecht) _____
4. (nett) _____
5. (kalt) _____
6. (heiß) _____
7. (langweilig) _____
8. (hübsch) _____
9. (freundlich) _____
10. (weit) _____
11. (nah) _____
12. (dumm) _____
13. (dick) _____
14. (groß) _____
15. (hoch) _____

When a superlative adjective modifies a noun directly, the adjective ending is determined by the number, gender, and case of the noun:

Masculine

Nom. der jüngste Mann	*the youngest man*	ihr jüngster Mann	*her youngest husband*
Acc. den jüngsten Mann		ihren jüngsten Mann
Dat. dem jüngsten Mann		ihrem jüngsten Mann
Gen. des jüngsten Mannes		ihres jüngsten Mannes

Feminine

Nom. die älteste Frau	*the oldest woman*	meine älteste Frau	*my oldest wife*
Acc. die älteste Frau		meine älteste Frau
Dat. der ältesten Frau		meiner ältesten Frau
Gen. der ältesten Fraueiner		meiner ältesten Frau

Neuter

Nom. dieses netteste Kind	*this nicest child*	ihr nettestes Kind	*her nicest child*
Acc. dieses netteste Kind		ihr nettestes Kind
Dat. diesem nettesten Kind		ihrem nettesten Kind
Gen. dieses nettesten Kindes		ihres nettesten Kindes

Plural

Nom. jene kleinsten Katzen	*those smallest cats*
Acc. jene kleinsten Katzen	
Dat. jenen kleinsten Katzen	
Gen. jener kleinsten Katzen	
Nom. seine kleinsten Katzen	*his smallest cats*
Acc. seine kleinsten Katzen	
Dat. seinen kleinsten Katzen	
Gen. seiner kleinsten Katzen	

Say It Out Loud

Read each sentence out loud, paying attention to the declension of the superlative adjectives:

Ich glaube, dass unsere Mannschaft am stärksten ist.	*I believe that our team is the strongest.*
Sie fragt, ob dieser Wolkenkratzer am höchsten ist.	*She asks whether this skyscraper is the tallest.*
Der längste Fluss in Deutschland ist der Rhein.	*The longest river in Germany is the Rhine.*
Seine besten Studenten kommen aus Kanada.	*His best students come from Canada.*
Der größte Berg ist wahrscheinlich in den Alpen.	*The biggest mountain is probably in the Alps.*
Der neueste Schüler sagt, dass er kein Deutsch kann.	*The newest student says that he cannot understand any German.*
Das schlechteste Wetter ist immer im Frühling.	*The worst weather is always in spring.*
Ihr längstes Kleid ist sehr altmodisch.	*Her longest dress is very old fashioned.*
Ist der Flughafen die nächste Station?	*Is the airport the nearest (next) station?*
Warum ist mein bestes Hemd so schmutzig?	*Why is my best shirt so dirty?*

Wondering About This? *er kann kein Deutsch*

Look again at this sentence: **Der neueste Schüler sagt, dass er kein Deutsch kann.** The verb **können** means *can* or *be able to*. When used with languages, it is used alone, but certain other verbs are understood. For example:

Er kann kein Deutsch.	*He cannot <u>understand</u> German.*
Kannst du Englisch?	*Do you <u>know</u> English?*
Wir können gut Spanisch.	*We can <u>speak</u> Spanish well.*

Exercise 18.4

Change the adverb or adjective provided to the superlative. Then fill in the blank with the superlative and any needed ending. For example:

(schön) Meine Schwester is am *schönsten*.

1. (weit) Der letzte Bahnhof ist am _____.

2. (gut) Die _____ Schriftstellerin war eine Deutsche.

3. (langweilig) Haben Sie seinen _____ Roman gelesen?

4. (bald) Der Zug nach München kam am
   _____.

5. (warm) Unser _____ Zimmer ist wahrscheinlich die Küche.

6. (ehrlich) Der _____ Mann war der Richter.

7. (hübsch) Die italienische Schauspielerin war am
   _____.

8. (nah) Ist der Flughafen am _____?

9. (intelligent) Man sagt, dass das _____ Tier (*animal*) der Delphin (*dolphin*) ist.

10. (billig) Die _____ Reise kostet €675.

 **Let's Read**

Read the following dialogue and determine its meaning on your own.

TINA: Wohin reist du nächste Woche? Nach Rom?

MAX: Nein, ich reise nach Zürich. Zürich ist viel näher.

TINA: Kommt dein Bruder mit?

MAX: Werner? Nein, er ist am faulsten. Er bleibt zu Hause.

TINA: Am faulsten? Aber Werner ist der beste Sportler der Fußballmannschaft.

MAX: Ja, er spielt viel besser als ich. Aber er ist der faulste Student in der Klasse.

Review Quiz 18

Choose the letter of the word or phrase that best completes each sentence.

1. Ist mein Fahrrad _____ als dein Fahrrad?
   a. sauber
   b. neuer
   c. teuer
   d. langweilig

2. Meine Freundin singt viel besser _____ ich.
   a. dass
   b. als
   c. ob
   d. den

3. Karin wohnt ein bisschen _____ von hier.
   a. schöner
   b. am nächsten
   c. weiter
   d. wohin

4. Wessen Mannschaft spielte _____?
   a. guter
   b. längste
   c. bald
   d. besser

5. Der _____ Fluss in Südamerika ist der Amazonas.
   a. längste
   b. am kürzesten
   c. schöner
   d. nah

6. Die _____ Leute sagen oft Dummheiten.
   a. deutsche
   b. am klügsten
   c. langweilige
   d. intelligentesten

7. Meine Frau spricht Deutsch _____ als ich.
   a. schlechter
   b. am besten
   c. langsam
   d. schnellste

8. Das _____ Zimmer ist immer mein Schlafzimmer.
   a. kälteste
   b. wärmer
   c. größtes
   d. am längsten

9. Der _____ Flughafen ist viel weiter von der Stadt.
   a. neue
   b. ältesten
   c. nächster
   d. großer

10. Heute ist die Temperatur in bisschen _____.
    a. schöne
    b. am kältesten
    c. warmer
    d. höher

New Vocabulary

altmodisch	*old fashioned*
bald	*soon*
Delphin (*m.*)	*dolphin*
einsam	*lonely*
Flughafen (*m.*)	*airport*
früh	*early*
Frühling (*m.*)	*spring*
hoch	*high, tall*
leicht	*light, easy*
Mannschaft (*f.*)	*team*
Schlips (*m.*)	*necktie*
schwer	*heavy, hard*
Station (*f.*)	*station*
Tier (*n.*)	*animal*
wahrscheinlich	*probably*
zusammenwohnen	*live together*

19

Imperatives and Double Infinitives

This chapter is devoted to the explanation of the German imperative forms of verbs. In addition, double infinitive structures will be introduced.

Some questions that will be answered are:

✓ How is the German imperative of verbs formed?
✓ How does the German imperative differ from English?
✓ What verbs besides modal auxiliaries have a double infinitive structure?

Commands

A command is given in English by using the imperative form of a verb. This is quite a simple process in English because the imperative is the same verb as the infinitive. For example:

Infinitive	Imperative
be	*be*
look	*look*
be able to	*be able to*

In a sentence, the imperatives look like this:

Please be on time tomorrow.

Look both directions before you cross the street.

Be able to translate the first paragraph.

Have a good time at the party.

Imperative verbs do not have a tense as such. They are commands to the second person (*you*) and imply an action that should take place now or in the future. For example:

> Come for a visit. (now)
>
> Come for a visit next week some time. (in the future)

Nearly all verbs can be used in the imperative; however, there are a few auxiliaries that never form imperatives: *must, can, will, should, have to, may,* and *might*. In general, just about all transitive and intransitive verbs can be formed as commands.

Step 1: The German Imperative

Just as an English imperative is directed at the second person (*you*), so too is it in German. But remember that German has three forms of *you*: **du** (informal singular), **ihr** (informal plural), and **Sie** (formal singular or plural). For that reason, German has three forms of imperative, one for each pronoun *you*.

Sie

You have already encountered a few imperatives for **Sie**. They are formed by the plural conjugation of the verb followed by **Sie**. For example:

Bleiben Sie da!	*Stay there.*
Geben Sie mir bitte das Buch!	*Please give me the book.*
Fahren Sie um ein Uhr ab!	*Depart at one o'clock.*

The only slight irregularity occurs with the verb **sein**. It becomes **seien**:

Seien Sie bitte ruhig!	*Please be quiet.*
Seien Sie nicht ungeduldig!	*Don't be impatient.*
Seien Sie mein ewiger Freund!	*Be my eternal friend.*

Say It Out Loud

Read each sentence out loud, paying attention to the imperative verb:

Bleiben Sie bitte vor dem Spiegel stehen!	*Please remain standing in front of the mirror.*
Zeigen Sie mir bitte Ihren Pass!	*Please show me your passport.*

Warten Sie ein paar Minuten im Wartesaal!	*Wait a couple of minutes in the waiting room.*
Helfen Sie meinem Vater mit den Koffern!	*Help my father with the suitcases.*
Bitte beeilen Sie sich!	*Please hurry.*
Am Montag sehen Sie mit uns fern!	*On Monday watch television with us.*
Bestellen Sie Pommes frites und Spätzle dazu!	*Order French fries and spaetzle with it.*
Verderben Sie ihm doch nicht seinen Spaß!	*Don't go ruining (spoiling) his fun.*

Ihr

The second person informal plural (**ihr**) uses the conjugation of the verb without the pronoun. For example:

Infinitive	Present Tense	Imperative	
einschlafen	ihr schlaft ein	Schlaft ein!	*Fall asleep*
gehen	ihr geht	Geht schneller!	*Go faster*
verkaufen	ihr verkauft	Verkauft es!	*Sell it*

Say It Out Loud

Read each sentence out loud, paying attention to the imperative verb:

Steigt bitte an der nächsten Ecke aus!	*Get off at the next corner.*
Steigt in Bus Nummer zehn ein!	*Get on bus number 10.*
Bezahlt das Essen und die Getränke an der Kasse!	*Pay for the food and drinks at the cashier.*
Hört mir bitte zu!	*Please listen to me.*
Ladet die ausländischen Studenten ein!	*Invite the foreign students.*
Bereitet ein köstliches Essen für die Gäste vor!	*Prepare a delicious meal for the guests.*
Seht euch die wunderbare Aussicht an!	*Look at the wonderful view.*
Sammelt Briefmarken aus aller Welt!	*Collect stamps from around the world.*

Exercise 19.1

*Give the **ihr** and **Sie** imperative forms for the infinitives shown. For example:*

geben	*Gebt!*	*Geben Sie!*
	ihr	**Sie**

1. fragen   _____   _____

2. mitkommen   _____   _____

3. vergessen   _____   _____

4. sein   _____   _____

5. zumachen   _____   _____

6. empfehlen   _____   _____

7. zerstören   _____   _____

8. einnehmen   _____   _____

9. fernsehen   _____   _____

10. besuchen   _____   _____

Du

The second person informal singular (**du**) has both a regular and an irregular imperative form. The regular form comes from the stem of the verb. Although it can be optional, usually an **e** is added to the stem. For example:

Infinitive	Stem	Imperative	
singen	sing-	Singe! (Sing!)	*sing*
schreiben	schreib-	Schreibe! (Schreib!)	*write*
anrufen	ruf- . . . an	Rufe an! (Ruf an!)	*phone*
bestellen	bestell-	Bestelle! (Bestell!)	*order*

The verbs **haben**, **sein**, and **werden** do something a little unique:

haben	hab-	Habe! (Hab!)	*have*
sein	sei-	Sei!	*be*
werden	werd-	Werde!	*become*

A present tense irregularity occurs in the second person singular with certain verbs that have an umlaut vowel in the stem (**fahren** = **du fährst**,

laufen = du läufst). This irregularity is disregarded, and the stem of the verb is treated as regular when the imperative is formed. For example:

Infinitive	Stem	Imperative	
anfangen	fang- . . . an	Fang(e) an!	*begin*
fahren	fahr-	Fahr(e)!	*drive*
laufen	lauf-	Lauf(e)!	*run*
waschen	wasch-	Wasch(e)!	*wash*

Another present tense irregularity that affects the second person singular is the vowel change from **e** to **i** or **ie**. This same irregularity occurs in the imperative with **du**. An **e** is not added to this form of imperative:

Infinitive	Stem	Imperative	
ansehen	sieh- . . . an	Sieh an!	*look at*
ausgeben	gib- . . . aus	Gib aus!	*spend*
brechen	brich-	Brich!	*break*
vergessen	vergiss-	Vergiss!	*forget*

Exercise 19.2

*Give the present tense of the verb with **du** and the second person singular imperative of the verb. For example:*

fragen	*du fragst*	*Frage!*
	Present	**Imperative**
1. tragen	_____	_____
2. bekommen	_____	_____
3. einschlafen	_____	_____
4. trinken	_____	_____
5. essen	_____	_____
6. lesen	_____	_____
7. mitnehmen	_____	_____
8. fliegen	_____	_____
9. sich beeilen	_____	_____
10. aussteigen	_____	_____

Say It Out Loud

Read each sentence out loud, paying attention to the imperative verb forms:

Bitte sprich ein bisschen lauter!	*Please speak a little louder.*
Hör sofort damit auf!	*Stop that immediately.*
Kinder, es ist spät. Beeilt euch!	*Children, it is late. Hurry.*
Steigen Sie bitte in den Zug ein!	*Please get on the train.*
Bleiben Sie während der Fahrt zurück.	*Please stay back during the trip.*
Halte meine Hand und küsse mich!	*Hold my hand and kiss me.*
Beschreiben Sie bitte Ihre letzte Reise nach Ägypten.	*Please describe your last trip to Egypt.*
Esst die Suppe und trinkt ein Glas Milch!	*Eat the soup, and drink a glass of milk.*
Bitte komm um halb neun vorbei!	*Please come by at eight-thirty.*
Sei geduldig und bring mir meine Tabletten!	*Be patient, and bring me my pills.*
Bleib unter der warmen Decke und werde bald gesund.	*Stay under the warm blanket, and get well soon.*

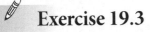

Exercise 19.3

Fill in the blanks with two of the missing imperative forms. For example:

Du: Komm sofort nach Hause!

Ihr: *Kommt sofort nach Hause!*

Sie: *Kommen Sie sofort nach Hause!*

1. Du: Sei nicht so ungeduldig!

   Ihr: _____

   Sie: _____

2. Du: _____

   Ihr: Besucht uns im Dezember!

   Sie: _____

3. Du: _____

   Ihr: _____

   Sie: Sprechen Sie mit dem jungen Schriftsteller!

4. Du: Fahr um Viertel vor elf ab!

   Ihr: _____

   Sie: _____

5. Du: _____

   Ihr: Gebt dem armen Mann ein paar Euro!

   Sie: _____

Double Infinitives

There are many similarities between English and German grammar, particularly in the area of verbs. But *double infinitive structures* are exclusive to German.

Where German can use a double infinitive, English sometimes uses a present participle (*singing, laughing, writing*). Let's look at some English sentences that illustrate this:

> *I watched the boys <u>playing</u> softball.*
>
> *We can hear the orchestra <u>practicing</u> in the theater.*
>
> *Did you see Mark and Jane <u>kissing</u> in the park?*

Although German has present participles, they are not used in the same way as English uses them.

Step 2: Present Perfect and Future Tenses

You are already familiar with the present perfect and future tenses. The former is formed with the auxiliary **haben** or **sein** and a past participle, and the latter is formed with the auxiliary **werden** and an infinitive. For cxample:

Present perfect:	Ich habe es gelesen.	*I read it.*
Future:	Ich werde es lesen.	*I will read it.*
Present perfect:	Wir sind schnell gelaufen.	*We ran fast.*
Future:	Wir werden schnell laufen.	*We will run fast.*

The present perfect and future tenses are important because they are the tenses in which a double infinitive can be used. Not just any verb can be used in this way. The largest group of verbs that can form double infinitives is the modal auxiliaries.

In the present and past tenses, a modal auxiliary is accompanied by an infinitive. For example:

Present:	Ich kann es nicht verstehen.	*I cannot understand it.*
Past:	Ich konnte es nicht verstehen.	*I could not understand it.*
Present:	Hans will nach Hause gehen.	*Hans wants to go home.*
Past:	Hans wollte nach Hause gehen.	*Hans wanted to go home.*

There are two more basic tenses in which modal auxiliaries can be conjugated: the present perfect and future tenses. When the modal auxiliaries are used in these tenses, they form double infinitive structures. They are exactly what they sound like; they are composed of two infinitives standing side by side. For example:

Present:	Ich kann es nicht verstehen.	*I cannot understand it.*
Present perfect:	Ich habe es nicht <u>verstehen können</u>.	*I could not understand it.*
Future:	Ich werde es nicht <u>verstehen können</u>.	*I will not be able to understand it.*
Present:	Hans will nach Hause gehen.	*Hans wants to go home.*
Present perfect:	Hans hat nach Hause <u>gehen wollen</u>.	*Hans wanted to go home.*
Future:	Hans wird nach Hause <u>gehen wollen</u>.	*Hans will want to go home.*

Notice that the modal auxiliary is the last verb in the double infinitive and that the double infinitive does not affect the normal translation of the present perfect and future tenses.

Say It Out Loud

Read each sentence out loud, paying attention to the double infinitive structures:

Wie lange werden wir warten müssen?	*How long will we have to wait?*
Sie hat mit dem schrecklichn Mann nicht zusammenwohnen können.	*She was not able to live together with the terrible man.*

Werden Sie da im Irrgarten spazieren wollen?	*Will you want to go strolling the maze?*
Karl hat die neuen Sätze übersetzen müssen.	*Karl had to translate the new sentences.*
Wird sie sich jetzt besser benehmen können?	*Will she be able to behave herself better now?*
Ihr habt euch die Hände waschen sollen.	*You should have washed your hands.*
Die Fluggäste werden während des Flugs nicht rauchen dürfen.	*The passengers will not be allowed to smoke during the flight.*
Er hat keine ausländischen Bücher lesen mögen.	*He did not like reading foreign books.*
Das wird niemand in der Kirche machen dürfen.	*No one will be allowed to do that in church.*
Mutti hat die Kinder davor warnen wollen.	*Mom wanted to warn the children about it.*

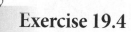

Exercise 19.4

Reword each sentence in the missing three tenses. For example:

Present: Ich will zu Hause bleiben.

Past: *Ich wollte zu Hause bleiben.*

Present perfect: *Ich habe zu Hause bleiben wollen.*

Future: *Ich werde zu Hause bleiben wollen.*

1. Present: Diese Jungen können nicht schwimmen.

   Past: _____

   Present perfect: _____

   Future: _____

2. Present: _____

   Past: Die Ausländerin konnte die Bibliothek benutzen (*use*).

   Present perfect: _____

   Future: _____

3. Present: _____

   Past: _____

   Present perfect: Man hat fleißiger arbeiten sollen.

   Future: _____

4. Present: _____

   Past: _____

   Present perfect: _____

   Future: Wer wird unseren Spaß verderben wollen?

5. Present: Warum muss ich mit ihnen zusammenwohnen?

   Past: _____

   Present perfect: _____

   Future: _____

Step 3: *Helfen, hören, lassen,* and *sehen*

German has four more verbs that form a double infinitive structure in the present perfect and future tenses: **hören, helfen, lassen,** and **sehen. Lassen** is a new verb for you and means *let* when used *without an accompanying infinitive.* For example:

Hast du den Hund in die Wohnung gelassen? *Did you let the dog into the apartment?*

The verb **lassen** as well as the other three verbs are conjugated normally when accompanied by an infinitive. But in the present perfect and future tenses, they form a double infinitive structure. The verb **lassen**, however, now means *get* or *have* something done. For example:

lassen

Ich lasse mein Fahrrad reparieren.	*I get my bicycle repaired.*
Ich ließ mein Fahrrad reparieren.	*I got my bicycle repaired.*
Ich habe mein Fahrrad <u>reparieren lassen</u>.	*I got my bicycle repaired.*
Ich werde mein Fahrrad <u>reparieren lassen</u>.	*I will get my bicycle repaired.*

helfen

Max hilft die Koffer tragen.	*Max helps carry the suitcases.*
Max half die Koffer tragen.	*Max helped carry the suitcases.*
Max hat die Koffer <u>tragen helfen</u>.	*Max helped carry the suitcases.*
Max wird die Koffer <u>tragen helfen</u>.	*Max will help carry the suitcases.*

hören

Er hört uns singen.	*He hears us singing.*
Er hörte uns singen.	*He heard us singing.*
Er hat uns <u>singen hören</u>.	*He heard us singing.*
Er wird uns <u>singen hören</u>.	*He will hear us singing.*

sehen

Siehst du die Frauen arbeiten?	*Do you see the women working?*
Sahst du die Frauen arbeiten?	*Did you see the women working?*
Hast du die Frauen <u>arbeiten sehen</u>?	*Did you see the women working?*
Wirst du die Frauen <u>arbeiten sehen</u>?	*Will you see the women working?*

Say It Out Loud

Read each sentence out loud, paying attention to the use of the double infinitive structures:

Niemand hilft mir die Küche saubermachen.	*No one helps me clean the kitchen.*
Hast du die Touristen auf der Straße sprechen hören?	*Did you hear the tourists talking on the street?*
Sah Frau Reimer die Kinder auf der Terasse spielen?	*Did Ms. Reimer see the children playing on the terrace?*
Ich werde meinen Wagen waschen lassen.	*I will get my car washed.*
Wir ließen das Haus von einer neuen Baufirma bauen.	*We had our house built by a new construction company.*
Sie hat ihren Eltern das Haus streichen helfen.	*She helped her parents paint the house.*
Erik wird die olympischen Sportler trainieren sehen.	*Erik will see the Olympic athletes training.*
Max hörte eine Frau hinter der Kunsthalle schreien.	*Max heard a woman screaming behind the art museum.*
Meine Mutter hat ein Kleid von Frau Benz nähen lassen.	*My mother had a dress made by Ms. Benz.*
Ich habe ein paar Jugendliche flüstern hören.	*I heard a couple of young people whispering.*

Exercise 19.5

Reword each sentence in the missing three tenses. For example:

Present: Ich will zu Hause bleiben.

Past: *Ich wollte zu Hause bleiben.*

Present perfect: *Ich habe zu Hause bleiben wollen.*

Future: *Ich werde zu Hause bleiben wollen.*

1. Present: Ich lasse die Fenster reparieren.

   Past: _____

   Present perfect: _____

   Future: _____

2. Present: _____

   Past: Sahen sie Tina und Max von der Kunsthalle zurückkommen?

   Present perfect: _____

   Future: _____

3. Present: _____

   Past: _____

   Present perfect: Wir haben die Kinder auf der Terasse flüstern hören.

   Future: _____

4. Present: _____

   Past: _____

   Present perfect: _____

   Future: Wir werden ihr nähen helfen.

5. Present: Können Sie die Jugendlichen fotografieren?

   Past: _____

   Present perfect: _____

   Future: _____

6. Present: _____

   Past: Ich ließ ein Bild von dem Künstler (*artist*) malen (*paint*).

   Present perfect: _____

   Future: _____

7. Present: _____

Past: _____

Present perfect: Hast du das Gedicht auswendig (*poem, learn by heart*) lernen müssen?

Future: _____

8. Present: _____

Past: _____

Present perfect: _____

Future: Ihr werdet die Tiere im Zoo fressen sehen.

9. Present: Niemand hört unseren Nachbar klopfen.

Past: _____

Present perfect: _____

Future: _____

10. Present: _____

Past: Ich half ihr aufstehen.

Present perfect: _____

Future: _____

Some Useful Phrases

The noun **der Spaß** means *fun* and is used in several expressions that come in handy. For example:

Das macht Spaß.	*That is fun.*
Die Jugendlichen hatten alle viel Spaß.	*The young people all had a good time.*
Das hat mir gar keinen Spaß gemacht.	*That was no fun for me at all.*
Oma versteht keinen Spaß.	*Granny cannot take a joke.*
Mein Job macht mir keinen Spaß.	*I don't enjoy my job.*

The nouns **der Hunger** and **der Durst** mean *hunger* and *thirst*, respectively. They can be used with **haben** when you wish to say that *you are hungry* or *thirsty*:

Wo ist das Café? Ich habe Hunger.	*Where is the café? I am hungry.*
Ein Glas Wasser bitte! Ich habe Durst.	*A glass of water please. I'm thirsty.*

Exercise 19.6

Add an appropriate line to each short dialogue:

1. WERNER: Sind wir zu spät angekommen?

   MARIANNE: _____

   WERNER: Hoffentlich spielt der Diskjockey die neuesten Hits.

2. TINA: Es ist eine wunderbare Geburtstagsparty, Max.

   MAX: _____

   TINA: Als Geschenk, deine erste Flasche Rotwein.

3. ERIK: Warum haben Sie eine neue Garage bauen lassen?

   HERR BAUER: _____

   ERIK: Und die neue Garage ist sauber und warm.

Review Quiz 19

Choose the letter of the word or phrase that best completes each sentence.

1. _____ mir bitte ein Glas Wasser, Herr Reimer!
   - a. Gib
   - b. Geben Sie
   - c. Zeigt
   - d. Zeigten Sie

2. Max und Sonja, _____ viel Spaß in Berlin!
   - a. habt
   - b. seid
   - c. machen
   - d. werde

3. Nächste Woche _____ mit Bus Nummer elf!
   - a. fahren
   - b. fährt
   - c. fährst
   - d. fahr

4. Ich habe mit ihm nicht zusammenwohnen _____.
   - a. will
   - b. sollte
   - c. können
   - d. hören

5. Hör sofort damit _____!
   - a. müssen
   - b. auf
   - c. kann
   - d. lassen

6. Wann hast du die Tür _____ lassen?

    a. gebrochen   c. trainiert

    b. reparieren   d. bauten

7. Hast du eine Suppe gekocht? Ich _____.

    a. kann helfen   c. habe Hunger

    b. will es   d. sah sie saubermachen

8. _____ Sie hier im Wartesaal!

    a. Setzten   c. Aßen

    b. Erwarteten   d. Warten

9. Vati wird ihr den Koffer tragen _____.

    a. helfen   c. konnten

    b. gelassen   d. muss

10. In diesem Zimmer wird man nicht _____.

    a. rauchen dürfen   c. wohnen zusammen

    b. gehört hat   d. spielen Karten

New Vocabulary

Aussicht (*f.*)	*view*
aussteigen	*get off* (*transportation*)
auswendig	*by heart*
Baufirma (*f.*)	*construction company*
sich beeilen	*hurry up*
sich benehmen	*behave oneself*
benutzen	*use*
bezahlen	*pay*
Briefmarke (*f.*)	*stamp*
Durst (*m.*)	*thirst*
einsteigen	*get on, in* (*transportation*)
Essen (*n.*)	*food*
ewig	*eternal*
Flug (*m.*)	*flight*
Fluggast (*m.*)	*passenger* (*airplane*)
flüstern	*whisper*
Gedicht (*n.*)	*poem*

Getränk (*n.*)	*drink, beverage*
Hunger (*m.*)	*hunger*
Irrgarten (*m.*)	*maze*
Jugendliche (*m.*)	*young person*
Kunsthalle (*f.*)	*art museum*
Künstler (*m.*)	*artist*
malen	*paint (pictures)*
Oma (*f.*)	*granny*
Pass (*m.*)	*passport*
Pommes frites (*pl.*)	*French fries*
rauchen	*smoke*
reparieren	*repair*
ruhig	*quiet, calm*
sammeln	*collect*
saubermachen	*clean*
schrecklich	*terrible*
schreien	*scream*
Spaß (*m.*)	*fun*
Spätzle (*pl.*)	*spaetzle, dumplings*
streichen	*paint*
Terasse (*f.*)	*terrace*
trainieren	*train, work out*
übersetzen	*translate*
ungeduldig	*impatient*
verderben	*spoil*
warnen	*warn*
Wartesaal (*m.*)	*waiting room*
Welt (*f.*)	*world*
wunderbar	*wonderful*
Zoo (*m.*)	*zoo*
zusammenwohnen	*live together*

20

Using All the Cases and
All the Tenses

This chapter provides a review of all the cases and practice using a variety of verbs in all the tenses you have learned. Independent clauses will also be explained.

Some of the questions that will be answered are:

✓ What new patterns occur as nouns change case?
✓ How are different kinds of verbs conjugated in the various tenses?
✓ How are dependent clauses different from independent clauses?

Cases and Declensions

Except when nouns change to the plural or the possessive, English nouns do not have declensional changes. The subject of a sentence, the direct object, the indirect object, and the object of a preposition all look the same. For example:

Subject:	*My relatives have a house in the mountains.*
Direct object:	*I rarely visit my relatives.*
Indirect object:	*Mary gave my relatives a welcome home party.*
Object of preposition:	*The letter I got from my relatives was good news.*
Possessive:	*My relatives' house finally sold.*

Because English nouns are used in this relatively simple way, it is sometimes hard to grasp the idea that German is quite different: nouns decline in the various cases.

English pronouns have declensions when they are objects. But when they form a possessive, a *possessive adjective is formed*. For example:

Subject:	*I*	*you*	*he*	*we*
Direct object:	*me*	*you*	*him*	*us*
Indirect object:	*me*	*you*	*him*	*us*
Object of preposition:	*about me*	*for you*	*to him*	*of us*
Possessive:	*my*	*your*	*his*	*our*

Step 1: German Declensions of Nouns and Pronouns

The four German cases have specific functions. They signal that a noun is being used in a certain way and requires the appropriate declension of articles and adjectives. In addition, the gender of the noun must be taken into consideration to make the correct declension. You need to ask two questions when declining nouns:

1. How is the noun being used in the sentence (subject, direct object, indirect object, object of a preposition, or possessive)?

2. What is the gender and number of the noun (masculine, feminine, neuter, singular, or plural)?

Nominative

The subject of a German sentence or the predicate nominative is in the nominative case. In this case, the gender of the noun determines what kind of ending the article and adjective that modify the noun will have. The **der**-words (definite articles and **dieser, jener, jeder, welcher**) must be differentiated from the **ein**-words (indefinite articles and **mein, dein, sein, ihr, unser, euer, Ihr, kein**).

With **der**-words, the gender of the noun is identified in the **der**-word, and the adjective ending is **-e**. With **ein**-words, the gender of the noun is identified in the adjective, and the **ein**-word is either **ein/eine** in the singular or **keine/Ihre** in the plural. Plural adjectives always end in **-en**. For example:

Der-Words

Masculine	Feminine	Neuter	Plural
der kleine Wagen	die schöne Dame	das große Haus	die jungen Leute
jener blaue Mantel	diese weiße Bluse	jedes kleine Kind	jene netten Frauen

Ein-Words

Masculine	Feminine	Neuter	Plural
ein kleiner Wagen	eine schöne Dame	ein großes Haus	keine jungen Leute
sein blauer Mantel	meine weiße Bluse	Ihr kleines Kind	deine netten Kinder

Accusative

Direct objects and objects of the accusative prepositions (**bis, durch, für, gegen, ohne, wider, um**) are in the accusative case. Only masculine nouns have a new declension in this case: all modifiers end in **-en**. The feminine, neuter, and plural make no changes from the nominative.

Der-Words

Masculine	Feminine	Neuter	Plural
den kleinen Wagen	die schöne Dame	das große Haus	die jungen Leute
jenen blauen Mantel	diese weiße Bluse	jedes kleine Kind	jene netten Frauen

Ein-Words

Masculine	Feminine	Neuter	Plural
einen kleinen Wagen	eine schöne Dame	ein großes Haus	keine jungen Leute
seinen blauen Mante	meine weiße Bluse	Ihr kleines Kind	deine netten Kinder

Say It Out Loud

Read each sentence out loud, paying attention to the case and the function that calls for that case:

Ist mein neues Handy im Schlafzimmer?	*Is my new cell phone in the bedroom?*
Wissen Sie, was ihre Telefonnummer ist?	*Do you know what her telephone number is?*
Er ging langsam durch das dunkle Zimmer.	*He went through the dark room slowly.*

Dieser hübsche Soldat kommt aus Südamerika.	This handsome soldier comes from South America.
Sind diese Tabletten für den kranken Jungen?	Are these pills for the sick boy?
Welche weißen Tabletten muss ich einnehmen?	Which white pills do I have to take?
Der Mann war ein guter Freund von Thomas.	The man was a good friend of Thomas.

Exercise 20.1

In the blank provided, use the letter S if the underlined noun phrase is the subject of the sentence. Use the letters PN if it is a predicate nominative. Use the letters DO if it is the direct object. Use the letter O if it is the object of a preposition. For example:

S Seine neue Freundin ist Deutsche.

DO Kennen Sie diesen jungen Sportler?

1. _____ Diese Leute sind gegen den neuen Richter.

2. _____ Ist dein neues Handy teuer gewesen?

3. _____ Ich habe ein kleines Haus in den Bergen.

4. _____ Martin hat ein paar Blumen für seine alten Verwandten.

5. _____ Meine Kinder waren keine fleißigen Schüler.

6. _____ Welche roten Äpfel hast du gegessen?

7. _____ Ich möchte eine große Tasse Tee trinken.

8. _____ Ist sie wieder ohne ihren neuen Mann gekommen?

9. _____ Der letzte Zug kommt um elf Uhr an.

10. _____ Wissen Sie, wo die reiche Dame wohnt?

Dative

In the dative case, all nouns make declensional changes. The dative case identifies indirect objects, objects of dative prepositions (**aus, außer, bei, mit,** nach, seit, von, zu), and objects of dative verbs (such as **helfen** and **glauben**). The declensions are the same for **der**-words and **ein**-words.

Masculine	Feminine	Neuter	Plural
dem kleinen Wagen	der schönen Dame	dem großen Haus	den jungen Leuten
jenem blauen Mantel	dieser weißen Bluse	jedem kleinen Kind	jenen netten Frauen

Ein-Words

Masculine	Feminine	Neuter	Plural
einem kleinen Wagen	einer schönen Dame	einem großen Haus	keinen jungen Leuten
seinem blauen Mantel	meiner weißen Bluse	Ihrem kleinen Kind	deinen netten Kindern

Say It Out Loud

Read each sentence out loud, paying attention to the case and the function that calls for that case.

Ich zeige den amerikanischen Gästen die Bilder.

I show the American guests the pictures.

Wohnen sie noch bei ihren deutschen Verwandten?

Do they still live with their German relatives?

Ich konnte meinem neuen Nachbarn nicht glauben.

I could not believe my new neighbor.

Wer schenkte deiner jungen Tochter einen Ring?

Who gave your young daughter a ring?

Wir haben diesen armen Leuten geholfen.

We helped these poor people.

Wird er mit dem letzten Bus kommen?

Will he come on the last bus?

Geben Sie dem kranken Mann ein Glas Wasser!

Please give the sick man a glass of water.

Exercise 20.2

In the blank provided, use the letters IO if the underlined noun phrase is the indirect object. Use the letters DV if it is the object of a dative verb. Use the letter O if it is the object of a preposition. For example:

IO Ich sende <u>einem alten Freund</u> ein Telegramm.

1. _____ Können Sie <u>meiner neuen Wirtin</u> dieses Geld geben?

2. _____ Der Kellner bringt <u>unseren russischen Gästen</u> eine Flasche Wein.

3. _____ Wir helfen <u>jenen alten Touristen</u> damit.

4. _____ Erik hat <u>seiner jungen Tochter</u> einen Brief geschickt.

5. _____ Werden die Kinder <u>ihren neuen Freunden</u> glauben?

6. _____ Warum antwortest du <u>dem großen Polizisten</u> nicht?

7. _____ Nach <u>seiner letzten Klasse</u> ist er nach Hause gegangen.

8. _____ Ist sie mit <u>ihrem zweiten Mann</u> gekommen?

9. _____ Außer <u>meiner deutschen Cousine</u> ist die Familie in der Stadt geblieben.

10. _____ Ich werde <u>der reichen Dame</u> für das Geschenk danken.

Genitive

In the genitive case, all nouns make declensional changes. The genitive case identifies possessives and objects of genitive prepositions (**anstatt, trotz, während, wegen**). The declensions are the same for **der**-words and **ein**-words.

Masculine	**Feminine**	**Neuter**
des kleinen Wagens	der schönen Dame	des großen Hauses
jenes blauen Mantels	dieser weißen Bluse	jedes kleinen Kindes

Plural

der jungen Leute

jener netten Frauen

Ein-Words

Masculine	**Feminine**	**Neuter**
eines kleinen Wagens	einer schönen Dame	eines großen Hauses
seines blauen Mantels	meiner weißen Bluse	Ihres kleinen Kindes

Plural

keiner jungen Leute

deiner netten Kinder

Pronouns

The personal pronouns are declined in three of the cases but form possessive adjectives in place of the genitive case. For example:

Nom.	ich	du	er	sie	wir	ihr	Sie	sie
Acc.	mich	dich	ihn	sie	uns	euch	Sie	sie
Dat.	mir	dir	ihm	ihr	uns	euch	Ihnen	ihnen
Poss.	mein	dein	sein	ihr	unser	euer	Ihr	ihr

The same functions for the four cases that affect nouns also affect pronouns in the same way:

Subject:	<u>Er</u> lernt Deutsch.	*He learns German.*
Direct object:	Kennen Sie <u>ihn</u>?	*Do you know him?*
Indirect object:	Martin gibt <u>ihm</u> zwei Euro.	*Martin gives him two euros.*
Object of preposition:	Wir kommen mit <u>ihm</u>.	*We come with him.*

Say It Out Loud

Read each sentence out loud, paying attention to the case and the function that calls for that case:

Haben Sie die Rede des neuen Präsidenten gehört?	*Did you hear the new president's speech?*
Wo hast du sie kennen gelernt?	*Where did you make her acquaintance?*

Das Haus seiner englischen Verwandten ist klein.	*His English relatives' house is small.*
Wegen eines langen Krieges blieben sie in Europa.	*Because of a long war, they stayed in Europe.*
Die Musik der alten Oper ist ganz schön.	*The music of the opera is quite pretty.*
Was ist der Titel ihres ersten Romans?	*What is the title of her first novel?*
Haben Sie mit ihm gesprochen?	*Did you speak with him?*
War Tina die Freundin des komischen Ausländers?	*Was the funny foreigner's girlfriend Tina?*
Ist Frau Keller eine Freundin von Ihnen?	*Is Ms. Keller a friend of yours?*
Außer eines freundlichen Matrosen hat ihm niemand geholfen.	*Except for a kind sailor, no one helped him.*

 ## Exercise 20.3

In the blank provided, use the letter P if the underlined noun phrase is a genitive possessive. Use the letter O if it is the object of a genitive preposition. For example:

P Wo ist das Haus <u>deines neuen Freundes</u>?

1. _____ Ich möchte die Familie <u>meiner amerikanischen Verwandten</u> besuchen.

2. _____ Während <u>des heißen Sommers</u> fahren wir nach Schweden.

3. _____ Er hat trotz <u>einer langen Krankheit</u> gearbeitet.

4. _____ Hast du die Bücher <u>deines toten Onkels</u> gefunden?

5. _____ Gudrun lernte den Rechtsanwalt <u>einer reichen Richterin</u> kennen.

Exercise 20.4

Use the word or phrase in parentheses to complete each sentence. Various cases are involved. For example:

(meine kleine Schwester)

Ich liebe *meine kleine Schwester*.

Er hat mit *meiner kleinen Schwester getanzt*.

Wo ist *meine kleine Schwester* gewesen?

(dieses alte Museum)

1. Wir wollen _____ besuchen.

2. Warum sind sie durch _____ gelaufen?

3. Die Fenster _____ sind alle kaputt.

4. Wie alt ist _____?

(sein langweiliger Roman)

5. Hast du _____ gelesen?

6. Nach _____ will er einen interessanten Roman schreiben.

7. Wegen _____ bin ich schnell eingeschlafen.

8. Sie kam ohne _____ ins Klassenzimmer.

(eine hässliche Hexe)

9. Niemand wollte mit _____ sprechen.

10. _____ hat in den Bergen gewohnt.

11. Die schwarze Katze _____ wartet an der Tür.

12. Ich habe _____ einen Sack Gold gegeben.

(kein reicher Ausländer)

13. _____ hat in dieser Straße gewohnt.

14. Wir haben _____ Geld geschickt.

15. Nein, sie hat _____ angerufen.

16. Herr Bellini ist _____.

(er)

17. Monika darf _____ kaufen.

18. _____ war zu teuer.

19. Wo haben Sie _____ gefunden?

20. Hat _____ den Mädchen gefallen?

Tenses

It is important to remember that English has two forms of each tense. One describes a habitual or repeated action, and the other describes an incomplete or ongoing action. For example:

Habitual	Incomplete
I work at a factory.	*I am working at a factory.*
She has a party every Saturday.	*She is having a party on Saturday.*
My children go to school.	*My children are going to school.*

This concept is found in all the tenses.

German does not distinguish between these two concepts. Either one is translated in German in one form:

I work in a factory.	Ich arbeite in einer Fabrik.
I am working in a factory.	Ich arbeite in einer Fabrik.

Step 2: Varieties in the German Tenses

There are basic endings to know for each of the four tenses you have learned (present, past, present perfect, and future). Sometimes there are irregularities in the verbs that can occur in any of the tenses. Let's look at how German verbs are conjugated in the four tenses.

Present Tense

The basic conjugational endings for the present tense are:

ich -e	wir -en
du -st	ihr -t
er -t	Sie -en
	sie *pl.* -en

The conjugation of a regular verb like **machen** (*make, do*) looks like this with these endings: **ich mache, du machst, er macht, wir machen, ihr macht, Sie machen**, and **sie machen**. If the endings follow certain consonants such as -**t** and -**d**, an extra -**e**- is added before the second person singular and plural and the third person singular ending, for example, **ich rede, du red<u>e</u>st, er red<u>e</u>t, wir reden, ihr red<u>e</u>t, Sie reden**, and **sie reden**.

Some verbs have an irregularity in the present tense. It occurs most often in the second and third person singular. A vowel shift is one form of irregularity, and the addition of an umlaut is another form. For example:

geben (*give*) = ich gebe, du g<u>i</u>bst, er g<u>i</u>bt, wir geben, ihr gebt, Sie geben, sie geben

fahren (*drive*) = ich fahre, du f<u>ä</u>hrst, er f<u>ä</u>hrt, wir fahren, ihr fahrt, Sie fahren, sie fahren

The verbs **haben** (*have*), **sein** (*be*), and **werden** (*become*) are also irregular in the present tense.

ich	habe	bin	werde
du	hast	bist	wirst
er	hat	ist	wird
wir	haben	sind	werden
ihr	habt	seid	werdet
Sie	haben	sind	werden
sie	haben	sind	werden

The modal auxiliaries have a unique present tense conjugation with the singular having one stem form and the plural having another. For example, **wollen** = **ich will, wir wollen** and **können** = **ich kann, wir können**. Review Chapter 15 for another look at the modal auxiliaries.

Wondering About This? *ich will, ich möchte*
The two verb phrases **ich will** and **ich möchte** can both be used to express a desire. If you use a form of **wollen** (**ich will, wir wollen**), the desire is expressed directly and is often considered blunt and almost rude. If you use the conjugation of **möchten** (**ich möchte, wir möchten**), the desire is polite

and more respectful. Even the translation of the two verbs expresses this difference. For example:

Ich will nach Hause gehen.	*I want to go home.*
Ich möchte nach Hause gehen.	*I would like to go home.*
Sie wollen diese Hemden anprobieren.	*They want to try on these shirts.*
Sie möchten diese Hemden anprobieren.	*They would like to try on these shirts.*

Consider the circumstances in which you find yourself when deciding which of these two verbs to use.

Say It Out Loud

Read each sentence out loud, paying attention to the present tense conjugation of the verbs:

Wir schreiben einen Artikel.	*We are writing an article.*
Kauft der reiche Mann oft ein neues Handy?	*Does the rich man often buy a new cell phone?*
Warum antwortest du langsam?	*Why do you answer slowly?*
Hast du heute Nachmittag eine Klasse?	*Do you have a class this afternoon?*
Wir müssen in einem Hotel übernachten.	*We have to stay overnight in a hotel.*
Deine Schwester sieht wirklich hübsch aus.	*You sister really looks beautiful.*
Weißt du, wann der Zug kommt?	*Do you know when the train is coming?*
Meine Eltern kennen Herr Bauer nicht.	*My parents don't know Mr. Bauer.*
Wie lange dauert die Reise dorthin?	*How long does the trip there take?*
Mein kleiner Bruder liest schon sehr gut.	*My little brother already reads very well.*
Willst du Schach spielen?	*Do you want to play chess?*

Past Tense

The regular past tense uses the following endings:

ich -te		wir -ten	
du -test		ihr -tet	
er -te		Sie -ten	
		sie *pl.* -ten	

The conjugation of a regular verb like **machen** (*make, do*) looks like this on the past tense with these endings: **ich machte, du machtest, er machte, wir machten, ihr machtet, Sie machten,** and **sie machten.** If the past tense endings follow certain consonants such as **-t** and **-d,** an extra **-e-** is added, for example, **ich redete, du redetest, er redete, wir redeten, ihr redetet, Sie redeten,** and **sie redeten.**

The three most important irregular verbs (**haben, sein, werden**) are irregular in the past tense. **Haben** becomes **ich hatte, du hattest. Sein** becomes **ich war, du warst. Werden** becomes **ich wurde, du wurdest.**

There are numerous irregular past tense verbs. A complete list of them is provided in Appendix B. Most irregular verbs form a new past tense stem, and the following endings are then added:

ich -		wir -en	
du -st		ihr -t	
er -		Sie -en	
		sie *pl.* -en	

For example, **helfen** (*help*) = **ich half, du halfst, er half, wir halfen, ihr halft, Sie halfen,** and **sie halfen.**

A few verbs make a vowel change and then add the *regular past tense endings,* among which are the modal auxiliaries (**können, mögen, müssen, wollen,** and **sollen**). For example:

	wissen *know*	nennen *name, call*	können *can, be able to*
ich	wusste	nannte	konnte
du	wusstest	nanntest	konntest
er	wusste	nannte	konnte
wir	wussten	nannten	konnten
ihr	wusstet	nanntet	konntet
Sie	wussten	nannten	konnten
sie	wussten	nannten	konnten

Say It Out Loud

Read each sentence out loud, paying attention to the past tense conjugation of the verbs:

Ihr Mann brachte ihr jeden Tag Blumen.	*Her husband brought her flowers every day.*
Wer machte die Fenster zu?	*Who closed the windows?*
Wann waren die Kinder beim Arzt?	*When were the children at the doctor?*
Es wurde wieder kalt und regnerisch.	*It became cold and rainy again.*
Gestern fuhren sie in die Berge.	*Yesterday they drove into the mountains.*
Vor einem Jahr wohnte Max in der Hauptstadt.	*A year ago Max lived in the capital.*
Er versprach uns, pünktlich zu sein.	*He promised us he'd be punctual.*

Exercise 20.5

Reword each present tense sentence in the past tense. Reword each past tense sentence in the present tense. For example:

Mutti kaufte ein paar Äpfel.

Mutti kauft ein paar Äpfel.

1. Seid ihr gute Freunde?

   _____

2. Die Studenten gehen auf eine Party.

   _____

3. Die kranke Frau blieb zu Hause.

   _____

4. Martin wollte ihr einen schönen Ring kaufen.

   _____

5. Wir bestellen Würstchen und Bier.

   _____

6. Niemand aß die kalte Suppe.

   _____

7. Ich habe wirklich keine Zeit.

_____

8. Am Donnerstag ging Tina schlittschuhlaufen.

_____

9. Der Schauspieler singt auch gut.

_____

10. Wer sendet dieses Telegramm?

_____

Present Perfect

The present perfect tense is made up of the auxiliary **haben** or **sein** and a regular or irregular past participle. Regular past participles use the stem of a verb with the prefix **ge-** and the suffix **-t**. For example, **suchen = haben gesucht** and **reisen = sein gereist**.

The irregular present perfect tense also uses **haben** or **sein** as its auxiliary, but many of its past participles have an **-en** suffix. For example, **sehen = haben gesehen** and **kommen = sein gekommen**. Verbs such as **wissen** and **rennen** make a vowel change when forming a past participle but use the **-t** suffix. For example, **wissen = haben gewusst** and **rennen = sein gerannt**.

Inseparable and separable prefixes play a role in the formation of the past participles. Inseparable prefixes replace the **ge-** prefix, and separable prefixes begin the participle and are followed by the participle with a **ge-** prefix. For example, **versprechen = haben versprochen** and **abfahren = sein abgefahren**.

Future

The future tense is the easiest to form. The verb **werden** is conjugated and is followed at the end of the sentence by an accompanying infinitive. For example:

Ich werde hier blieben.	_I will stay here._
Wer wird dem Mann helfen?	_Who will help the man?_

When a modal auxiliary is in the present perfect tense or the future tense, it follows the accompanying infinitive at the end of the sentence and forms a _double infinitive_. It is translated normally into English. For example:

Ich habe mit ihm sprechen wollen.	_I wanted to speak with him._
Ich werde mit ihm sprechen wollen.	_I will want to speak with him._
Niemand hat ihr helfen können.	_No one could help her._

Niemand wird ihr helfen können.	*No one will be able to help her.*
Haben Sie nach London fliegen müssen?	*Did you have to fly to London?*
Werden Sie nach London fliegen müssen?	*Will you have to fly to London?*

When a modal auxiliary is in the present perfect tense and is accompanied by a verb of motion, remember that it is the modal that is being conjugated, not the accompanying infinitive. That is why the present perfect tense auxiliary for all modals is **haben**, even when the accompanying infinitive would use **sein** if it were the conjugated verb:

<u>Haben</u> Sie nach London <u>fliegen</u> müssen?	*Did you have to fly to London?*
Ich <u>habe</u> nach Hause <u>gehen</u> wollen.	*I wanted to go home.*

Say It Out Loud

Read each sentence out loud, paying attention to the present perfect and future tense conjugations of the verbs:

Es ist endlich sehr warm geworden.	*It has finally become warm.*
Wirst du Flugbegleiterin werden?	*Will you become a flight attendant?*
Martin hat das Wochenende in Bremen verbracht.	*Martin spent the weekend in Bremen.*
Vati wird die kleine Waldhütte verkaufen.	*Dad will sell the little hut in the woods.*
Er hat in der Waldhütte bleiben müssen.	*He had to stay in the hut in the woods.*
Wirst du endlich nach Freiburg kommen können?	*Will you finally be able to come to Freiburg?*
Wir sind ziemlich oft wandern gegangen.	*We went hiking rather often.*
Habt ihr genug Zeit gehabt?	*Did you have enough time?*
Die Polizisten werden den Verbrecher verhaften.	*The police will arrest the criminal.*
Auf dem Fußballfeld ist sie sehr schnell gelaufen.	*She ran very fast on the soccer field.*
Die Kinder haben zu oft ferngesehen.	*The children watched TV too often.*

Exercise 20.6

Reword each verb in the present perfect and future tenses with the pronoun **er**. *For example:*

zumachen   *er hat zugemacht*   *er wird zumachen*

1. einschlafen _____   _____

2. mitkommen _____   _____

3. bestellen _____   _____

4. trinken _____   _____

5. lachen _____   _____

6. erwarten _____   _____

7. kennen _____   _____

8. wissen _____   _____

9. fernsehen _____   _____

10. sterben _____   _____

Exercise 20.7

Reword each sentence in the missing tenses. For example:

Present: *Ich mache das Fenster zu.*

Past: Ich machte das Fenster zu.

Present perfect: *Ich habe das Fenster zugemacht.*

Future: *Ich werde das Fenster zumachen.*

1. Present: Wer bekommt ein Geschenk von ihm?

   Past: _____

   Present perfect: _____

   Future: _____

2. Present: _____

   Past: Er wusste nicht, wo sie wohnt.

   Present perfect: _____

   Future: _____

3. Present: _____

   Past: _____

   Present perfect: Wir haben eine Flasche Wein bestellt.

   Future: _____

4. Present: _____

   Past: _____

   Present perfect: _____

   Future: Werden Sie bei einer Bank arbeiten?

5. Present: Der Präsident ist in der Hauptstadt.

   Past: _____

   Present perfect: _____

   Future: _____

6. Present: _____

   Past: Der müde Junge schlief auf dem Boden ein.

   Present perfect: _____

   Future: _____

7. Present: _____

   Past: _____

   Present perfect: Ich habe dorthin reisen müssen.

   Future: _____

8. Present: _____

   Past: _____

   Present perfect: _____

   Future: Wer wird damit helfen können?

9. Present: Gudrun liest drei Zeitungen.

   Past: _____

   Present perfect: _____

   Future: _____

10. Present: _____

   Past: _____

   Present perfect: _____

   Future: Der Ausländer wird auch mitkommen.

Review Quiz 20

Choose the letter of the word or phrase that best completes each sentence.

1. Vor einer Woche _____ wir im Park spazieren.
   - a. gegangen
   - b. fahren
   - c. werden
   - d. gingen

2. Sie haben _____ Haus in den Bergen.
   - a. ein großes
   - b. diese große
   - c. keinen großen
   - d. meines großen

3. Hat der Ausländer _____ getanzt?
   - a. mit dir
   - b. von ihnen
   - c. für wen
   - d. außer euch

4. Am Abend werde ich die Zeitung _____.
   - a. lesen
   - b. geschrieben
   - c. bleiben
   - d. zuhören

5. Um wie viel Uhr _____ die alte Dame gestorben?
   - a. haben
   - b. wird
   - c. ist
   - d. konnte

6. Meine Freundin lernte ihn _____.
   - a. genannt
   - b. kennen
   - c. wusste
   - d. dachte

7. Monika musste _____ ihren Verwandten wohnen.
   - a. für
   - b. bei
   - c. während
   - d. zu

8. Wegen _____ müssen die Jungen zu Hause Schach spielen.
   - a. es regnet
   - b. schneien
   - c. das letzte Jahr
   - d. des schlechten Wetters

9. Werner ist dorthin _____.
   - a. bekommen
   - b. laufen
   - c. gehabt
   - d. gefahren

10. Wie oft bist du _____ gefahren?
    - a. mit der Straßenbahn
    - b. jeden Tag
    - c. dem Zug nach Berlin
    - d. umsteigen

New Vocabulary

Artikel (*m.*)	*article*
dorthin	*there, to there*
einnehmen	*take (medicine)*
fernsehen	*watch television*
Fußballfeld (*n.*)	*soccer field*
Handy (*f.*)	*cell phone*
Musik (*f.*)	*music*
Präsident (*m.*)	*president*
Rede (*f.*)	*speech*
Tabletten (*pl.*)	*tablets, pill*
Telefonnummer (*f.*)	*telephone number*
Verbrecher (*m.*)	*criminal*
verhaften	*arrest*
Waldhütte (*f.*)	*hut in the woods*
ziemlich	*rather*

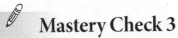

Mastery Check 3

This Mastery Check is provided to help you identify the areas of German covered in this book that you feel confident about or that you should review. Choose the letter of the word or phrase that best completes each sentence.

1. The first syllable of **Stühle** is pronounced _____.
   a. shpreh
   b. stoo
   c. stoe
   d. shtue

2. _____ dein Bruder in München?
   a. Wohin
   b. War
   c. Heißt
   d. Heißen

3. Meine _____ ist Lehrerin.
   a. Schwester
   b. Frau Schäfer
   c. Brüder
   d. Eltern

4. _____ schicken Sie diese Ansichtskarten?

   a. Euch   c. Sie *s*.

   b. Wem   d. Abend

5. Sie spielen nicht Karten, _____ sie spielen Schach.

   a. sondern   c. mussten

   b. oder   d. können

6. Der kleine Schüler _____ sich den Arm.

   a. antwortet   c. brach

   b. konnte   d. möchte

7. Kann Erik gut _____?

   a. schlittschuhlaufen   c. spielten Schach

   b. Tennis oder Fußball   d. gefahren

8. Der neue Arbeiter war wirklich sehr _____.

   a. faul   c. keine intelligente

   b. kluge   d. oft

9. Warum habt ihr _____ ausgegeben?

   a. ein bisschen Zeit   c. in Nordamerika

   b. so viel Geld   d. damit

10. Professor Bauer wollte zweihundert Euro _____.

   a. ausgegeben   c. zurückbekommen

   b. verbringen   d. retten

11. Der Junge wäscht sich die Hände _____.

   a. und putzt sich die Zähne   c. ob der Boden schmutzig ist

   b. dass wir es wussten   d. denn sie sind sauber

12. Unser Flugbegleiter war nicht so nett, _____.

   a. und er hat mir viel geholfen   c. dass wir Probleme hatten

   b. wie unser Pilot   d. wenn er ist in einer Fabrik

13. Er wollte einen Artikel über _____ schreiben.

   a. ihrem Geburtstag   c. diesen Fluggästen

   b. meine Familie   d. seinem Tod

14. Ich habe meine Handschuhe unter _____ gefunden.

   a. meinem Bett   c. die alte Katze

   b. ein Badetuch   d. den Esszimmern

15. Der _____ Fluss in Nordamerika ist der Mississippi.

    a. längste

    b. am kürzesten

    c. schöner

    d. nah

16. Der _____ Lehrer sagt oft Dummheiten.

    a. deutschen

    b. am klügsten

    c. langweiliger

    d. intelligenteste

17. Meine Kinder sprechen Englisch _____ als ich.

    a. besser

    b. am schlechtesten

    c. langsam

    d. schnellste

18. _____ Sie hier im Wartesaal!

    a. Warte

    b. Erwarteten

    c. Aßen

    d. Bleiben

19. Mein Sohn hat ihnen die großen Koffer tragen _____.

    a. muss

    b. gelassen

    c. konnten

    d. helfen

20. Wegen _____ mussten wir in der Waldhütte bleiben.

    a. es regnete

    b. schneien

    c. das schreckliche Gewitter

    d. des schlechten Wetters

21. Vor ein paar Tagen _____ wir im Wald spazieren.

    a. gegangen

    b. fahren

    c. werden

    d. gingen

22. Was _____ ihr noch tun?

    a. wird

    b. können

    c. willst

    d. müsst

23. _____, ob Herr Bauer hier wohnt?

    a. Erik fragt

    b. Weißt du

    c. Der Reporter berichtet

    d. Meine Tante hat geantwortet

24. Haben Sie nie _____ uns gedacht?

    a. ins

    b. auf

    c. vor

    d. an

25. Das _____ Zimmer war immer die Küche.

    a. kälter

    b. wärmste

    c. größten

    d. am längsten

Appendix A
Fraktur Alphabet (1600–1940)

Aa	𝕬a	Jj	𝕵i	Ss	𝕾s
Bb	𝕭b	Kk	𝕶f	Tt	𝕿t
Cc	𝕮c	Ll	𝕷l	Uu	𝖀u
Dd	𝕯d	Mm	𝕸m	Vv	𝖁v
Ec	𝕰c	Nn	𝕹n	Ww	𝖂w
Ff	𝕱f	Oo	𝕺o	Xx	𝖃x
Gg	𝕲g	Pp	𝕻p	Yy	𝖄y
Hh	𝕳h	Qq	𝕼q	Zz	𝖅z
Ii	𝕴i	Rr	𝕽r		

ß	𝕭
Ää	𝕬ä
Öö	𝕺ö
Üü	𝖀ü

Appendix B
The Principal Parts of Irregular Verbs

Only the second person and third person singular are shown in the present tense. In the past tense, the third person singular is provided. However, because of the number of irregularities in the conjugation, the full present tense conjugation of **sein** and **tun** is shown.

INDICATIVE				SUBJUNCTIVE
Infinitive	**Present**	**Past**	**Past Participle**	**Imperfect**
backen	bäckst bäckt	buk *or* backte	gebacken	büke *or* backte
befehlen	befiehlst befiehlt	befahl	befohlen	beföhle
befleißen	befleißt befleißt	befliss	beflissen	beflisse
beginnen	beginnst beginnt	begann	begonnen	begönne
beißen	beißt beißt	biss	gebissen	bisse
bergen	birgst birgt	barg	geborgen	bürge
bersten	birst birst	barst	geborsten	börste
betrügen	betrügst betrügt	betrog	betrogen	betröge

	INDICATIVE			SUBJUNCTIVE
Infinitive	**Present**	**Past**	**Past Participle**	**Imperfect**
bewegen	bewegst bewegt	bewog	bewogen	bewöge
biegen	biegst biegt	bog	gebogen	böge
bieten	bietest bietet	bot	geboten	böte
binden	bindest bindet	band	gebunden	bände
bitten	bittest bittet	bat	gebeten	bäte
blasen	bläst bläst	blies	geblasen	bliese
bleiben	bleibst bleibt	blieb	geblieben	bliebe
bleichen	bleichst bleicht	blich	geblichen	bliche
braten	brätst brät	briet	gebraten	briete
brechen	brichst bricht	brach	gebrochen	bräche
brennen	brennst brennt	brannte	gebrannt	brennte
bringen	bringst bringt	brachte	gebracht	brächte
denken	denkst denkt	dachte	gedacht	dächte
dingen	dingst dingt	dingte *or* dang	gedungen *or* gedingt	dingte
dreschen	drischst drischt	drasch	gedroschen	drösche
dringen	dringst dringt	drang	gedrungen	dränge

Infinitive	Present	Past	Past Participle	Imperfect
dürfen	darfst	durfte	gedürft	dürfte
	darf			
empfangen	empfängst	empfing	empfangen	empfinge
	empfängt			
empfehlen	empfiehlst	empfahl	empfohlen	empföhle
	empfiehlt			
empfinden	empfindest	empfand	empfunden	empfände
	empfindet			
erbleichen	erbleichst	erbleichte *or*	erbleicht *or*	erbleichte
	erbleicht	erblich	erblichen	erbliche
erlöschen	erlischst	erlosch	erloschen	erlösche
	erlischt			
erschrecken	erschrickst	erschrak	erschrocken	erschäke
	erschrickt			
erwägen	erwägst	erwog	erwogen	erwöge
	erwägt			
essen	isst	aß	gegessen	ässe
	isst			
fahren	fährst	fuhr	gefahren	führe
	fährt			
fallen	fällst	fiel	gefallen	fiele
	fällt			
fangen	fängst	fing	gefangen	finge
	fängt			
fechten	fichtest	focht	gefochten	föchte
	ficht			
finden	findest	fand	gefunden	fände
	findet			
flechten	flichtest	flocht	geflochten	flöchte
	flicht			
fliegen	fliegst	flog	geflogen	flöge
	fliegt			

INDICATIVE				SUBJUNCTIVE
Infinitive	**Present**	**Past**	**Past Participle**	**Imperfect**
fliehen	fliehst flieht	floh	geflohen	flöhe
fließen	fließt fließt	floss	geflossen	flösse
fressen	frisst frisst	fraß	gefressen	frässe
frieren	frierst friert	fror	gefroren	fröre
gären	gärst gärt	gor	gegoren	göre
gebären	gebierst gebiert	gebar	geboren	gebäre
geben	gibst gibt	gab	gegeben	gäbe
gedeihen	gedeihst gedeiht	gedieh	gediehen	gediehe
gehen	gehst geht	ging	gegangen	ginge
gelten	giltst gilt	galt	gegolten	gälte *or* gölte
genesen	genest genest	genas	genesen	genäse
genießen	genießt genießt	genoss	genossen	genösse
geraten	gerätst gerät	geriet	geraten	geriete
gewinnen	gewinnst gewinnt	gewann	gewonnen	gewänne *or* gewönne
gießen	gießt gießt	goss	gegossen	gösse
gleichen	gleichst gleicht	glich	geglichen	gliche

| INDICATIVE | | | | SUBJUNCTIVE |
Infinitive	Present	Past	Past Participle	Imperfect
gleiten	gleitest gleitet	glitt	geglitten	glitte
glimmen	glimmst glimmt	glomm *or* glimmte	geglommen *or* geglimmt	glömme *or* glimmte
graben	gräbst gräbt	grub	gegraben	grübe
greifen	greifst greift	griff	gegriffen	griffe
haben	hast hat	hatte	gehabt	hätte
halten	hältst hält	hielt	gehalten	hielte
hangen	hängst hängt	hing	gehangen	hinge
hauen	haust haut	hieb	gehauen	hiebe
heben	hebst hebt	hob	gehoben	höbe
heißen	heißt heißt	hieß	geheißen	hieße
helfen	hilfst hilft	half	geholfen	hülfe
kennen	kennst kennt	kannte	gekannt	kennte
klimmen	klimmst klimmt	klomm *or* klimmte	geklommen *or* geklimmt	klömme *or* klimmte
klingen	klingst klingt	klang	geklungen	klänge
kneifen	kneifst kneift	kniff	gekniffen	kniffe
kommen	kommst kommt	kam	gekommen	käme

INDICATIVE				SUBJUNCTIVE
Infinitive	**Present**	**Past**	**Past Participle**	**Imperfect**
können	kannst	konnte	gekonnt	könnte
	kann			
kriechen	kriechst	kroch	gekrochen	kröche
	kriecht			
laden	lädst *or* ladest	lud *or*	geladen *or*	lüde *or*
	lädt *or* ladet	ladete	geladet	ladete
lassen	lässt	ließ	gelassen	ließe
	lässt			
laufen	läufst	lief	gelaufen	liefe
	läuft			
leiden	leidest	litt	gelitten	litte
	leidet			
leihen	leihst	lieh	geliehen	liehe
	leiht			
lesen	liest	las	gelesen	läse
	liest			
liegen	liegst	lag	gelegen	läge
	liegt			
lügen	lügst	log	gelogen	löge
	lügt			
mahlen	mahlst	mahlte	gemahlen	mahlte
	mahlt			
meiden	meidest	mied	gemieden	miede
	meidet			
melken	melkst	melkte	gemelkt *or*	mölke
	melkt		gemolken (*adjective*)	
messen	misst	maß	gemessen	mässe
	misst			
mögen	magst	mochte	gemocht	möchte
	mag			
müssen	musst	musste	gemusst	müsste
	muss			

INDICATIVE				*SUBJUNCTIVE*
Infinitive	**Present**	**Past**	**Past Participle**	**Imperfect**
nehmen	nimmst	nahm	genommen	nähme
	nimmt			
nennen	nennst	nannte	genannt	nennte
	nennt			
pfeifen	pfeifst	pfiff	gepfiffen	pfiffe
	pfeift			
pflegen	pflegst	pflegte *or*	gepflegt *or*	pflegte *or*
	pflegt	pflog	gepflogen	pflöge
preisen	preist	pries	gepriesen	priese
	preist			
quellen	quillst	quoll	gequollen	quölle
	quillt			
raten	rätst	riet	geraten	riete
	rät			
reiben	reibst	rieb	gerieben	riebe
	reibt			
reißen	reißt	riss	gerissen	risse
	reißt			
reiten	reitest	ritt	geritten	ritte
	reitet			
rennen	rennst	rannte	gerannt	rennte
	rennt			
riechen	riechst	roch	gerochen	röche
	riecht			
ringen	ringst	rang	gerungen	ränge
	ringt			
rinnen	rinnst	rann	geronnen	rönne
	rinnt			
rufen	rufst	rief	gerufen	riefe
	ruft			
salzen	salzt	salzte	gesalzt *or*	salzte
	salzt		gesalzen (*figurative*)	

	INDICATIVE			SUBJUNCTIVE
Infinitive	**Present**	**Past**	**Past Participle**	**Imperfect**
saufen	säufst säuft	soff	gesoffen	söffe
saugen	saugst saugt	sog	gesogen	söge
schaffen	schaffst schafft	schuf	geschaffen	schüfe
schallen	schallst schallt	schallte	geschallt	schallte *or* schölle
scheiden	scheidest scheidet	schied	geschieden	schiede
scheinen	scheinst scheint	schien	geschienen	schiene
schelten	schiltst schilt	schalt	gescholten	schölte
scheren	schierst schiert	schor *or* scherte	geschoren *or* geschert	schöre *or* scherte
schieben	schiebst schiebt	schob	geschoben	schöbe
schießen	schießt schießt	schoss	geschossen	schösse
schinden	schindest schindet	schund	geschunden	schünde
schlafen	schläfst schläft	schlief	geschlafen	schliefe
schlagen	schlägst schlägt	schlug	geschlagen	schlüge
schleichen	schleichst schleicht	schlich	geschlichen	schliche
schleifen	schleifst schleift	schliff	geschliffen	schliffe
schleißen	schleißt schleißt	schliss	geschlissen	schlisse

INDICATIVE				SUBJUNCTIVE
Infinitive	**Present**	**Past**	**Past Participle**	**Imperfect**
schliefen	schliefst schlieft	schloff	geschloffen	schlöffe
schließen	schließt schließt	schloss	geschlossen	schlösse
schlingen	schlingst schlingt	schlang	geschlungen	schlänge
schmeißen	schmeißt schmeißt	schmiss	geschmissen	schmisse
schmelzen	schmilzt schmilzt	schmolz	geschmolzen	schmölze
schneiden	schneidest schneidet	schnitt	geschnitten	schnitte
schrecken	schrickst schrickt	schrak	geschrocken	schräke
schreiben	schreibst schreibt	schrieb	geschrieben	schriebe
schreien	schreist schreit	schrie	geschrieen	schriee
schreiten	schreitest schreitet	schritt	geschritten	schritte
schweigen	schweigst schweigt	schwieg	geschwiegen	schwiege
schwellen	schwillst schwillt	schwoll	geschwollen	schwölle
schwimmen	schwimmst schwimmt	schwamm	geschwommen	schwömme
schwinden	schwindest schwindet	schwand	geschwunden	schwände
schwingen	schwingst schwingt	schwang	geschwungen	schwänge
schwören	schwörst schwört	schwur	geschworen	schwüre

	INDICATIVE			SUBJUNCTIVE
Infinitive	**Present**	**Past**	**Past Participle**	**Imperfect**
sehen	siehst sieht	sah	gesehen	sähe
sein	bin bist ist sind seid sind	war	gewesen	wäre
senden	sendest sendet	sandte *or* sendete	gesandt *or* gesendet	sendete
sieden	siedest siedet	sott *or* siedete	gesotten	sötte *or* siedete
singen	singst singt	sang	gesungen	sänge
sinken	sinkst sinkt	sank	gesunken	sänke
sinnen	sinnst sinnt	sann	gesonnen	sänne
sitzen	sitzt sitzt	saß	gesessen	sässe
sollen	sollst soll	sollte	gesollt	sollte
spalten	spaltest spaltet	spaltete	gespalten *or* gespaltet	spaltete
speien	speist speit	spie	gespieen	spiee
spinnen	spinnst spinnt	spann	gesponnen	spönne
spleißen	spleißt spleißt	spliss	gesplissen	splisse
sprechen	sprichst spricht	sprach	gesprochen	spräche
sprießen	sprießt sprießt	spross	gesprossen	sprösse
springen	springst springt	sprang	gesprungen	spränge

	INDICATIVE			SUBJUNCTIVE
Infinitive	**Present**	**Past**	**Past Participle**	**Imperfect**
stechen	stichst sticht	stach	gestochen	stäche
stecken	steckst steckt	steckte *or* stak	gesteckt	steckte *or* stäke
stehen	stehst steht	stand	gestanden	stünde *or* stände
stehlen	stiehlst stiehlt	stahl	gestohlen	stöhle
steigen	steigst steigt	stieg	gestiegen	stiege
sterben	stirbst stirbt	starb	gestorben	stürbe
stieben	sticbst stiebt	stob *or* stiebte	gestoben *or* gestiebt	stöbe *or* stiebte
stinken	stinkst stinkt	stank	gestunken	stänke
stoßen	stößt stößt	stieß	gestoßen	stieße
streichen	streichst streicht	strich	gestrichen	striche
streiten	streitest streitet	stritt	gestritten	stritte
tragen	trägst trägt	trug	getragen	trüge
treffen	triffst trifft	traf	getroffen	träfe
treiben	treibst treibt	trieb	getrieben	triebe
treten	trittst tritt	trat	getreten	träte
triefen	triefst trieft	troff	getrieft	tröffe

INDICATIVE				SUBJUNCTIVE
Infinitive	**Present**	**Past**	**Past Participle**	**Imperfect**
trinken	trinkst trinkt	trank	getrunken	tränke
tun	tue tust tut tun tut tun	tat	getan	täte
verderben	verdirbst verdirbt	verdarb	verdorben	verdürbe
verdrießen	verdrießt	verdross	verdrossen	verdrösse
vergessen	vergisst vergisst	vergaß	vergessen	vergässe
verhehlen	verhehlst verhehlt	verhelte	verhehlt *or* verhohlen	verhelte
verlieren	verlierst verliert	verlor	verloren	verlöre
verwirren	verwirrst verwirrt	verwirrte	verwirrt *or* verworren (*adjective*)	verwirrte
wachsen	wächst wächst	wuchs	gewachsen	wüchse
wägen	wägst wägt	wog *or* wägte	gewogen	wöge *or* wägte
waschen	wäschst wäscht	wusch	gewaschen	wüsche
weichen	weichst weicht	wich	gewichen	wiche
weisen	weist weist	wies	gewiesen	wiese
wenden	wendest wendet	wandte *or* wendete	gewandt *or* gewendet	wendete
werben	wirbst wirbt	warb	geworben	würbe
werden	wirst wird	wurde	geworden	würde
werfen	wirfst wirft	warf	geworfen	würfe

INDICATIVE				SUBJUNCTIVE
Infinitive	**Present**	**Past**	**Past Participle**	**Imperfect**
wiegen	wiegst wiegt	wog	gewogen	wöge
winden	windest windet	wand	gewunden	wände
wissen	weißt weiß	wusste	gewusst	wüsste
wollen	willst will	wollte	gewollt	wollte
zeihen	zeihst zeiht	zieh	geziehen	ziehe
ziehen	ziehst zieht	zog	gezogen	zöge
zwingen	zwingst zwingt	zwang	gezwungen	zwänge

Some irregular verbs are used in impersonal expressions and are conjugated only with the third person.

INDICATIVE				SUBJUNCTIVE
Infinitive	**Present**	**Past**	**Past Participle**	**Imperfect**
dünken	dünkt *or* deucht	deuchte *or* dünkte	gedeucht *or* gedünkt	deuchte *or* dünkte
gelingen	gelingt	gelang	gelungen	gelänge
geschehen	geschieht	geschah	geschehen	geschähe
misslingen	misslingt	misslang	misslungen	misslänge
schwären	schwärt *or* schwiert	schwor	geschworen	schwöre
verschallen	verschillt	verscholl	verschollen	verschölle

Answer Key

Chapter 1 Pronunciation and Cognates
Review Quiz 1

1. b   2. a   3. a   4. d   5. d   6. c   7. a   8. c   9. a   10. d

Chapter 2 Gender and *heißen*
Exercise 2.1

(Sample answers are provided.)

1. Bruder   2. Vater   3. Tag   4. Auf   5. Onkel   6. Ihre Mutter   7. Peter   8. ist
9. Berlin   10. Mein

Exercise 2.2

1. der Onkel Ihr Onkel mein Onkel   2. die Tante Ihre Tante meine Tante   3. die Tasche Ihre Tasche meine Tasche   4. der Wagen Ihr Wagen mein Wagen   5. die Lehrerin Ihre Lehrerin meine Lehrerin   6. der Mantel Ihr Mantel mein Mantel   7. die Schwester Ihre Schwester meine Schwester   8. der Sohn Ihr Sohn mein Sohn   9. die Tochter Ihre Tochter meine Tochter

Exercise 2.3

1. die Mutter Ihre Mutter meine Mutter   2. das Buch Ihr Buch mein Buch   3. der Pilot Ihr Pilot mein Pilot   4. das Röslein Ihr Röslein mein Röslein   5. das Geld Ihr Geld mein Geld   6. der Jurist Ihr Jurist mein Jurist   7. die Lehrerin Ihre Lehrerin meine Lehrerin   8. die Tante Ihre Tante meine Tante   9. die Schwester Ihre Schwester meine Schwester   10. das Auto Ihr Auto mein Auto

Exercise 2.4

(Sample answers are provided.)

1. ist   2. heißen   3. Schwester   4. Ihr   5. Haus   6. Bruder   7. Wo   8. Ich
9. Student   10. Sie

Review Quiz 2

1. c   2. a   3. a   4. b   5. b   6. d   7. a   8. b   9. d   10. a

Chapter 3   Nominative Pronouns, *der*-Words, and the Verb *sein*

Exercise 3.1

1. sie   2. es   3. er   4. er   5. sie   6. es   7. es   8. sie   9. er   10. sie

Exercise 3.2

1. Der Mann ist jung.   2. Die Straße ist lang.   3. Das Auto ist rot.   4. Der Mantel
ist neu.   5. Die Vase ist schwarz.   6. Das Kleid ist klein.   7. Der Lehrer ist groß.
8. Die Bluse ist gelb.   9. Das Hemd ist blau.   10. Der Rock ist weiß.

Exercise 3.3

1. Wagen	der	welcher	dieser	jener	jeder
2. Küche	die	welche	diese	jene	jede
3. Mantel	der	welcher	dieser	jener	jeder
4. Bluse	die	welche	diese	jene	jede
5. Buch	das	welches	dieses	jenes	jedes
6. Garten	der	welcher	dieser	jener	jeder
7. Rock	der	welcher	dieser	jener	jeder
8. Bleistift	der	welcher	dieser	jener	jeder
9. Schule	die	welche	diese	jene	jede
10. Kind	das	welches	dieses	jenes	jedes

Exercise 3.4

1. Welche Farbe hat das Hemd? Es ist blau.   2. Welche Farbe hat die Bluse? Sie ist
grün.   3. Welche Farbe hat der Fotoapparat? Er ist schwarz.   4. Welche Farbe hat der
Wagen? Er ist rot.   5. Welche Farbe hat die Vase? Sie ist gelb.

Exercise 3.5

1. Seid   2. bin   3. ist   4. bist   5. sind   6. sind   7. sind
8. seid   9. Bist   10. Sind

Review Quiz 3

1. b   2. a   3. d   4. b   5. c   6. b   7. a   8. d   9. a   10. b

Chapter 4   *Ein*-Words, *haben*, and the Present Tense
Exercise 4.1

1. ein Student   2. eine Landkarte   3. eine CD   4. ein Mädchen   5. ein Stuhl
6. ein Tier   7. eine Stadt   8. eine Bibliothek   9. ein Telefon   10. ein Bleistift

Exercise 4.2

1. ein Student; der unser   2. die Landkarte; die seine   3. die CD; die deine   4. das
Kleid; das Ihr   5. der Stuhl; der ihr   6. das Tier; das ihr   7. die Stadt; die eure   8. die
Bibliothek; die unsere   9. das Telefon; das mein   10. der Bleistift; der dein

Exercise 4.3

1. hat   2. haben   3. habe   4. hat   5. Hast   6. Haben   7. Haben   8. hat
9. Haben   10. hat   11. Hat   12. Habt   13. hast   14. haben   15. habe

Exercise 4.4

1. seid   2. Hören   3. gehe   4. fliegen   5. Kaufst   6. verkauft   7. schreibt
8. trinkt   9. Versteht   10. lernen

Review Quiz 4

1. b   2. b   3. d   4. a   5. b   6. d   7. a   8. a   9. d   10. b

Chapter 5   Irregular Present Tense and *werden*
Exercise 5.1

1. geht   2. fahre   3. läuft   4. bin   5. fahren   6. kommt   7. hat   8. Läufst
9. kommen   10. Fahrt   11. hat   12. Ist   13. komme   14. fährst   15. läuft

Exercise 5.2

1. fährt   2. spricht   3. Kommt   4. Siehst   5. isst   6. Hat   7. geschieht   8. Lesen
9. empfiehlt   10. Habt   11. befiehlt   12. gebe   13. helfen   14. vergisst   15. essen

Exercise 5.3

1. Heute   2. wird   3. wird es   4. donnert   5. sie   6. Im Winter   7. krank
8. wieder   9. schneit   10. es

Exercise 5.4

1. Wie viel ist zwanzig weniger/minus acht? Zwanzig weniger/minus acht ist
zwölf.   2. Wie viel ist acht plus/und drei? Acht plus/und drei ist elf.   3. Wie viel ist
neunzehn weniger/minus achtzehn? Neunzehn weniger/minus achtzehn ist eins.
4. Wie viel ist drei plus/und vier? Drei plus/und vier ist sieben.   5. Wie viel ist
siebzehn weniger/minus fünfzehn? Siebzehn weniger/minus fünfzehn ist zwei.

Review Quiz 5

1. c   2. a   3. d   4. a   5. b   6. b   7. d   8. b   9. c   10. d

Chapter 6   Accusative Case: Direct Objects and Prepositions

Exercise 6.1

1. Was kaufe ich?   2. Wen besucht mein Bruder?   3. Wen hat Erik gern?   4. Was
küsst der Herr?   5. Was brauchen wir?   6. Was isst die Frau?   7. Wen sehen wir?
8. Was besuchen die Mädchen?   9. Wen besuchen sie?   10. Was trinke ich?

Exercise 6.2

1. Wer verkauft dieses Auto?   2. Wer verkauft diesen Wagen?   3. Meine Mutter
schreibt keine Postkarte.   4. Meine Mutter schreibt keinen Brief.   5. Die Männer
bauen eine Schule.   6. Die Männer bauen ein Theater.   7. Die Kinder verstehen
diesen Arzt nicht.   8. Die Kinder verstehen diese Lehrerin nicht.   9. Wir besuchen
unsere Tante in Österreich.   10. Wir besuchen unseren Sohn in Österreich.

Exercise 6.3

1. mich   2. uns   3. ihr   4. Sie   5. dich   6. wen   7. sie   8. ihn   9. es   10. ich

Exercise 6.4

1. Der Amerikaner arbeitet für mich. 2. Der Amerikaner arbeitet für deine Schwester. 3. Warum kommen die Jungen ohne dich? 4. Warum kommen die Jungen ohne den Sportler? 5. Niemand ist gegen uns. 6. Niemand ist gegen unsere Tochter. 7. Das Mädchen läuft durch das Haus. 8. Das Mädchen läuft durch die Straße. 9. Der Mann bittet um den Wein. 10. Der Mann bittet um ein Geschenk. 11. Was hast du für sie? 12. Was hast du für diese Dame? 13. Herr Braun kommt ohne sie. 14. Herr Braun kommt ohne seine Freundin. 15. Warum bitten Sie um einen Bleistift?

Exercise 6.5

1. die Brüder 2. die Onkel 3. der Junge 4. der Amerikaner 5. die Mäntel 6. der Brief 7. die Bleistifte 8. die Wagen 9. die Flüsse 10. der Schuh 11. die Männer 12. der Pullover 13. die Jungen 14. die Freunde 15. der Dieb

Review Quiz 6

1. b 2. c 3. a 4. a 5. a 6. d 7. d 8. c 9. c 10. a

Mastery Check 1

1. b 2. a 3. b 4. a 5. a 6. b 7. d 8. b 9. d 10. a 11. a 12. b 13. c 14. b 15. d 16. a 17. a 18. c 19. d 20. a 21. b 22. a 23. d 24. c 25. b

Chapter 7   Regular Past Tense and Interrogative Words

Exercise 7.1

1. machte 2. fragte 3. sagten 4. verkauftet 5. kauften 6. suchte 7. hörten 8. besuchte 9. reisten 10. wohntest

Exercise 7.2

1. Was machte Ihre Freundin? 2. Wir arbeiteten in Heidelberg. 3. Thomas spielte gern Fußball. 4. Wohntest du in München? 5. Meine Eltern hörten Radio. 6. Die alte Dame redete kein Wort. 7. Im Winter reiste seine Familie nach Italien. 8. Die Kinder lernten Mathematik. 9. Suchten Sie den Bahnhof? 10. Was bauten die Männer?

Exercise 7.3

1. Gestern warteten wir an der Ecke.   2. Gestern zeigten sie Frau Bauer den Wagen.   3. Die Eltern reisten nach Hamburg.   4. Vor einer Woche regnete es jeden Tag.   5. Vor drei Monaten wohnten Thomas und Tina in Berlin.

Exercise 7.4

1. Er verkaufte das Fahrrad, denn das Fahrrad ist alt.   2. Er fotografiert das Mädchen, denn das Mädchen ist schön.   3. Die Blumen kosten zwanzig Euro, denn die Blumen sind teuer.   4. Sie reiste nach Paris, denn ihre Freunde wohnten in Frankreich.   5. Sie versteht uns nicht, denn sie ist Amerikanerin.

Exercise 7.5

1. Wann besuchte er seinen Onkel in Hamburg?   2. Wann fahren sie gern in die Alpen?   3. Wie geht es Frau Schneider?   4. Wer lehrte Deutsch hier?   5. Wohin reisten viele Studenten?   6. Woher kommen die Touristen?   7. Warum ist Ihre Mutter heute zu Hause?   8. Wen fotografierte Martin?   9. Was möchten wir kaufen?
10. Für wen arbeitete unser Vater?

Exercise 7.6

1. die Touristinnen   2. die Frauen   3. die Bluse   4. die Schwestern   5. die Tante
6. die Zeitungen   7. die Uhren   8. die Postkarte   9. die Straßen   10. die Mütter

Exercise 7.7

(*Sample answers are provided.*)

1. MONIKA: Er ist zu Hause.   2. MONIKA: Nein, ich besuchte meine Tante.
3. MARTIN: Wie viele Brüder hast du?   4. MARTIN: Möchtest du nach Amerika reisen?   5. MARTIN: Das stimmt.

Review Quiz 7

1. a   2. d   3. a   4. b   5. d   6. b   7. a   8. b   9. d   10. b

Chapter 8   Irregular Past Tense and Neuter Plurals
Exercise 8.1

1. ich	trank	verstand	kam	hieß
2. du	trankst	verstandest	kamst	hießt
3. er	trank	verstand	kam	hieß

4. wir	tranken	verstanden	kamen	hießen
5. ihr	trankt	verstandet	kamt	hießt
6. Sie	tranken	verstanden	kamen	hießen
7. sie *pl.*	tranken	verstanden	kamen	hießen
8. Erik	trank	verstand	kam	hieß
9. wer	trank	verstand	kam	hieß
10. sie *s.*	trank	verstand	kam	hieß

Exercise 8.2

1. schrieb   2. verstanden   3. sangen   4. ging   5. hieß   6. Batest   7. Trankt
8. fuhr   9. flog   10. bekamen

Exercise 8.3

1. Ihr Geburtstag ist im Herbst.   2. Ihr Geburtstag ist am Dienstag.   3. Ihr Geburtstag ist im Januar.   4. Wo wohntet ihr im Oktober?   5. Wo wohntet ihr im Sommer?
6. Wo wohntet ihr (im Jahre) 2010?   7. Mein Sohn ist am Montag geboren.   8. Mein Sohn ist im Dezember geboren.   9. Ich besuchte meine Familie im Frühling.   10. Ich besuchte meine Familie im März.

Exercise 8.4

1. Er fragt, wer jetzt zwanzig Jahre alt ist.   2. Er fragt, wessen Bruder in der Schweiz wohnt.   3. Er fragt, wie diese Mädchen heißen.   4. Er fragt, wen die Touristen in München besuchten.   5. Er fragt, wie alt deine Tochter ist.   6. Er fragt, wann Sie nach Hause fahren möchten.   7. Er fragt, wohin die Jungen liefen.   8. Er fragt, was zweihundert Euro kostet.   9. Er fragt, woher diese Männer kamen.   10. Er fragt, wann ihr Geburtstag ist.

Exercise 8.5

1. Diese Länder sind sehr weit von hier.   2. Die Mädchen liefen sehr schnell.
3. Wo sind deine Häuser?   4. Sind die Theater an der Ecke neu?   5. Diese Bücher sind sehr alt.   6. Meine Hemden sind rot und weiß.   7. Die Kinder spielen im Garten.   8. Diese Büchlein sind alt.   9. Ihre Gesichter sind nicht schön.   10. Sind diese Lieder alt?

Review Quiz 8

1. b   2. b   3. c   4. d   5. a   6. a   7. b   8. c   9. b   10. a

Chapter 9   Dative Case and More Irregular Past Tense

Exercise 9.1

1. meiner Frau   2. seiner Schwester   3. Ihren Eltern   4. dem Mann   5. den Jungen
6. der Lehrerin   7. dem Richter   8. seinem Sohn   9. ihren Freundinnen   10. dem Geburtstagskind

Exercise 9.2

1. Wir kauften euren Kindern neue Handschuhe.   2. Wir kauften unserem Sohn neue Handschuhe.   3. Wir kauften der Dame neue Handschuhe.   4. Erik gibt seiner Freundin ein Geschenk.   5. Erik gibt dem Geburtstagskind ein Geschenk.
6. Erik gibt seinem Professor ein Geschenk.   7. Was schickten Sie Ihrer Tochter?
8. Was schickten Sie Ihren Eltern?   9. Was schickten Sie Ihrem Gast?   10. Was schickten Sie dem Mädchen?

Exercise 9.3

1. Was kaufen Sie mir?   2. Was kaufen Sie ihm?   3. Was kaufen Sie ihnen?
4. Der Kellner bringt dir eine Flasche Wein.   5. Der Kellner bringt ihr eine Flasche Wein.   6. Der Kellner bringt euch eine Flasche Wein.   7. Gibst du uns genug Geld?   8. Gibst du ihnen genug Geld?   9. Gibst du mir genug Geld?   10. Gibst du ihm genug Geld?

Exercise 9.4

1. Seine Eltern arbeiten bei einer Bank.   2. Seine Eltern arbeiten bei dieser Firma.
3. Seine Eltern arbeiten bei der Bahn.   4. Meine Großmutter sprach oft von ihrem Mann.   5. Meine Großmutter sprach oft von euch.   6. Meine Großmutter sprach oft von ihnen.   7. Die Kinder liefen aus dem Haus.   8. Die Kinder liefen aus der Schule.   9. Die Kinder liefen aus dem Kino.   10. Fahren Sie oft mit dem Bus?
11. Fahren Sie oft mit diesem Zug?   12. Fahren Sie oft mit Ihrem Auto?   13. Heute Abend gehen wir zu dem Arzt.   14. Heute Abend gehen wir zu unseren Eltern.
15. Heute Abend gehen wir zu einem Freund.

Exercise 9.5

1. Angela war eine alte Freundin von mir.   2. Hatte er viele Geschwister?   3. Im Winter wurde es sehr kalt.   4. Ich war leider wieder krank.   5. Sie hatte zwei Schwestern und einen Bruder.   6. Herr Schneider wurde Zahnarzt.   7. Warst du reich?   8. Der reiche Herr wurde arm.   9. Wart ihr im Esszimmer oder im Wohnzimmer?   10. Hatten Sie keine Zeit, Frau Schäfer?

Exercise 9.6

1. er	kennt	kannte
2. wir	kennen	kannten
3. sie *s.*	kennt	kannte
4. die Jungen	kennt	kannte
5. Sie	kennen	kannten
6. ich	weiß	wusste
7. ihr	wisst	wusstet
8. du	weißt	wusstest
9. sie *pl.*	wissen	wussten
10. wer	weiß	wusste

Review Quiz 9

1. c   2. a   3. a   4. a   5. d   6. b   7. a   8. b   9. d   10. c

Chapter 10   Dative Expressions and Conjunctions *aber, oder, und,* and *sondern*

Exercise 10.1

1. Ihnen   2. ihr   3. dem   Gastgeber   4. dem Hund   5. einer Katze   6. ihnen
7. den Lehrerinnen   8. euch   9. dir   10. diesen Männern

Exercise 10.2

1. Wir putzen uns die Nase.   2. Sie putzen sich die Nase.   3. Das Kind putzt sich die Nase.   4. Die Kinder waschen sich das Gesicht.   5. Du wäschst dich das Gesicht.   6. Man wäscht sich das Gesicht.   7. Mein Sohn wäscht sich das Gesicht.   8. Ihr brecht euch die Hände.   9. Sie brechen sich die Hände.
10. Wer bricht sich die Hände?

Exercise 10.3

1. Mein Bruder arbeitet bei einer Bank und meine Schwester arbeitet für einen Arzt.   2. Das Wetter war gut und die Kinder spielten im Park.   3. Hans spricht Italienisch, aber er versteht die Touristen nicht.   4. Ich wartete an der Ecke, aber kein Bus kam.   5. Tina möchte ins Kino gehen, aber sie hat nicht genug Geld.
6. Wart ihr in der Stadt, oder besuchet ihr Monika im Dorf?   7. Jeden Tag spielten

die Kinder Tennis, oder sie gingen ins Kino.   8. Dein Freund ist nicht klug, sondern er ist sehr dumm.   9. Andreas spricht kein Englisch, sondern er kann Russisch und Spanisch.   10. Nicht er tut es, sondern sie tut es.

Exercise 10.4

1. Karin kann so schön singen.   2. Können Sie mir zehn Euro geben?   3. Kannst du gut Schach spielen?   4. Die Studentinnen können im Fluss schwimmen.   5. Niemand kann diese Leute verstehen.   6. Muss man an einer Universität studieren?   7. Du musst ein bisschen lauter sprechen.   8. Andreas muss spät kommen.   9. Müsst ihr diesen alten Leuten helfen?   10. Ich muss dem kranken Mann ein Glas Wasser bringen.

Exercise 10.5

1. Wir mussten am Montag nach Hause fahren.   2. Konnte Erik Geige spielen? 3. Hans und Tina müssen vier Tage warten.   4. Hoffentlich konnte der Mann euch helfen.   5. Musstest du eine Woche in Russland bleiben?   6. Tina kann uns dreißig Euro geben.   7. Warum müssen wir nach London reisen?   8. Musstet ihr den alten Volkswagen verkaufen?   9. Ich konnte nur ein Jahr in Hamburg studieren.   10. Konnten Sie ihnen ein paar Briefe schreiben?

Review Quiz 10

1. d   2. a   3. a   4. c   5. b   6. a   7. b   8. d   9. b   10. c

Chapter 11   Regular Present Perfect Tense

Exercise 11.1

1. gefragt   2. gelacht   3. gewartet   4. gestellt   5. gedankt   6. geantwortet 7. geschmeckt   8. gelernt   9. gelehrt   10. gekauft   11. gehört   12. gedeckt 13. gebadet   14. geglaubt   15. gekostet

Exercise 11.2

1. Haben die Würstchen gut geschmeckt?   2. Ich habe spät am Abend gebadet. 3. Haben Sie einen alten BMW gekauft?   4. Was hat Frau Schneider geantwortet? 5. Tina und Hans haben den Tisch gedeckt.   6. Meine Freunde haben laut gelacht. 7. Wohin hat sie die Lampe gestellt?   8. Hat man viel Geld gebraucht?   9. Der Professor hat mit uns geredet.   10. Was hat Frau Braun gelehrt?

Exercise 11.3

1. Die Suppe hat wunderbar geschmeckt.   2. Am Montag sind wir nach Hause gereist.   3. Die Kinder sind zum Park marschiert.   4. Der kranke Mann hat nicht geantwortet.   5. Karl ist mit dem Zug gefahren.   6. Wann bist du ins Restaurant gekommen?   7. Wer hat den Tisch gedeckt?   8. Wohin sind sie gereist?   9. Die Soldaten sind durch die Stadt marschiert.   10. Im Sommer sind wir nach Holland gefahren.

Exercise 11.4

1. PAST: Wir lernten Italienisch. PRESENT PERFECT: Wir haben Italienisch gelernt.
2. PRESENT: Martin fährt in die Stadt. PRESENT PERFECT: Martin ist in die Stadt gefahren.   3. PAST: Die Soldaten marschierten durch einen Tunnel. PRESENT PERFECT: Die Soldaten sind durch einen Tunnel marschiert.   4. PRESENT: Wann kommt Frau Becker nach Hause? PAST: Wann kam Frau Becker nach Hause?   5. PAST: Wie oft reistest du in die Schweiz? PRESENT PERFECT: Wie oft bist du in die Schweiz gereist?

Exercise 11.5

1. elfte   2. vierundzwanzigste   3. erste   4. zweite   5. dreißigste   6. vierten
7. dreizehnten   8. dritten   9. ersten   10. fünften

Exercise 11.6

1. PAST: Wer beantwortete die Frage? PRESENT PERFECT: Wer hat die Frage beantwortet?
2. PAST: Die rote Bluse gehörte ihr. PRESENT PERFECT: Die rote Bluse hat ihr gehört.
3. PAST: Mein Nachbar versuchte es zu verstehen. PRESENT PERFECT: Mein Nachbar hat versucht es zu verstehen.   4. PAST: Tina errötete vor Scham. PRESENT PERFECT: Tina ist vor Scham errötet.   5. PAST: Sie entfernten meinen Sohn aus der Schule. PRESENT PERFECT: Sie haben meinen Sohn aus der Schule entfernt.

Exercise 11.7

(Sample answers are provided.)

1. TINA: Nein, ich bin mit der Straßenbahn gefahren.   2. HERR BRAUN: Haben Sie sein neues Buch gekauft?   3. SONJA: Ich habe mein Auto hier gekauft.

Review Quiz 11

1. b   2. c   3. d   4. a   5. a   6. b   7. b   8. a   9. a   10. c

Chapter 12   Adjective Endings and Separable Prefixes
Exercise 12.1
(Sample answers are provided.)

1. Ihre Kinder sind sehr müde.   2. Früh am Morgen ist die Sonne hell.   3. In der Nacht war mein Schlafzimmer dunkel.   4. Nach ein paar Wochen wurde sie wieder krank.   5. Meine Nachbarn waren immer nett.   6. Warum bist du so stark?   7. Am Nachmittag ist der Himmel oft blau.   8. Ihre Söhne sehen blass aus.   9. Seid ihr froh?   10. Man muss immer fleißig sein.

Exercise 12.2

1. dunkle   2. sauber   3. schöne   4. stille   5. komischen   6. fleißige   7. kalten   8. krank   9. schwach   10. hässliche

Exercise 12.3

1. die erste Frage   2. diese schönen Damen   3. den letzten Satz   4. jene langen Sätze   5. Welchen warmen Mantel   6. Die fleißigen Schüler   7. jeden amerikanischen Gast   8. das stille Klassenzimmer   9. jene alte Bibliothek   10. den deutschen Komponisten   11. die sauberen Handschuhe   12. die neuen Bücher   13. Jedes dunkle Hotelzimmer   14. jenen muskulösen Sportler   15. der komische Mann

Exercise 12.4

1. ich sehe aus/sah aus   2. du siehst aus/sahst aus   3. er sieht aus/sah aus   4. ihr macht zu/machtet zu   5. Sie machen zu/machten zu   6. wer macht zu/machte zu   7. wir stehen auf/standen auf   8. sie *s.* steht auf/stand auf   9. du stehst auf/standest auf   10. sie *pl.* laufen weg/liefen weg   11. ich laufe weg/lief weg   12. es läuft weg/lief weg   13. er geht zurück/ging zurück   14. ihr geht zurück/gingt zurück   15. Tina geht zurück/ging zurück

Exercise 12.5

1. Der Rechtsanwalt muss sehr spät ankommen.   2. Wir können ein paar Engländer einladen.   3. Kannst du auch mitkommen?   4. Erik musste den großen Koffer aufmachen.   5. Die Touristen aus Afrika können hier umsteigen.   6. Ich muss der jungen Lehrerin zuhören.   7. Wann mussten sie zurückgehen?   8. Das müde Kind kann schnell einschlafen.   9. Müsst ihr früh aufstehen?   10. Meine Freundin konnte am Mittwoch ankommen.

Review Quiz 12

1. c   2. a   3. a   4. a   5. d   6. b   7. c   8. b   9. b   10. d

Chapter 13   Irregular Present Perfect Tense and Prefixes

Exercise 13.1

1. du hast geschrieben   2. wir haben getrunken   3. ich habe gegeben   4. wer hat gelesen   5. ihr seid gegangen   6. niemand hat gestanden   7. das Kind hat geheißen   8. er ist gefallen   9. Erik hat gestohlen   10. ich habe gesehen   11. sie *pl.* haben getragen   12. der Sportler hat gebrochen   13. du bist gelaufen   14. Tina hat gefangen   15. die Jungen haben gesungen

Exercise 13.2

1. Wir haben ihr ein paar Blumen gebracht.   2. Ich habe es nicht gewusst.
3. Warum hat ein Licht im Wohnzimmer gebrannt?   4. Die Kinder haben langsam gegessen.   5. Wir haben diesen Matrosen gut gekannt.   6. Wohin habt ihr die Geschenke gesandt?   7. Sie haben an ihre Eltern gedacht.   8. Die Mutter hat ihren Sohn Johann genannt.   9. Wer hat diesen Artikel geschrieben?   10. Die Jungen sind in die Bibliothek gerannt.

Exercise 13.3

1. er starb, wir sind gestorben, sie *pl.* starben, ihr seid gestorben   2. ich war, du bist gewesen, Sie waren, wir sind gewesen   3. er kannte, sie hat gekannt, du kanntest, wer hat gekannt   4. er hatte, wir haben gehabt, sie *pl.* hatten, ich habe gehabt   5. ihr dachtet, er hat gedacht, sie *s.* dachte, du hast gedacht

Exercise 13.4

1. Wir sind um zehn Uhr zurückgegangen.   2. Haben Sie die Zeitung gelesen?
3. Meine Tante hat mir diesen Ring versprochen.   4. Niemand hat den russischen Matrosen gekannt.   5. Wer hat den Kuchen gegessen?   6. Viele Mädchen sind auf die Party mitgekommen.   7. Haben sie Gäste erwartet?   8. Wo sind sie umgestiegen? 9. Mein alter Hund ist gestorben.   10. Ich bin in den Alpen gewesen.   11. Im April ist es oft regnerisch geworden.   12. Habt ihr es schon gewusst?   13. Der arme Mann hat wieder Pech gehabt.   14. Um wie viel Uhr ist der Zug angekommen?   15. Diese Jungen haben meinen Garten zerstört.

Review Quiz 13

1. c   2. a   3. d   4. a   5. a   6. c   7. a   8. c   9. c   10. b

Mastery Check 2

1. d   2. d   3. b   4. a   5. d   6. b   7. a   8. a   9. a   10. b   11. a   12. c   13. b   14. c   15. d   16. a   17. b   18. b   19. a   20. a   21. c   22. c   23. a   24. d   25. a

Chapter 14   Genitive Case and Antonyms

Exercise 14.1

1. dieser Dame   2. Ihrer Kinder   3. des Hauses   4. jeder Wirtin   5. Frau Bauers
6. eines Glases   7. Sonjas   8. keiner Leute   9. meines Fahrrads   10. der Oper

Exercise 14.2

1. ausländischen   2. hübschen   3. langen   4. polnischen   5. alten   6. großen
7. musikalischen   8. reichen   9. kurzen   10. freundlichen

Exercise 14.3

1. eine Tafel Schokolade   2. ein Stück Kuchen   3. eine Scheibe Käse   4. eine Tasse
Kaffee   5. eine große Flasche Limonade   6. einen Teller Gulasch   7. eine Scheibe
Brot mit Butter   8. eine ganze Tüte Chips   9. zwei Dosen Erbsen   10. einen Korb
Äpfel

Exercise 14.4

(Sample answers are provided.)

1. eines neuen Pullovers   2. des schlechten Wetters   3. des heißen Sommers
4. einer langen Krankheit   5. unserer neuen Nachbarn   6. der regnerischen Tage
7. meines letzten Konzerts   8. des starken Windes

Exercise 14.5

1. kleine   2. langes   3. langweilig   4. gestorben   5. leise   6. zugemacht
7. hell   8. sauberes   9. weit   10. langsam

Exercise 14.6

(Sample answers are provided.)

1. Jeden Tag gehe ich mit ihr joggen.   2. Gingen Sie im Wald wandern?   3. Er ist
in den Alpen klettern gegangen.   4. Heute gehen die Kinder fischen.   5. Gingst du
auch tauchen?   6. Ich bin zum Park Fußball spielen gegangen.   7. Im Winter gehen
sie oft schlittschuhlaufen.   8. Ging Monika heute Morgen einkaufen?   9. Wir sind
am See spazieren gegangen.   10. Ich gehe um ein Uhr segeln.

Review Quiz 14

1. a   2. c   3. b   4. b   5. d   6. a   7. b   8. d   9. a   10. a

Chapter 15   Future Tense and Modal Auxiliaries
Exercise 15.1

1. Übermorgen bleibt Werner zu Hause und arbeitet. / Morgen wird Werner zu Hause bleiben und arbeiten.   2. Übermorgen verbringen wir einen ganzen Tag in der Stadt. / Morgen werden wir einen ganzen Tag in der Stadt verbringen. 3. Übermorgen zieht meine Familie nach Schweden. / Morgen wird meine Familie nach Schweden ziehen.   4. Übermorgen bekommt Stefan viele Geschenke zum Geburtstag. / Morgen wird Stefan viele Geschenke zum Geburtstag bekommen. 5. Übermorgen verkauft Vati das alte Haus im Osten. / Morgen wird Vati das alte Haus im Osten verkaufen.   6. Übermorgen landet das Flugzeug in Südafrika. / Morgen wird das Flugzeug in Südafrika landen.   7. Übermorgen gibt er seiner Frau einen teuren Ring. / Morgen wird er seiner Frau einen teuren Ring geben. 8. Übermorgen stehen die Studenten pünktlich auf. / Morgen werden die Studenten pünktlich aufstehen.   9. Übermorgen wird mein Großvater hundert Jahre alt. / Morgen wird mein Großvater hundert Jahre alt werden.   10. Übermorgen haben die Zwillinge Geburtstag. / Morgen werden die Zwillinge Geburtstag haben. 11. Übermorgen bin ich endlich im Norden in Russland. / Morgen werde ich endlich im Norden in Russland sein.   12. Übermorgen wartet der Hund vor dem Tor. / Morgen wird der Hund vor dem Tor warten.   13. Übermorgen fotografiert sie die Elefanten. / Morgen wird sie die Elefanten fotografieren.   14. Übermorgen findet jemand einen Sack Gold. / Morgen wird jemand einen Sack Gold finden. 15. Übermorgen zeigt der Direktor den Touristen die alten Bilder. / Morgen wird der Direktor den Touristen die alten Bilder zeigen.

Exercise 15.2

1. Die Soldaten marschierten durch das Dorf. / Die Soldaten sind durch das Dorf marschiert. / Die Soldaten werden durch das Dorf marschieren.   2. Wir wohnten im Nordwesten. / Wir haben im Nordwesten gewohnt. / Wir werden im Nordwesten wohnen.   3. Wo verbrachten Sie die Ferien? / Wo haben Sie die Ferien verbracht? / Wo werden Sie die Ferien verbringen?   4. Waren eure Eltern gesund? / Sind eure Eltern gesund gewesen? / Werden eure Eltern gesund sein?   5. Wie viel gab er für die Jacke aus? / Wie viel hat er für die Jacke ausgegeben? / Wie viel wird er für die Jacke ausgeben?   6. Vati schnitt ein paar Scheiben Käse ab. / Vati hat ein paar Scheiben Käse abgeschnitten. / Vati wird ein paar Scheiben Käse abschneiden.   7. Wir gingen oft im Wald wandern. / Wir sind oft im Wald wandern gegangen. / Wir werden oft im Wald wandern gehen.   8. Wann wurdest du einundzwanzig Jahre alt? / Wann bist du einundzwanzig Jahre alt geworden? / Wann wirst du einundzwanzig Jahre alt werden? 9. Spielte der Matrose Klavier? / Hat der Matrose Klavier gespielt? / Wird der Matrose Klavier spielen?   10. Zwei Flugzeuge starteten um halb acht. / Zwei Flugzeuge sind um halb acht gestartet. / Zwei Flugzeuge werden um halb acht starten.

Exercise 15.3

1. Darf er ein Stück Kuchen abschneiden?   2. Ich kann den ganzen Monat im Süden verbringen.   3. Der Tourist will sein Geld zurückbekommen.   4. Ihr Sohn mag wirklich sehr jung sein.   5. Sollst du so viel Geld ausgeben?   6. Um wie viel Uhr muss der Jumbo-Jet landen?   7. Heute mag der erste Mai sein.   8. Viele Leute können Deutsch sprechen.   9. Wollt ihr diese Jeans anprobieren?   10. Darf ich in der dritten Reihe sitzen?

Exercise 15.4

1. Sie durfte den alten Hund nicht streicheln.   2. Ich sollte meinen Verwandten damit helfen.   3. Herr Schneider mochte keinen Rotwein.   4. Musste deine Familie wirklich nach Amerika ziehen?   5. Der Verkäufer konnte ihnen damit helfen.   6. Unsere Nichte wollte Flugbegleiterin werden.   7. Durften Sie in der Parade marschieren?   8. Wir konnten ein paar Tage in der Hauptstadt verbringen.   9. Mussten die Flugzeuge sofort landen?   10. Die Studentinnen wollten hier bleiben und arbeiten.

Review Quiz 15

1. b   2. b   3. c   4. d   5. a   6. c   7. b   8. b   9. c   10. a

Chapter 16   Dependent Clauses and Conjunctions

Exercise 16.1

(Sample answers are provided.)

1. Wir waren nicht reich, aber wir waren sehr froh.   2. Musst du auf deine Freundin warten, oder kannst du jetzt einkaufen gehen?   3. Mein Bruder ist im Bett geblieben, und meine Schwester ist schwimmen gegangen.   4. Wir können an den See fahren, denn das Wetter ist wieder angenehm.   5. Wir haben die Tür nicht zugemacht, sondern wir haben sie aufgemacht.   6. Es ist heute heiß, aber es ist sehr regnerisch geworden.   7. Ich werde bei meiner Tante wohnen, oder ich werde nach Oldenburg ziehen.   8. Ich wohnte im Studentenheim, und Tina wohnte bei ihren Verwandten.   9. Max muss bis Samstag warten, denn ich habe am Wochenende Zeit.   10. Sie ist nicht mit dem Zug gefahren, sondern sie ist mit dem Bus gefahren.

Exercise 16.2

1. Als er ankam, sah er seine Frau auf dem Bahnsteig.   2. Bevor Gudrun weinte, hat er sie geküsst.   3. Bis es fünfzehn Uhr ist, habe ich drei Briefe geschrieben.   4. Nachdem sie die Fenster zumachte, hörte es auf zu regnen.   5. Seitdem ich dir eine Gitarre kaufte, spielst du gar nicht mehr.   6. Ich suchte sie im Studentenheim, während ich an der Uni

war.　7. Wir kaufen oft nichts, wenn wir einkaufen gehen.　8. Wir haben eine fremde Stimme gehört, als wir ferngesehen haben.　9. Die Eltern müssen mehr verdienen, ehe Sie eine Europareise machen können.　10. Er fand viele alte Bilder, seit sein Großvater starb.

Exercise 16.3

1. Da die Frau sehr müde ist, fährt sie sofort ins Hotel.　2. Ich lerne jeden Abend, damit ich gute Noten bekomme.　3. Mein Kollege kommt vorbei, falls er Zeit hat. 4. Obwohl der Ring sehr schön ist, ist er wirklich zu teuer.　5. Gudrun muss eine Brille tragen, weil sie nicht gut sehen kann.　6. Wir haben ihnen geholfen, in dem wir ihnen €100 (hundert Euro) gaben.　7. Soviel sie weiß, geht es ihren Verwandten noch gut.　8. Seine Romane sind nicht so schlecht, wie seine Gedichte.　9. Der Student ist vor seinen Büchern eingeschlafen, weil er sehr müde ist.　10. Der Harz ist nicht so hoch, wie die Alpen.

Exercise 16.4

(Sample answers are provided.)

1. Meine Kollegen fragen mich, ob ich das Problem verstehe.　*2.* Seine Cousine sagt, dass sie den Dom besichtigen möchte.　3. Weißt du, ob der Chef schon nach Berlin gereist ist?　4. Der Schüler antwortet, dass sein Aufsatz zu Hause ist.　5. Ich lese, dass das Wetter sehr schlecht wird.

Review Quiz 16

1. b　2. b　3. c　4. d　5. a　6. b　7. a　8. d　9. d　10. b

Chapter 17　Dative-Accusative Prepositions

Exercise 17.1

1. ihrer neuen Decke, seinen Büchern, einem braunen Korb　2. unserer neuen Schule, dem großen Einkaufszentrum, uns　3. dem hohen Fernsehturm, den schmutzigen Fenstern, mir　4. einem langen Fluss, diesem See, dem Ende der Straße　5. dem hohen Baum, der Straße, dem Dach　6. dem jungen Chef, seiner Freundin, euch　7. einer dicken Decke, diesen kleinen Betten, der Bettcouch　8. dem Arzt und der Krankenschwester, den Stühlen, uns　9. einem kleinen Zimmer, seinem Wartesaal, der dunklen Garage　10. der neuen Bibliothek, einem kleinen Berg, ihr.

Exercise 17.2

1. vor ihm   2. darin   3. daran   4. zwischen ihnen   5. darüber   6. darauf
7. vor ihm   8. darunter   9. neben ihnen   10. davor

Exercise 17.3

1. eine alte Brücke, den großen Baum, darunter   2. deine Töchter, diese hübsche
Ausländerin, sie   3. diesen Verbrecher, seine unehrlichen Verwandten, Sie   4. Ihre
Geburtstagsparty, seine nächste Rede, darauf   5. ein Stück Kuchen, eine heiße Tasse
Tee, darum   6. diesen fremden Mann, einen italienischen Matrosen, ihn   7. seine
Probleme, diesen langen Krieg, darüber   8. den starken Wind, die fremde Frau an
der Ecke, sie   9. das Gewitter, einen furchtbaren Unfall, uns   10. dieses Problem,
die neue Chefin, mich

Exercise 17.4

1. Fluss   2. Kanal   3. Meer   4. Amazonas   5. Wüste   6. Frankreich   7. Moskau
8. Norden   9. Oder   10. Frankreich   11. Gletscher   12. Liechtenstein
13. Europa   14. Wüste   15. Regenwald

Review Quiz 17

1. a   2. a   3. b   4. d   5. b   6. c   7. a   8. b   9. b   10. b

Chapter 18   Comparative and Superlative

Exercise 18.1

1. größeren   2. schönere   3. dümmerer   4. reicheren   5. stärkerer
6. komischeren   7. schnelleren   8. schlechteren   9. längeren
10. helleren

Exercise 18.2

(Sample answers are provided.)

1. Ihr seid einsamer als ich.   2. Der Kellner arbeitet langsamer als die Kellnerin.
3. Meine Tochter schreibt besser als mein Sohn.   4. Diese Straße ist länger als
Schillerstraße.   5. Der Professor redet lauter als sein Kollege.   6. Der Düsenjäger fliegt
höher als der Jumbo-Jet.   7. Der Bus kommt später als der Zug an.   8. Wir fahren
eher als unsere Eltern ab.   9. Im Januar ist das Wetter kälter als im September.
10. Thailand ist weiter als Österreich.

Exercise 18.3

1. am schmutzigsten   2. am besten   3. am schlechtesten   4. am nettesten
5. am kältesten   6. am heißesten   7. am langweiligsten   8. am hübschesten
9. am freundlichsten   10. am weitesten   11. am nächsten   12. am dümmsten
13. am dicksten   14. am größten   15. am höchsten

Exercise 18.4

1. weitesten   2. beste   3. langweiligsten   4. ehesten   5. wärmstes   6. ehrlichste
7. hübschesten   8. nächsten   9. intelligenteste   10. billigste

Review Quiz 18

1. b   2. b   3. c   4. d   5. a   6. d   7. a   8. a   9. a   10. d

Chapter 19   Imperatives and Double Infinitives

Exercise 19.1

1. Fragt! Fragen Sie!   2. Kommt mit! Kommen Sie mit!   3. Vergesst! Vergessen
Sie!   4. Seid! Seien Sie!   5. Macht zu! Machen Sie zu!   6. Empfehlt! Empfehlen
Sie!   7. Zerstört! Zerstören Sie!   8. Nehmt ein! Nehmen Sie ein!   9. Seht fern!
Sehen Sie fern!   10. Besucht! Besuchen Sie!

Exercise 19.2

1. trägst Trag(e)!   2. bekommst Bekomm(e)!   3. schläfst ein Schlaf(e) ein!   4. trinkst
Trink(e)!   5. ißt Iß!   6. liest Lies!   7. nimmst mit Nimm mit!   8. fliegst Flieg(e)!
9. beeilst dich Beeil(e) dich!   10. steigst aus Steig(e) aus!

Exercise 19.3

1. Ihr: Seid nicht so ungeduldig! Sie: Seien Sie nicht so ungeduldig!   2. Du: Besuch
uns im Dezember! Sie: Besuchen Sie uns im Dezember!   3. Du: Sprich mit dem
jungen Schriftsteller! Ihr: Sprecht mit dem jungen Schriftsteller!   4. Ihr: Fahrt um
Viertel vor elf ab! Sie: Fahren Sie um Viertel vor elf ab!   5. Du: Gib dem armen
Mann ein paar Euro! Sie: Geben Sie dem armen Mann ein paar Euro!

Exercise 19.4

1. PAST: Diese Jungen konnten nicht schwimmen. PRESENT PERFECT: Diese Jungen
haben nicht schwimmen können. FUTURE: Diese Jungen werden nicht schwimmen

können. 2. PRESENT: Die Ausländerin kann die Bibliothek benutzen. PRESENT PERFECT: Die Ausländerin hat die Bibliothek benutzen können. FUTURE: Die Ausländerin wird die Bibliothek benutzen können. 3. PRESENT: Man soll fleißiger arbeiten. PAST: Man sollte fleißiger arbeiten. FUTURE: Man wird fleißiger arbeiten sollen. 4. PRESENT: Wer will unseren Spaß verderben? PAST: Wer wollte unseren Spaß verderben? PRESENT PERFECT: Wer hat unseren Spaß verderben wollen? 5. PAST: Warum musste ich mit ihnen zusammenwohnen? PRESENT PERFECT: Warum habe ich mit ihnen zusammenwohnen müssen? FUTURE: Warum werde ich mit ihnen zusammenwohnen müssen?

Exercise 19.5

1. PAST: Ich ließ die Fenster reparieren. PRESENT PERFECT: Ich habe die Fenster reparieren lassen. FUTURE: Ich werde die Fenster reparieren lassen. 2. PRESENT: Sehen sie Tina und Max von der Kunsthalle zurückkommen? PRESENT PERFECT: Haben sie Tina und Max von der Kunsthalle zurückkommen sehen? FUTURE: Werden sie Tina und Max von der Kunsthalle zurückkommen sehen? 3. PRESENT: Wir hören die Kinder auf der Terasse flüstern. PAST: Wir hörten die Kinder auf der Terasse flüstern. FUTURE: Wir werden die Kinder auf der Terasse flüstern hören. 4. PRESENT: Wir helfen ihr nähen. PAST: Wir halfen ihr nähen. PRESENT PERFECT: Wir haben ihr nähen helfen. 5. PAST: Konnten Sie die Jugendlichen fotografieren? PRESENT PERFECT: Haben Sie die Jugendlichen fotografieren können? FUTURE: Werden Sie die Jugendlichen fotografieren können? 6. PRESENT: Ich lasse ein Bild von dem Künstler malen. PRESENT PERFECT: Ich habe ein Bild von dem Künstler malen lassen. FUTURE: Ich werde ein Bild von dem Künstler malen lassen. 7. PRESENT: Musst du das Gedicht auswendig lernen? PAST: Musstest du das Gedicht auswendig lernen? FUTURE: Wirst du das Gedicht auswendig lernen müssen? 8. PRESENT: Ihr seht die Tiere im Zoo fressen. PAST: Ihr saht die Tiere im Zoo fressen. PRESENT PERFECT: Ihr habt die Tiere im Zoo fressen sehen. 9. PAST: Niemand hörte unseren Nachbarn klopfen. PRESENT PERFECT: Niemand hat unseren Nachbarn klopfen hören. FUTURE: Niemand wird unseren Nachbarn klopfen hören. 10. PRESENT: Ich helfe ihr aufstehen. PRESENT PERFECT: Ich habe ihr aufstehen helfen. FUTURE: Ich werde ihr aufstehen helfen.

Exercise 19.6

(Sample answers are provided.)

1. MARIANNE: Nein, es ist zwanzig Uhr, und niemand ist im Lokal. 2. MAX: Danke. Endlich bin ich einundzwanzig Jahre alt. 3. HERR BAUER: Das Dach der alten Garage war kaputt.

Review Quiz 19

1. b 2. a 3. d 4. c 5. b 6. b 7. c 8. d 9. a 10. a

Chapter 20   Using All the Cases and All the Tenses

Exercise 20.1

1. O   2. S   3. DO   4. P   5. PN   6. DO   7. DO   8. O   9. S   10. S

Exercise 20.2

1. IO   2. IO   3. DV   4. IO   5. DV   6. IO   7. O   8. O   9. O   10. DV

Exercise 20.3

1. P   2. O   3. O   4. P   5. P

Exercise 20.4

1. Wir wollen dieses alte Museum besuchen.   2. Warum sind sie durch dieses alte Museum gelaufen?   3. Die Fenster dieses alten Museums sind alle kaputt.   4. Wie alt ist dieses alte Museum?   5. Hast du seinen langweiligen Roman gelesen?   6. Nach seinem langweiligen Roman will er einen interessanten Roman schreiben.   7. Wegen seines langweiligen Romans bin ich schnell eingeschlafen.   8. Sie kam ohne seinen langweiligen Roman ins Klassenzimmer.   9. Niemand wollte mit einer hässlichen Hexe sprechen.   10. Eine hässliche Hexe hat in den Bergen gewohnt.   11. Die schwarze Katze einer hässlichen Hexe wartet an der Tür.   12. Ich habe einer hässlichen Hexe einen Sack Gold gegeben.   13. Kein reicher Ausländer hat in dieser Straße gewohnt.   14. Wir haben keinem reichen Ausländer Geld geschickt.   15. Nein, sie hat keinen reichen Ausländer angerufen.   16. Herr Bellini ist kein reicher Ausländer. 17. Monika darf ihn kaufen.   18. Er war zu teuer.   19. Wo haben Sie ihn gefunden? 20. Hat er den Mädchen gefallen?

Exercise 20.5

1. Wart ihr gute Freunde?   2. Die Studenten gingen auf eine Party.   3. Die kranke Frau bleibt zu Hause.   4. Martin will ihr einen schönen Ring kaufen.   5. Wir bestellten Würstchen und Bier.   6. Niemand isst die kalte Suppe.   7. Ich hatte wirklich keine Zeit.   8. Am Donnerstag geht Tina schlittschuhlaufen.   9. Der Schauspieler sang auch gut.   10. Wer sandte dieses Telegramm?

Exercise 20.6

1. er ist eingeschlafen er wird einschlafen   2. er ist mitgekommen er wird mitkommen   3. er hat bestellt er wird bestellen   4. er hat getrunken er wird trinken   5. er hat gelacht er wird lachen   6. er hat erwartet er wird erwarten 7. er hat gekannt er wird kennen   8. er hat gewusst er wird wissen   9. er hat ferngesehen er wird fernsehen   10. er ist gestorben er wird sterben

Exercise 20.7

1. PAST: Wer bekam ein Geschenk von ihm? PRESENT PERFECT: Wer hat ein Geschenk von ihm bekommen? FUTURE: Wer wird ein Geschenk von ihm bekommen? 2. PRESENT: Er weiß nicht, wo sie wohnt. PRESENT PERFECT: Er hat nicht gewusst, wo sie wohnt. FUTURE: Er wird nicht wissen, wo sie wohnt. 3. PRESENT: Wir bestellen eine Flasche Wein. PAST: Wir bestellten eine Flasche Wein. FUTURE: Wir werden eine Flasche Wein bestellen. 4. PRESENT: Arbeiten Sie bei einer Bank? PAST: Arbeiteten Sie bei einer Bank? PRESENT PERFECT: Haben Sie bei einer Bank gearbeitet? 5. PAST: Der Präsident war in der Hauptstadt. PRESENT PERFECT: Der Präsident ist in der Hauptstadt gewesen. FUTURE: Der Präsident wird in der Hauptstadt sein. 6. PRESENT: Der müde Junge schläft auf dem Boden ein. PRESENT PERFECT: Der müde Junge ist auf dem Boden eingeschlafen. FUTURE: Der müde Junge wird auf dem Boden einschlafen. 7. PRESENT: Ich muss dorthin reisen. PAST: Ich musste dorthin reisen. FUTURE: Ich werde dorthin reisen müssen. 8. PRESENT: Wer kann damit helfen? PAST: Wer konnte damit helfen? PRESENT PERFECT: Wer hat damit helfen können? 9. PAST: Gudrun las drei Zeitungen. PRESENT PERFECT: Gudrun hat drei Zeitungen gelesen. FUTURE: Gudrun wird drei Zeitungen lesen. 10. PRESENT: Der Ausländer kommt auch mit. PAST: Der Ausländer kam auch mit. PRESENT PERFECT: Der Ausländer ist auch mitgekommen.

Review Quiz 20

1. d   2. a   3. a   4. a   5. c   6. b   7. b   8. d   9. d   10. a

Mastery Check 3

1. d   2. b   3. a   4. b   5. a   6. c   7. a   8. a   9. b   10. c   11. a   12. b   13. b   14. a   15. a   16. d   17. a   18. b   19. d   20. d   21. d   22. d   23. b   24. d   25. b